Shooting the
Executive Rapids

Shooting the Executive Rapids

The First Crucial Year of a New Assignment

John D. Arnold

McGraw-Hill Book Company

New York   St. Louis   San Francisco   Auckland
Bogotá   Hamburg   Johannesburg   London   Madrid
Mexico   Montreal   New Delhi   Panama   Paris
São Paulo   Singapore   Sydney   Tokyo   Toronto

Library of Congress Cataloging in Publication Data

Arnold, John D, date.
  Shooting the executive rapids.

  Includes index.
  1. Executives.   I. Title.
HF5500.2.A76   658.4   80-23408
ISBN 0-07-002312-3

1234567890   DODO   8987654321

The editors for this book were William R. Newton and Tobia L.
Worth, the designer was Mark E. Safran, and the production supervisor
was Sally L. Fliess. It was set in Garamond by The Kingsport Press.

Printed and bound by R. R. Donnelley & Sons.

TO: The American and Canadian executives who, in our early days—before our approach and methods were widely known—sought our counsel, applied our methods, and accelerated achievement of their goals.

Contents

Preface

When I first began writing a book for executives in new assignments, some people thought I was crazy. "Aren't there already a million books about how to succeed in business?" they asked. Some added, "What about all those thick volumes crammed full of 'management principles?'"

True enough, there are plenty of both kinds of books on the market or gathering dust on library shelves.

But between the "success-formula" books, which dispense generalized advice on how to achieve fame and fortune, and the traditional management guides, both specialized and general, there is a significant gap: a book that answers the distinctive needs of executives in new assignments.

For thirteen years, my company, John Arnold ExecuTrak® Systems, Inc., of Waltham, Massachusetts, has been helping executives meet new challenges. Some are parachuted into a new company, others promoted from within the ranks, and still others—executives for years—are receiving challenging new assignments. In all three situations, we have been struck by the similarity of the challenges facing executives in their first year.

Whether they control multinational conglomerates or family-owned businesses, produce products or sell services, staff government agencies, or administer nonprofit organizations—all executives face certain common needs: to establish a strong sense of direction and a firm grasp of their new responsibilities; to quickly come to grips with the key issues and opportunities they face; to gain the respect of their managers; to develop a common vision of what needs to be done and a viable plan to do it; and to accelerate the organizational "pulse rate" to make the right things happen faster.

In the process, they will face a host of tough decisions—planning and budgeting, marketing, product development, investment, diversification, human and organizational challenges, among others—many of which they will have to make while still learning their jobs and struggling to understand the company, group, or division, or governmental/nonprofit agency culture.

There are, of course, differences in the challenges to the new chief executive of, say, a multinational container company, who has been our client; the founder-president of a new medical laboratory; or a new managing partner of a law firm whom we have also served. But the differences are of scope and complexity, not of substance or kind. What's more, the challenges the small-laboratory executive faces are every bit as critical to his success as those that confront the multinational CEO are to him.

Hence, this book. It distills more than a decade of intensive counseling experience to relate—as vividly as I can (while maintaining the confidentiality of our clients)—the pressures, problems, challenges, pitfalls, opportunities, rewards, and, I hope, the feeling of excitement, anxiety, and exhilaration of a new assignment.

If this book succeeds, it will provide you, the reader, with an insider's view of the executive suite rarely seen by people even at middle-management levels. It should provide insight and enlightenment (maybe even some entertainment), not only for new and experienced executives, but for any man or woman who aspires to reach the pinnacle of an organization.

It's written also for wives, husbands, college students, and others with an interest in understanding the challenges, the rewards, and the frustrations of leadership. We hope that younger readers will be able to make more informed career choices from the insights they will gain from this book.

I chose the title *Shooting the Executive Rapids* because the first year of an executive's new assignment is a perilous period. As if he were riding the rapids, an executive in his first year embarks on a journey to a destination he cannot discern, carried by a current he cannot completely control, and aboard a boat manned by people he may hardly know and on whom his daily mode of living and success depend.

My company serves executives negotiating these rapids as a navigational guide. To the new executive, these may be uncharted waters, but we've traveled them many times. He must set his own destination. It's his ship, after all. He must steer it. But we can show him where the shoals are and how to steer when the white waters begin to roil. In a word, the new executive must choose his own course; we provide the compass—and a map.

In keeping with the nature of our services, this is *not* a technical book. It is a guidebook. It provides principles, procedures, and guidelines drawn from our clients' experiences. Those clients include many Fortune 1000 companies as well as smaller firms in the United States, Canada, Latin America, and Europe. Because this book is based on actual experiences of the author, the names of companies and individuals—and often of industries and locations—have been changed to preserve client confidentiality.

The book contains practical, "nuts and bolts" advice on mastering such business challenges as:

- Turning around depressed earnings
- Developing a viable strategic team plan
- Revitalizing a business
- Accelerating product and service development
- Increasing marketing and sales effectiveness
- Revamping the organizational structure
- Managing acquisitions
- Managing relationships with the board of directors and with key constituencies (i.e., customers, vendors, bankers, investment community, trade associations, government agencies, etc.)

En route to meeting these challenges, you will learn how to:

1. Find the right executive job and negotiate the best compensation package.
2. Assure your new job is a "win" for your family as well as yourself.
3. Establish realistic goals for your first 30 days, 90 days and year in a new assignment.
4. Get your management team on *your* wavelength.
5. Cope with day-to-day problems, chronic crises, and delicate personnel matters while still "learning the ropes."
6. Make the best use of your manpower and material resources.
7. Develop realistic action plans and translate them into *early* bottom-line results.
8. Assure that your boss recognizes your accomplishments.
9. Increase your organizational impact and expand your responsibilities.
10. Know when it's time to move up—or out.

Book "personalities" you will read about include:

1. *Clarence ("Reel") Reed,* an empire builder with an instinct for success—and a desire to exert total control over the lives of his subordinates.
2. *Harry Wilson,* a marketing genius and "honest Christian," who accepted Reel's promises at face value and saw his career blocked—until he finally "got the message."
3. *Ben Wyman,* the young president of a huge communications conglomerate, whose appointment from outside the industry created a confrontation with his inherited staff and a comment by one of its members, "You'll be dead within a month!"

4. *Roger Foss,* a brilliant, hard-driving manager who made major inroads against the competition in record time—but almost drove his managers to mutiny.

5. *Jim Doyle,* a sales wiz whose promotion brought with it responsibilities he didn't know how to shoulder—until he arrived at a new understanding with his boss.

6. *Nicholas Troubat,* a meticulous scientist and elegant host whose tyrannical management methods and violent temper made him a latter-day Dr. Jekyll and Mr. Hyde—and almost cost him his job.

There are several overall principles that guide our work with these and other executives. One is "win-win." We consistently find that organizations operate more effectively—and in the case of companies, more profitably—when managers develop a *process* enabling them to pursue solutions that benefit *all* parties, whether they involve strategic team planning, developing new products, identifying profit improvement opportunities, responding to customer complaints, bidding on new contracts, solving difficult organizational and "people problems," or making major diversification and investment decisions.

Another is "planning with people." Today's corporations are blamed for a multitude of sins: inferior products, indifferent service, disdain for what customers really want, a public-be-damned attitude, environmental neglect, conformism, red tape, profiteering, an "anything-for-a-buck" mentality—the list is endless.

Many of these criticisms—and the practices that give rise to them—would disappear if the decision process of business, industrial, governmental, and even nonprofit service organizations were broadened to give systematic consideration to the information, values, and feelings of those persons and publics most affected by their decisions.

Our own process combines a disciplined approach to opportunity detection and analysis, planning, decision making, problem solving, and communications, with procedures for assuring *high-quality* involvement of managers (and, as appropriate, other employees, customers, vendors, and the public) in critical determinations.

If we have accomplished nothing else in the past decade, we've been told that we have developed distinctive methods that permit organizations to *tap* the collective motivation, energy, and wisdom of their management groups and work forces, *focusing* these on developing better, more creative solutions to critical problems and opportunities.

Through this book, I hope we can open *your* opportunity lens to new ways of utilizing the talents—and realizing the potential—of your most important resource as an executive: People.

Acknowledgments

To Mark Arnold, whose valued counsel and craftsmanship in helping me structure and write this book, make it, I hope, a significant contribution to the management profession.

Also, to Bert Tompkins, whose dedication, perceptive eye, and counsel have been a source of strength to ExecuTrak Systems, Inc.; and to Anne Mooradian, my Administrative Assistant, who offered valuable encouragement and criticism, and—with Sandra Shulman—produced the manuscript.

John D. Arnold

About the Author

John D. Arnold, 46, is president of John Arnold ExecuTrak® Systems, Inc., decision/planning/communications and business effectiveness counselors, and president of ExecuTrak® Ltd., specialists in making and managing acquisitions. For the past decade, he has served as personal counselor to presidents and other top executives of multinational corporations, and as a catalyst/"integrating mechanism" with their management groups.

Shooting the Executive Rapids: The Crucial First Year in a New Assignment, Mr. Arnold's second book, will be published by McGraw-Hill in January 1981. It draws on John Arnold's role during the past decade as personal counselor and "integrating mechanism" for senior executives of major North American corporations.

Born and raised in Newton, Massachusetts, and a graduate of Harvard in 1955, he lives in Wayland, Massachusetts. His avocations include skiing, tennis, playing various African instruments, and investments.

Shooting the Executive Rapids

Chapter 1
"What Am I in For?"

(Your Challenges in a New Assignment)

Some of the most common situations we face in life, we face without guidance: Adjusting to marriage. Bringing up children. Beginning a new job.

There are plenty of books on how to get "the right" job. But there are none at all about how to succeed in it during those first critical months when you are trying to feel your way, get clear direction, establish your leadership—and make your mark.

My company earns a major portion of its livelihood helping executives succeed in new assignments. In the course of counseling hundreds of them, newly promoted or "parachuted in," we have developed some methods of universal application.

This is a book about those methods—a "how to" book about succeeding in your new assignment.

America is a mobile society, partly by choice (Americans seem to pride themselves on comparing notes on where they once lived), partly by necessity. Our vocabulary encapsulates our meandering lifestyle: "Up and out"; "Here today, gone tomorrow." Old IBM hands quip that the name of their company stands for "I've Been Moved."

Businesses relocate an estimated 470,000 managers and other employees annually, according to Merrill-Lynch's home-buying/selling subsidiary. Perhaps an equal number—it's impossible to know for sure—change companies and locations on their own in any given year.

The problems of the relocated family are well known. In contrast, the problems of the relocating executive are barely studied. But one thing is obvious: Some executives will succeed at their new assignments, and some will not.

What distinguishes most winners from most losers is not—as some popular books would have you believe—the way they dress *(Dress for Success)*, the extent to which they can intimidate others *(Winning through Intimida-*

tion), or simply their ability to match the "chemistry" of their superiors.

I believe that the distinguising characteristic is *their ability to quickly establish realistic and ambitious goals, strategies, and plans—and to manage and organize time, information, and people to achieve them.*

This is a book on how to do that.

First, some benchmarks.

We recently polled a group of executives from a dozen companies with annual sales from $10 million to over $1 billion about the challenges they encountered in their first year in a new assignment. What they had to say may provide some guidelines for setting *your own* goals and expectations.

Essentially, this is the way they look back on their first-year challenges:

- First 30 days: Know the turf (understand how the company operates and, if you don't already, the dynamics of the business).
- Next 30 days: Know the players (your superiors, key peers, and subordinates).[1]
- First 6 months: Establish a business plan and a supporting organizational plan (develop and translate your priorities into a plan and organize your people into an effective force).
- First 12 months: "Work the plan" and "make the plan work" (overcome external and internal obstacles to its effectiveness).

A key suggestion from those surveyed: After only 1 year, the new executive should be able to demonstrate *tangible* results from his leadership.

We asked the executives whether they enjoyed a "honeymoon" period and, if so, how long it endured. Fifty percent said they had a honeymoon period; the others said they did not.

Significantly, the half who did enjoy a honeymoon period said it was cut short *prematurely*—by the necessity to meet some crisis or organizational resistance to the moves they planned. Most of the "honeymooners" had expected it to last between 3 and 6 months, which it *didn't!*

Some challenges proved greater than they had anticipated. Among those cited:

- Understanding the company's financial system
- Learning the company culture
- Making tough personnel decisions
- Gaining commitment by subordinates to organizational changes
- Acting on critical issues (including turning around money-losing operations and eliminating obsolete products, programs, and projects)

---

[1] In practice, you will probably be learning the turf and the players simultaneously.

Eighty percent said they felt they were "firmly in control" within 6 months. The rest said it took them up to 18 months to feel in control. Significantly, however, most felt they had won the confidence and support of their direct superior earlier—even before they felt in control. Half the group felt they had the support and confidence of their superior from the *outset* of their assignment. For those who had to work to gain this confidence, they won it by "demonstrating control," "making difficult decisions," "improving communications," and—according to 25 percent—"eliminating surprises."

Common mistakes made by executives in new assignments were cited as:

- Trying to do too much too soon
- Misjudging people and their resistance to change
- Not understanding the limits of their authority and "the way the system works"

Almost all have advice to offer you as an executive in a new assignment. Here are some of their responses:

- "Avoid sweeping changes before you know the ropes."
- "Promote open communications both up and down the line."
- "Think through all the consequences of your intended course of action before proceeding."
- "Listen, learn, probe, and challenge—then proceed."
- "Keep your superior fully informed, obtain his guidance and counsel to ensure his support."
- "Make the rules and the *process* by which you will operate clearly understood."
- "Know your people, their potential, and their strengths and weaknesses."

Many executives starting a new assignment with an open calendar find themselves almost immediately immersed in meetings, reviews, and road shows (to regional offices, plants, customers, etc.). The temptation to learn as much as you can as fast as you can is natural. But let's face it, you can't know everything—and you can wear yourself out trying.

One executive we know was working 15 hours a day, 7 days a week, during his first 3 months on a new job. He attended more than 125 meetings, which occupied 60 percent of his total work time. He was also receiving 400 pages of documents a week to read.

"I was mired in 'meetingitis' and paperwork, and when I went on the road, it was good getting to know the people, but they were looking for answers from me and I was too new to have anything but questions."

Our experience suggests that while it's important to gain the perspectives and insights of your "troops" and customers in your first few weeks on the job, it's not important—unless you face some "crisis of confidence" that requires your actual presence—to try to cover *all* the bases in person. In fact, it's downright wasteful of your time to try to do so.

An outside resource who is sensitive to the needs and priorities of newly appointed senior executives can tap the accumulated wisdom of those who know your challenges best and distill this information for you while you're investing your critical first few weeks in ways that can help achieve your business objectives. There'll be plenty of time to make the rounds later—when you have, or can develop with others, the answers people are looking for.

How should you spend your time the first few weeks?

In Chapter 4, we'll help you establish your own 30-day goals and strategy. For now, the most important thing for you to do initially is to ask the right questions. Here are four questions to start with:

1. *Why?* Why are we here? What's our reason for being—as a business and as each function?

2. *What?* What are we doing? What products or services do we offer in pursuit of that reason for being? What new products or services are we developing?

3. *How?* How do we do what we do? What's the process by which decisions are made and executed?

4. *How well?* How profitably do we do what we do—overall and for each product or service line?

In your own new assignment, you will face distinct specific challenges. But if you can relate them to the larger questions raised here and establish a *process* for dealing with them systematically and a *mechanism* that galvanizes the whole organization to address what truly are the key issues and opportunities facing your enterprise, you will have made a superior start in your job.

In the end, there are only two types of issues you need be concerned with:

• Business issues

• People issues

This book will help you organize your own attack to deal effectively with both.

Chapter 2
"But Is It for Me?"
(Getting the Right Job— and the Job Right)

This is not primarily a book about how to get the right executive position. It *is* a book about how to achieve distinguished performance once you get the right executive position.

Many executives, however, are dissatisfied with the position they hold— they may not be holding down the right job. And many others, while on the whole content with their position, are plagued by a host of on-the-job frustrations such as superiors who just can't let go of the reins, lack of senior executive commitment to corporate excellence, constant travel, and uncertain authority. These people may have the right job, but they don't have the job right.

Therefore, we are including some general observations—and then some specific guidelines—to increase your chances of getting the right position and getting the position right. These observations, based on our own clients' experiences, are meant not to be comprehensive but rather to fill in some important gaps in the conventional treatment of these subjects.

By the time a man or woman reaches executive status, he or she can probably dispense with advice on "how to write a résumé," "looking out for number one," "conducting job interviews," and the hundreds of other job-hunting or self-improvement tips—some helpful, many not—whose invention has made the givers of such advice considerably more wealthy than the recipients.

Accordingly, this chapter focuses on providing answers to three questions that almost all executives face at one or more points in their career:

1. How do I know when it's time to move on?

2. Where should I look for opportunities (including *within* my company)?

3. How can I negotiate the best deal?

5

When to Make a Move

How long you stay in your present position depends on your own objectives. Every executive should establish a set of career objectives and a timetable for reaching them. He should review the objectives and timetable periodically, measure them against his performance, and weigh his options. In doing so, he should consider the following questions:

- What kind of track am I on?
- How am I doing at my present job?
- What's my future with the company?
- How "marketable" am I?

What Kind of Track Are You On?

There are, essentially, two tracks an executive can follow to get ahead. Alex Goodwin, a principal of MBA/Corporate Resources, Inc., a fast-growing New York–Chicago executive recruiting firm, describes these as the track of the "hired gunslinger" and the track of the "long-term employee." He explains:

"The long-term employee knows how long it takes to reach a certain level of upper management of the company. Based on past performance, he can measure his progress according to that timetable. The hired gunslinger is someone who is working for one company today, but recognizes that if it will help his career, he'll move to another company tomorrow. His skills are transferable from one company to another, and he is continually on the lookout for new opportunities."

The long-term employee has the benefit of stability. He can set down roots and pace his life in a way that permits him to establish a comfortable balance between his job and his family and outside responsibilities. His life is ordered and predictable.

The gunslinger, on the other hand, recognizes that his ambitions require considerable mobility, constant attention to achieving results that will impress his next employer, and often the sacrifice of many personal and family responsibilities.

The long-term employee essentially leaves his future in the hands of others, unless he becomes dissatisfied—in which case he takes on some of the characteristics of the gunslinger. The gunslinger is opportunistic in outlook, short-term-oriented, and always alert for new options, which he tries to leverage or parlay to his advantage.

The essential difference between them, in my view, is that the gunslinger switches tracks frequently whereas the long-term employee pins his hopes on the expectation that the track he is on will take him to his chosen destination. In either case, however, it is important for an executive to periodically undertake a reassessment of his situation and options.

Whichever track you are on, periodically review your timetable and measure your progress against your plan.

How Are You Doing at Your Present Job?

We advise clients to gauge their performance at least once a year by drawing up a "Key Contributions Scorecard." This can become the basis for a performance review with your superior and/or a discussion about your prospects for company advancement.

To compile a Key Contributions Scorecard, take a blank sheet of paper and draw a line down the center, separating the sheet into two vertical columns. Title the left-hand column "Key Performance Areas (in priority)." Title the right-hand column "Major Contributions."

In the first (left-hand) column, list your major responsibilities (key performance areas) in order of priority. Opposite each responsibility listed, enter in the second column a short description of your major contributions during the period of your assessment.

In drafting your Key Contributions Scorecard, don't concentrate on the activities in which you engaged (e.g., "visited each advertising agency at least three times") or on unquantifiable results ("achieved better understanding by agencies of our needs"). Rather, concentrate on the *impact on the business* (e.g., "initiated ad campaign that achieved consumer-acceptance-level impact of X and Y—highest in division history").[1]

One of our clients, the vice president of marketing of a major health care company, identified 10 key performance areas in 1979. He listed these as follows:

1. Product marketing
2. Profitability and growth rate
3. Management and development
4. Market research
5. Market intelligence
6. Organizational structure
7. Customer satisfaction
8. Internal communications
9. Personal development
10. Public relations

[1] For a fuller description of how to draw up a Key Contributions Scorecard, see Chapter 20, "How Am I Doing?" (Assessing Your First Year).

In filling out his Key Contributions Scorecard, he identified some of his contributions as follows:

Key performance areas (In priority)	Major contributions
1. Product marketing	A. Successfully introduced 3 new products in test market which achieved targeted share in 12 months.
	B. Met volume objectives on all ongoing products.
	C. Stayed within budget restrictions of 1979 plan.
2. Profitability and growth rate	A. Achieved targeted 10% growth in sales.
	B. Delivered bottom-line profit exceeding 10% ROA as targeted in marketing plan.
And so forth.	

Compiling your Key Contributions Scorecard tells you *how you think* you're doing. The next step is to find out *how your boss thinks* you're doing.

Most companies, of course, hold periodic performance reviews of their executives and managers. Drawing up your contributions scorecard to present at such a meeting enables you to present your record in the most positive light. It also demonstrates to your boss that you are consciously and systematically setting priorities and evaluating your performance against goals. It may impress him with the need to be equally disciplined in his assessment of you.

Whether or not your superior's evaluation is favorable enough to satisfy you, you may want to ask him to discuss your future with the organization— either then or there, or, preferably, at a future meeting.

What's Your Future If You Stay?

In preparing for this discussion, you will want to clarify your objectives with the company to determine the responsibilities, challenges, and compensation levels you want to achieve. Here are some points to consider in advance of such a meeting:

1. What's happening to the company? Is it growing? Is the atmosphere developmental or reductive? Are the pay scales low or high?

2. What's happening to the industry?

3. If I stay, am I expanding my opportunities for growth and development—or restricting them?

4. Within the company, what job offers the opportunity for maximum growth and development? What other opportunities might there be for me here?

5. Are openings, in fact, occurring, or are they likely to occur, at these levels if I stay?

6. Does the company tend to fill top positions from inside or from outside?

   In some companies, the longer your service, the less leverage you may be able to exert for a position—unless the company is one that promotes virtually entirely from within.

7. How do I stack up against other potential candidates for promotion?

   Assess your own age, energy, performance level, and "political support" against those of any potential rivals for the position. Ask yourself: "In top management's eyes, am I the leading candidate for promotion to _____?"

8. If I am not the leading candidate, what can I do to make myself the leading candidate?

   Explore whether it would be advisable to attend an advanced management program, work toward an additional degree, and/or become more active in trade, industry, and civic associations—both for the contacts and the broader perspective it would give you.

9. How much clout or leverage do I have within the company?

   A good way to measure this is to ask yourself: "How hard do I have to press to get what I want?" Compare this with how hard you used to have to press and how hard others in a similar situation have to press.

10. How can I make my boss look good and improve his performance in the eyes of *his* superiors?

    Generally, the more your boss recognizes your value to him, the more apt he will be to see you as his protégé and to advance you if/ as he advances.

11. What's my deadline?

    Set yourself a deadline for moving—*up* or *out.* If you are not able to move ahead because your superior is not moving, then perhaps you should be looking elsewhere.

How Marketable Are You?

In all fairness to yourself, your decision on whether or not to stay with the company should probably involve an assessment—however discreet and limited—of your prospects outside the company. In making this assessment, bear in mind that the grass often does look greener on the other side of the street; it may not be quite so green when you get close to it.

Make a list of your *career* accomplishments or contributions and of your strengths—both those that are being utilized in your present position and those that are not. Ask yourself such questions as:

1. What are the other ways to utilize my strengths and my accomplishments in this company? In what other industries or organizations? In what kinds of positions?

2. What do I want to *achieve, preserve,* and *avoid* by any possible change in my position?

3. What are my weaknesses, liabilities, or gaps from the point of view of a prospective employer? How serious are they in terms of finding other employment? How can I overcome them or minimize their adverse impact on my prospects?

In clarifying your outside options, it may be advisable to try for a position where you can view a new business as a whole, preferably from the top or a perch near the top. A position as assistant to the president, for example, gives you better perspective—and probably more leverage—than a line function that gives you only a view of one aspect of the business. Moreover, the more top management can see you function, the better position you are in to impress them with your performance and to recognize opportunities as they arise.

You may also want to check with friends, trusted colleagues, and perhaps an executive recruiter (see below) to help assess how marketable your skills are.

Where to Move

Where you move is a function of the objectives you establish—that is, what you are looking for in a new job and where you want (or are willing to resign yourself) to live. In specifying your objectives, distinguish between those that are essential or absolute (i.e., those that any job *must* satisfy to be worthwhile) and those that you consider desirable but not essential. These objectives or criteria will serve as a way of both focusing your research and evaluating offers when they come.[2]

Here are some criteria set by a client of ours—a 34-year-old communications executive who found his career blocked in the company where he had spent the previous 8 years:

Criteria for a New Executive Position

Absolute Requirements:

1. A minimum 20 percent increase in compensation

2. Greater responsibility than I now have

---

[2] For a fuller discussion of goal setting, establishment of criteria, and priorities, see John D. Arnold, *Make Up Your Mind*, AMACOM, New York, 1978. This book devotes three chapters to clarifying career objectives and obtaining the right position.

3. A fast-growing business (sales increasing 10 percent or more a year)

4. A boss who believes in and *practices* motivating people—not undercutting and second-guessing them.

Desirable Objectives:

1. Live in a major metropolitan area

2. Work in a field where I can capitalize on my existing expertise and contacts

3. Travel no more than 30 percent of my time

4. Achieve a generous compensation package

5. Have responsibility for a department of the company with sales in excess of $500 million

6. Have status commensurate with my responsibilities (title, staff, perquisites)

7. Work for a company known for its creative atmosphere and encouragement of initiative

8. Have good advancement potential, based on the movement of others of my age and qualifications

9. Work for a company with good industry reputation

Once you have set your criteria for any job change, you can actively begin your search.

You may want to seek out the services of an executive search firm to help clarify your options. Typically, a good search firm can cast a wider net to identify job openings than you could on your own. In addition, the chances of maintaining confidentiality are better if you work through a reputable search firm than if, for example, you were to mail your résumé to numerous companies.

In lining up the right executive search firm, seek advice from other executives who have recently changed companies. Get the name of a key counselor in whatever firm you think you may want to work and call for an appointment.

At the meeting, you will, of course, discuss your job needs, career objectives, and qualifications. You should also ask the counselor for an assessment of what your prospects are, the likely timetable for results, and the process he will use. You will probably want to stress the need for *utmost* discretion, so that your employer does not prematurely discover that you are seeking another job.

Any executive recruiter worth his salt knows that his professional reputation rests on his ability not only to find the right job for you but also to safeguard the confidentiality of your relationship. Even so, discuss thoroughly what the ground rules should be for the search and make sure they allow *you* to control the search process.

Working through an executive recruiter saves you time, since he will take the responsibility for determining to which companies to send your résumé, screen the initial inquiries, and ultimately help negotiate the deal. Even better, it will cost you nothing, since the employer pays the costs (typically 30 to 35 percent of your first year's compensation).

Researching—and Negotiating—a New Position

Before you have your first interview with a prospective employer, do some initial research on the company. The quickest way is to get several recent annual reports; the latest quarterly report; and financial analyst research reports comparing the company with its competitors. Annual reports, although projecting a Pollyanna-ish picture of the company, provide useful background data and information on the company's self-image and introduce you to the "key players."

At a minimum, you should read the letter to shareholders from the most recent three annual reports, beginning with the earliest. Look for plans that were announced one year and not mentioned the next. If you find such discrepancies (and you often can), this gives you a talking point in your interview ("You know, Mr. Smith, I was thumbing through some recent annual reports and I wonder whatever happened to the plan to . . . ?"). Whether there are discrepancies or not, by asking a question or two based on your reading of the annual reports, you show that you have done your homework.

If the initial negotiations look promising, you will want to make further checks on the company. The best sources of information—according to an ExecuTrak® survey of 3000 chief executives in 1978—are present company executives, consultants, and trade and industry sources.

You will also want to nail down the specifics of the job itself with a series of probing questions. We have developed a list of 25 key questions to aid in determining whether *their* needs match *your* talents. Among them are:

- What qualities is the company looking for in a new executive?
- What specifically are the responsibilities of the job?
- How will performance be measured, according to what criteria, and at what intervals?
- What are the major challenges of the job—both short and longer term?
- Are there any particular problems—interdepartmental, personality, etc.— that you should be aware of?
- What happened to the last two incumbents who held this position?

Later, you may want to ask some of these questions, if you are seriously interested in the position:

- How well understood—and accepted—is the position in the organization?
- What should be the likely reaction of subordinates to your appointment?
- What guidelines could you adopt in the way you handle yourself to minimize any possible frictions?
- Are there any "sacred cows" or "hot buttons" that you should be aware of?
- Are there any significant weaknesses in the management competence of subordinates?
- If all goes well, where would the job be likely to lead? When?

The answers to these and other questions we've developed in our counseling work with executives will help clarify your suitation and give you a better basis for determining if you will be comfortable in the job or not. Some of them will be difficult for the new organization to answer. You may also feel that by asking them, you run the risk of asking too many questions and thus being labeled a "troublemaker." While you are the final judge as to how appropriate these questions may be to your situation, the experience of our clients suggests that prospective employers respect people who ask tough questions. They take them more seriously than they do those who meekly follow the lead of company interviewers. After all, the job of a senior executive is to *lead*—and the employment interview is a good test of this!

Conducting the Interview

Before you go into a serious interview, in addition to researching the company, you should:

1. Clarify in your own mind your objectives for the meeting—what you want to *achieve, preserve,* and *avoid* by the interview.
2. Design a strategy and a discussion guide to turn the interview to your advantage.
3. Draw up a "shopping" list of compensation demands (euphemistically called "compensation needs"), though you probably should keep it to yourself as long as possible. The list should enumerate all the benefits of your present job, including salary, bonus, profit sharing, stock option, vacation, expense accounts, perquisites, life insurance, medical, dental, and disability insurance, and any other benefits provided by your employer. It should also include your objectives in each of these areas and in any new areas—what you hope to gain from a new job.

4. Outline a tentative presentation that relates your strengths and experience to the prospective employer's needs. You may have to adapt this as the discussion evolves, but it gives you a firm platform from which to speak, if necessary.

Having prepared yourself for the meeting, you should seek to make the session conform to your strategy. Most good interviews—as seen from the perspective of the job seeker—have five stages:

1. Feeling each other out—breaking the ice
2. Tentative probing
3. Finding out what the employer wants
4. Keying your pitch to his needs, without, of course, shading the truth
5. Talking money

1. Breaking the ice   When you enter the interviewer's office, take a moment to look around. You will inevitably see indications of his interests or hobbies—perhaps a trophy on the wall or a picture of his family at a summer resort. Ask him about something that catches your eye and try to relate your own experiences or vacations or hobbies to his. Most successful interviews begin with an initial period of small talk to set the mood for serious negotiations. By taking the initiative to set the climate, you help establish yourself as "his kind of guy." If he's like most people, he enjoys talking about himself, particularly about things he is proud enough to display in his office.

2. Tentative probing   After the initial pleasantries have been exchanged and the ice broken, the interviewer will probably ask you a general open-ended question. Many job seekers grab this opportunity and run with the ball by expounding for 10 to 30 minutes about their own accomplishments. It's almost always a mistake to do so. George Webb, director in the New York office of Owen, Webb, Bacci, Bennett, Inc., executive recruiting consultants, calls this "firing shots all over the room before you know what you should really be aiming at."

"What you want at this point is to find out what *his* needs are, not to let him find out what you can do."

Accordingly, answer the interviewer's initial question—which may ask what you've been doing or why you are looking for a job—in no more than two or three sentences, resisting the temptation to embellish your own goals or capabilities at the outset of the meeting.

Then, ask him a correspondingly gentle question to turn the spotlight on him. For example, you might ask, "I understand you're going through a rather exciting period here at Flexatron, Inc., these days. Can you tell me a little about it?"

He will respond either at length or—if he is a smart interviewer—as briefly as you did, and then ask you a more probing question. You should, once again, give an equally brief response and ask him an equally probing question back!

The purpose of parrying his thrusts and turning them back on him is to make him play your game. Says one executive job counselor for job interviews: "I've never had an employer who could survive more than four exchanges of questions. He folds and starts playing it your way—answering your questions."

A number of professional recruiters—as well as our own counseling experience—suggest that, contrary to popular belief, if you as the job seeker have properly prepared yourself, you can control the interview situation, for several reasons.

First, you have a game plan and the interviewer probably doesn't. Moreover, the interviewer usually feels uncomfortable asking probing questions. What he feels most comfortable talking about is *his* business and that's what you're trying to get him to focus on. In addition, he knows you need to know about his business sooner or later, so he is less reluctant to discuss it when you ask.

Finally, he is usually not as well prepared for the interview as you are— if you have done your homework, clarified your objectives for the interview, and developed a strategy.

3. Finding out what the employer wants   The purpose of this polite and subtle parrying is to get the interviewer to outline the company's needs *before* you begin to expound on your capabilities. The more information you are able to smoke out about the job requirements and challenges, the better platform you are able to build for your own presentation.

The questions outlined above ("Researching—and Negotiating—a New Position") will also help to bring the new position into focus.

4. Keying to his needs   Once you feel you have a good fix on the challenges of the job, it's your turn to step up to the bar. Wait until the interviewer has completed his discourse, while casually reviewing your notes and the main points you want to make. Then introduce your presentation by saying something like, "If I hear you right, Joe, your principal needs and concerns are these." Then tick them off—1, 2, 3, 4, 5, etc.—and watch for his reaction.

Summarizing his discourse demonstrates that you have indeed been listening and that you and he are on the same wavelength. If your summary is not entirely accurate, he'll correct you. Unless your summary has missed the target completely, however, you'll have demonstrated to him that you are an effective listener.

When you feel he is comfortable with *your* understanding of his needs and concerns, you have properly laid the groundwork for your own presentation. Begin it by saying something like: "It occurs to me, Joe, there's a striking parallel between some of the problems we were facing 3 years ago and what Flexatron is facing now."

You have then positioned your sales pitch for maximum impact, because you have tailored your presentation to his specific needs, which your strategy has effectively smoked out.

5. Talking money The basic rules in negotiating compensation are:

- Never bring up your demands until you have a sign of his definite interest.
- Use all past compensation as leverage.
- Establish criteria for performance.
- Provide for termination benefits.
- Get it now!
- Get it in writing.

The prospective employer will seek to have you talk about your compensation needs as early as possible. That's precisely when you don't want to discuss the subject. He will be preoccupied with what you're going to cost him.

Later, when you have him interested, he will be considerably more receptive to your needs. Therefore, you want to postpone talking money as long as possible. There are two exceptions to this rule:

1. When you have strong doubts about his willingness to pay what you require

2. When you are so secure and happy in your present job that you want him to know he will have to pay dearly to woo you away

If you have any doubts that it is worth your while to negotiate seriously, then you may want to say very early on, "I like what you're saying, but just to set the ground rules straight, I really can't consider something like this for less than X amount. Are we in the same ballpark?"

This strategy may save you time, but it risks breaking off the negotiations prematurely. Under most circumstances, therefore, it is best not to mention money until after you're reasonably sure the company wants to hire you. Explains one recruiter: "Prospective employers, like anxious suitors, do not think expansively until they're deeply in love. Once they are, anything is possible!"

If you're asked about compensation before you think it's timely to discuss it, try to diplomatically set the subject aside. For example, you might say: "Quite frankly, Joe, there are some assignments I wouldn't consider for several times what I'm now making. Possibly, somewhere there may be something I would be interested in for not too much more than I'm making now. It's really hard to answer until I know more about the specifics of the assignment you have in mind."

Use All Present Compensation as Leverage

Don't be afraid of pegging your demands too high. If you plan your strategy right and the employer is "in love," he'll bend over backwards to pay you what you want. A common mistake executives make in negotiating for new positions is to peg their demands too low. A case in point:

An actuary in a small actuarial firm was approached by a large investment house which was seeking to establish an actuarial consulting firm and wanted someone to head it. The actuary was making $54,000 at the time. After an initial interview with the personnel director of the company, the actuary met with the CEO, who confirmed the company's interest in his availability to head the new consulting firm.

"What kind of money are you interested in?" the CEO asked. The actuary took a deep breath, and decided he would "go for broke."

"I'd like to have $65,000." He reasoned that it would be several years before the small company he worked for generated enough sales to pay him $65,000.

The next day, having received the offer, he called a close friend to boast about his terrific offer. The friend, who headed an executive search firm, surprised the actuary by replying that he had made a crucial tactical error. "First of all," he said, "you should never have discussed your compensation needs so early in the game. Secondly, $65,000 is far below what you should be asking."

The executive recruiter went on to note that 80 percent of the assignments his firm fills are for increases in cash compensation of between 30 and 50 percent. He proceeded to outline a strategy for the actuary to use in subsequent negotiations with the company.

At the next meeting with the CEO, when the $65,000 figure came up, the actuary said, matter-of-factly: "Of course, $65,000 is the base, it doesn't include the bonus plan which I assume you would be offering." And he went on to list a number of other compensation objectives, drawing on the package he was receiving in his present job and the security he would be leaving behind to head a new venture that would inevitably entail some amount of risk on his part.

A bonus figure was agreed upon, at which point the actuary suggested that he and the CEO jointly establish criteria for "par performance." This, he pointed out, would enable him to know exactly what was expected of him. He also said that if he should do better than par performance, as he would expect to do, he should get a larger bonus—perhaps, he suggested, 30 percent of his base salary.

After some initial sparring, the prospective employer agreed on an additional 20 percent bonus, which would be pegged to "clearly superior performance."

By the time he finished, the actuary had negotiated a guaranteed first-year compensation package of $88,000. At the end of the first year, he in fact has earned almost $93,000.

Giving him added leverage in his bargaining was the fact that he was the only candidate being considered for the job. By making his demands ambitious, he not only assured himself of a higher income than he would otherwise have received; he also forced his new boss to take him more seriously. In addition, he may have increased his own motivation to make a success of the new venture.

Throughout your negotiations, keep your antenna up. Try to discover what other people are earning in the company at your level and above. Where do you fit in relationship to them? What kinds of benefits does the company offer? Are there three bonus plans or one? What are they called? How big are they normally? What perquisites come with executive jobs (club memberships, cars, theater tickets, tickets to sporting events, etc.)? Demonstrating your knowledge of how the company works will only increase a prospective employer's respect for your alertness and resourcefulness.

Of course, you may not want to ask for all the items on your shopping list. If you sense resistance or resentment on the interviewer's part—if he really thinks you're "asking for the moon"—you may want to back off. Be certain at all times that you "read" his reactions. Look for clues as to his comfort level. If a particular demand shows signs of making a prospective employer lose interest in you, you may want to quickly drop it from your shopping list. Or you might use it as a bargaining chip, suggesting that it's something to put on the back burner pending disposition of other elements in the negotiating package.

Nevertheless, the basic principle of negotiation—as true in salary negotiations as it is in collective bargaining—is "the more you ask for, the more you get." A corollary is that the higher your aspirations, the more you are motivated to achieve. If you're not inclined to make demands, take that lesson to heart and reevaluate your strategy.

Provide for Termination Benefits

When you're negotiating for a new position, you might think it tactless or negative to bring up the subject of "what happens if this job doesn't work out?"

On the other hand, if it should not work out, you obviously want to be protected long enough to seek another job without worrying about how you're going to pay the montly bills. Says one recruiter: "It's a difficult thing for a guy with a big mortgage to run a good campaign if he has to worry about missing a house payment. Some people are forced to jump too quickly in order to meet their financial obligations. That's not the kind of pressure you should be feeling if you want to take the time to find the best job."

But how, you may wonder, can you initiate a discussion of termination benefits with an employer who hasn't even hired you yet and whom you are trying to convince that you'll succeed on the new job? The answer lies in getting him "hooked" and then, in the course of your negotiations about compensation, casually raising the question of possible termination. One way to do it is as follows:

> One of the things I would like to get agreement on is what happens if, for whatever reason, things shouldn't work out the way you and I both want them to. I don't anticipate that happening, and I'm sure you don't either, or we wouldn't be sitting here together talking. But I think there's some merit in troubleshooting what could go wrong with the new position and seeing how we can minimize the hardships that might result.

> One idea I'd like to suggest is that my salary be protected long enough for me to get relocated in a new job if for any reason that should be necessary. I'm sure that if you were in my shoes, you'd be looking for some kind of protection. Of course, I'm not interested in a windfall, just enough to tide my family over and make sure we can still pay our bills.

Some executives ask for a year's severance if they are taking a significant risk by leaving a secure job. Others ask for 6 months' or less. One way to resolve this problem is to suggest a contingency arrangement, providing for a set period of termination pay, less if another job is found before that time.

In negotiating for termination benefits, bear in mind that many executives at the middle and higher echelons who lose their positions often go for more than 6 months before they find the right new job. Bear in mind too that when you're deeply in love, it's hard to conceive of anything going wrong. That's the time to negotiate a severance agreement, because the employer doesn't believe it will cost him anything.

Get It Now!

The chances are you'll never again be in as good a negotiating position with your new employer as you are when you stand on the threshold of joining his organization. This is the time of your greatest leverage. To capitalize on it, you must take the point of view that the benefits you don't negotiate now you may never get. Thus "Get it now!" should be the watchword for any negotiations. This refers not only to compensation but to responsibilities and timetable for advancement (on the basis of superior performance), relationships with your superiors and staff support, etc.

The most common source of disillusionment in a new job, we find, is management's failure to deliver what it promises. It may be added responsibilities, increases in compensation or stock, authority to do the job you're hired to do, or the commitment of promised resources.

Often an executive is told, "We need somebody to come in here and coordinate the different departments. We think you're the best man to do that." That kind of arrangement can work only if the CEO makes it clear to all the divisions how it's going to be. Otherwise, when they resist, as they inevitably will, the new executive gets caught short.

Another common problem occurs in highly centralized entrepreneurial companies, in which the owner-president brings in a new executive because he has decided that the time has come to delegate more authority and begin easing himself out of the picture. While many entrepreneurs have that intention, few follow through without great hardship. It often happens that as soon as the new man begins to assert himself—in ways that the owner would not have—the new man's wings are clipped.

Above all, beware of employers who tell you, "Come on in and we'll work out the details later." Once the door closes behind you, you've lost your bargaining power.

Get It in Writing

Get your boss to spell out significant elements of your agreement in a letter of understanding. It needn't be a contract. An exchange of letters in which each spells out his understanding of the job is sufficient, as long as the two understandings are in agreement. The agreement—specifying your responsibilities, performance criteria, compensation details, etc.—states the ground rules on which you will operate. There's nothing wrong with your offering to draft a letter setting forth your understanding, if he pleads lack of time or doesn't see the importance of doing so—as long as he agrees to the points that you have listed.

Such an agreement gives you something to guide you as you do your job. Equally important, if the job doesn't work out, you'll look better to a new employer for having a record of what you were promised. According to George Webb:

> From time to time, we encounter an executive who, for one reason or another, decides to join a smaller organization after having spent 10 or 15 years with a fine company like a General Electric or a General Foods. Sometimes, the new organization doesn't deliver on its promises, and the executive finds himself in a different kind of situation from the one he thought he was getting into.

Should he decide to leave, a prospective employer may incorrectly conclude that he is leaving because he couldn't hack it on his last job. If, however, he has a letter that spells out what he was promised, he can use it to support his claim that the company just didn't do what it said it was going to.

Weighing an Offer

In the final analysis, there is something more important in seeking a new job than the responsibilities, the compensation level, or any of the other factors that we have dealt with in this chapter. That is your *comfort level.*

One client of ours, an executive with a young, small electronics firm, was tempted to accept an offer with a larger, more stable company. The new job would provide responsibilities fully in keeping with his background, good prospects for advancement, and an extremely generous compensation package.

The executive, an extremely able manager, felt he had gone as far as he could in his present company and needed to "change horses." Yet as he considered the offer, he found himself troubled for reasons he could not understand. It was a question by a friendly colleague in whom he confided that brought him back to reality.

"Do you think you'll be as happy doing that as you are doing this?" the colleague asked. The more he thought about it, the more he became convinced that he would never achieve the challenge and satisfaction in the new job that he felt in the old.

As a result of that one question, and after renewed soul-searching, he decided not to take the offer, despite the benefits that he could readily see on paper. In this instance, he preferred to be happy than to be "better off."

In weighing an offer, ask yourself:

1. What "value added" do I represent? What contributions can I realistically expect to make in the new company?

2. What other options are open to me, and how do they stack up against this one?

3. What is the probability of success if I take this offer? Am I really hoping for a "long shot" (e.g., "to turn the business around") or are there reasonable prospects for success?

4. What questions and concerns remain after all the research and soul-searching I have done? How likely are these to be a serious obstacle in my performance or satisfaction?

To sum up, the keys to getting the right job and getting the job right are as follows:

1. Establish a career timetable.
2. Monitor your progress against your plan.
3. Explore your options.
4. Evaluate them against your own periodically updated objectives.
5. Develop a job-winning strategy.
6. Set your compensation sights high.
7. Avoid prematurely tipping your hand.
8. Get it now!
9. Get it in writing!
10. Examine the comfort level of the offer.

Following the steps outlined in this chapter does not guarantee that you will, in fact, land the right executive position. But it should substantially increase the likelihood that you will. In addition, it raises the prospects that, having found the right position, you will get the position right.

Chapter 3
"What's in It for Us, Dad?"
(Integrating Your Family with Your Job)

Alex Spector was ecstatic. Just when he was beginning to fear he might be stymied for life as market research vice president of a computer software company that offered no opportunity for advancement, his résumé was snapped up by a young, fast-growing competitor in another state.

He had interviewed the company and a number of others several months ago. Now here was the president of that company on the phone, saying, "Alex, sorry to be so long getting back to you. We want you as our vice president for marketing services. It's a new job that would involve pulling together market research, media buying, and other staff services. We've interviewed more than a dozen candidates, and we think you're the best man for the job. We'd like you to come in on the ground floor, help us grow, and grow with us."

It was indeed a temptation. More than a temptation, it was the opportunity of a lifetime, Alex thought. The money was good, the benefits included a generous stock option plan. And, at age 48, there might not be many future opportunities for him if he didn't grab this one. Besides, he reasoned, the family would be better leaving the congestion of northern New Jersey for a medium-size New England town with lots of open space.

He told the president he would get back to him with an answer within 24 hours. As far as he was concerned, the answer was yes. But he had not reckoned on the reactions of Becky, his wife, and the couple's three children: Ken, 15, Lucy, 14, and Julie, 7.

When Alex broke the news at dinner that night, Ken was the first to register his feelings.

"Why can't we stay here?" he asked. "Who wants to live out in the sticks?" Chimed in Lucy: "What about us? We don't know anybody there." And Julie burst into tears at the news, sobbing: "Don't make us move, Daddy. This is our home."

Even Becky had misgivings. "I know it's a good thing for you, Alex," she said, trying to appear calm. "But for the kids and me, it means starting all over again."

This scene is repeated, with variations, in thousands of American households every year. Changing jobs—and particularly changing job locations—inevitably creates tensions within families. Some problems are unavoidable. But many can be overcome or minimized by proper foresight and sensitivity. The key to successful relocation lies in anticipating the problems and jointly working with the family to resolve them in an atmosphere in which the family breadwinner recognizes not only the benefits but also the sacrifices that may result from relocation.

In this chapter, we will outline the major problems that confront the wives and children of mobile executives and suggest techniques for successfully coping with them. In working through your own relocation challenges, bear in mind that you must bring into balance both your own ambitions and the well-being of your family to operate at peak effectiveness in a new job. You must also consider, of course, the likely impact on your career if your company asks you to transfer and you reject the offer.

Interviews with corporate wives and the experiences of our own clients suggest there are four stages to a family's successful relocation: accepting the change, phasing out current activities and obligations, making the transition, and getting reestablished. Each stage presents distinct challenges, and since the challenges typically fall squarely on the shoulders of the wife, it is with her perspective that we shall begin.

The Wife

Many executives can't understand their family's misgivings when asked to move. When they encounter resistance they get defensive. One executive recalls thinking: "Here I am busting my ass day in and day out for them, and nobody appreciates it. They pay lip service to wanting things to be better for us but when the chips are down, they bury their heads in the sand and say, 'let's not go.'"

Often, however, what an executive may interpret as rejection of a move is really just an expression of fear of the unknown. Says the charming and very supportive wife of the president of a large electronics company: "Everytime we move, there's always a major upheaval in the family's life."

This wife and others we spoke with describe the distress they feel at the prospect of being separated from friends, activities, and sometimes jobs that have been a source of satisfaction. "As a music teacher and choral director," says one wife, "I knew that wherever we went, I'd find my talents could be used to advantage. But the emotional investment I had made in my former church and school would be lost. I remember wondering: 'Could it ever be as good somewhere else?' Luckily for me it was, but I really had to work at it."

It's commonly believed that executives who move around a lot have families who learn to adjust to moving. In fact, it rarely works out that way. A wife who has gone through eight major moves in less than 25 years to widely varying locations of the country makes this observation: "After the fourth move, people say to me, 'Well, you're used to it. It must get easier each time you move.' Actually, it doesn't, it gets harder and you almost get numb to it. I sort of look upon living here now as if I'm on a long stay. I don't really feel like this is my home and I've been here almost 4 years—longer than we ever spent anywhere else."

Considering the intensity with which corporate wives talk of their misgivings about moving, it is surprising that more of them don't openly object to their husband's first suggestion of a possible new location, or at least voice some loud concern about a move. Many do, of course. More than one "marriage made in heaven" has foundered on the rocks of a job change which the wife decided not to make.

But in many instances, it is clear that the family will benefit from the shift—for example, if the family circumstances will be substantially improved, if they're moving from an undesirable location to a desirable one, if they're moving to an area where they have friends or if they have no strong ties to the area they're leaving.

Most of the corporate moves within our experience, however, do involve stresses and strains on family relationships. At best, these strains cause one or more family members anxiety, heartache, and a few tears. At worst, they may indeed require that one partner or the other decide which is more important, the family or the new job.

Increasingly, corporations find that executives are balking at new assignments that may require moving their families. A leading moving company recently estimated that of the 200,000 to 300,000 executives who would be asked to move in any given year, nearly half would decline the assignment. A decade ago, the firm observed, the refusal rate was no more than 10 percent. Accordingly, corporate recruiters complain that hiring talented people is now more difficult than it was then as executives become more reluctant to trade the known for the unknown.

To some extent, changes in life values account for the resistance to relocating. People simply won't go as far as they once would—literally—to climb the career ladder or increase their income. Changes in lifestyles are an important factor too. As more women begin pursuing their own careers, they are less willing to subordinate their aspirations to those of their husbands.

One corporate husband learned the lesson the hard way. He lost his job in a Washington, D.C., suburb, and after weeks of pounding the pavement, obtained a similar job at higher salary in New York City. His wife, who held down a job that was as important to her as her husband's was to him, refused to move. "Would he want to move if I were the one with an offer in New York?" she reasoned. "Hell, no. We each have our careers. It's a fact of life he has to recognize."

Rather than go their separate ways—or live in different cities and meet on weekends (as many young couples are doing)—the husband stayed put and eventually obtained work nearer home.

With more women entering the work force each year, the attitude of this career woman may become increasingly common. Today, however, most wives still elect to "grin and bear" a corporate move in the interests of their husband's advancement.

"You have to suffer if you care about your husband's career," says the wife of one mobile executive. "So you face a dilemma: You don't want to move, though that would make him happy. And you don't want him to be unhappy on his job because you refused to move. It's a frustration, and sometimes it comes down to a choice between staying even if it means separation or divorce, or going and being miserable for a while. I've always come down on the side of, 'Hey, I don't want to feel responsible for holding up his career,' so I go. But it takes more effort on my part each time."

The problems do not, of course, end with a family's accepting the need to relocate. In many ways, that's when they just begin for the wife. Though circumstances vary, often the responsibility for negotiating and supervising the move rests with her. She has to line up a buyer or a realtor to sell the house, to arrange for a mover, to organize the packing, to find a new house in a new and strange community with very little time to look.

In addition, she must often hire workmen, register the children in new schools, locate competent doctors and dentists, and cope with the constant stream of details, interruptions, mishaps, worries, and frustrations that attend a major move. All the while, her husband may be demanding a higher measure of emotional support to cope with the growing pains of his new job.

The wife's burden may be heavier if, as frequently happens, her husband assumes his new post before the family actually relocates. Even if the job and family moves are made simultaneously, however, executives' wives complain they find themselves competing for his attention—at a distinct disadvantage.

One wife observes: "When you're going to a new location is frequently the time that the family needs the husband's emotional support and attention the most. But this is also a time when the demands of his job are tremendous. Later on, when he's settled into his job, he will have more time for his family. Yet the crucial time when they first move—that's when they need him most and when he is least available."

"During this transition period," says another woman, "the family often begins to feel that 'Dad's work comes first and his family second,' and that's very demoralizing. A wife may begin to wonder why she's hanging in there at all. I have one friend who served notice on her husband after their last move, when she found him so distracted by his new job: 'That's it. I'm not moving again. The next time you go, you go alone.'"

Adjusting to a new community brings a different set of problems for an executive's wife. "It takes 2 full years before you really feel like you belong," says one wife and mother who has moved frequently. "I could draw a curve. The first year, you go out and join everything and do everything you can to become involved in a new community. And by the end of the second year, if you're fortunate to have joined some groups in which you function well, you start feeling part of things. Husbands have trouble realizing how hard it is. My husband's moves have almost all been within the same company, so he's moving within a context of people and associations that are familiar to him. But I am not and the children are not. For us, it's back to square one every time."

One woman comments on the differences between moving as a military family and moving as an executive's family.

"The military has built up a support system to help people who move a lot." she observes. "There are the officers' wives clubs. I have a friend whose husband is in the Navy, and she performs very important services for the wives of other men when they are at sea for 6 months at a time. A woman always has a choice of not becoming part of these groups, but at least it's there. Somebody is saying, 'Welcome, we know how you must feel, come cry on my shoulder, and I'll tell you where to shop and where the best bargains are, and who's a good doctor.'"

"But there's none of that when you're a corporate wife. Just move in and you're on your own!"

Moreover, many communities seem to practice a kind of subtle discrimination toward mobile families, who may be "here today, but gone tomorrow." Says a wife who has successfully integrated her family into several communities over the years—but not in the old, established town to which she and her husband moved 4 years ago:

"I do a lot of things in the community and have friends now because I get out and get involved. I play tennis, golf, am active in my church. But I still don't feel part of the community. This community belongs to people who've been here 10 or 20 years, not fly-by-nights who will be gone in 2 or 3 years."

The problems of assimilation can be intensified if the wife is pregnant or has one or more infants at the time of the move. The enforced reduction in her mobility is likely to postpone opportunities for meaningful involvement in activities outside the home. On the other hand, when her children become involved in school (even nursery school or day care), she may find herself suddenly presented with new opportunities for forming friendships with other women.

Even so, in retrospect, some wives insist that the benefits of frequent moves outweigh the frustrations inevitably associated with them. "There's no way we could have seen so much of the country and even the world if we hadn't been willing to get up and go," says one woman. "And everywhere we've gone, we've made some friends."

"I'd hate to think," she adds, "that if we hadn't lived in Texas, I wouldn't know the people there that mean so much to me. When you stay in one place, you only have time for a few friends who really matter to you. But when you move around a lot as we have, you have two or three friends in each place that really matter. It makes you feel very wealthy. Through the years, we stay in touch. It's what relieves the pain of moving."

The Children

School-age children are apt to share the same concerns as their mothers in contemplating a move. They find it equally wrenching to say goodbye to friends and neighbors, to part with cherished possessions. One family recalls its 7-year-old daughter standing in her empty bedroom as the movers locked the family's belongings in the van. She was staring out the window into the backyard, saying: "Goodbye swing set, goodbye birdies, goodbye garden, goodbye fence. . . ."

Some families advise sending the children on ahead if at all possible before the house is "taken apart." Explains one mother who had her children flown up to stay with grandparents in the city to which the family was moving: "I wanted their last mental picture of the house to be of its family memories rather than of its emptiness."

Withdrawing or phasing out activities is especially difficult for children, and it can be even more so if others decide to phase *them* out. "One thing our older children found," one mother reports, "is that as soon as they announced they were moving, their relationship with their peers changed. They weren't invited to as many parties. People started eliminating them from their lives." Another mother tells of her children pleading with her, upon being informed of an impending move: "Please, Mom, don't tell anybody we're going until the last minute."

Most of the families we talked with find that the tensions of readjustment are considerably eased if the mother takes a positive attitude toward the move. Even so, the transition is usually easier for children of preschool or elementary school age than for youngsters in junior or senior high school.

The problems associated with transplanting adolescents can take on critical proportions. One wife who had moved enough times to draw comparisons among all her children at the same ages confided:

"When the children were young and we were under 35 or 40, moving offered a chance to grow and the children would quickly find friends and become part of the new community. When they entered junior high, the moves began to become a bad experience. By then, it's important for a youngster to feel part of a group. If you are an outsider at that age, it's hard to break down the walls. They're too young to realize that it's not them as *persons* that a group of kids may be objecting to; it's just the fact that they weren't part of the group when it was formed. People that age can be awfully cliquey."

By the time youngsters are in high school, some mothers counsel it is almost impossible to make a smooth adjustment—so well established are the friendships and so defensive the prevailing teenage view toward outsiders. "I would never again relocate when I had kids who are teenagers," one mother says flatly.

A mother of four—two in high school and two in grade school—reports:

"When they are young and in the first grade, they can make a very successful adjustment. But in high school, they sit alone at lunch and they ride on the bus and no one sits beside them. They're just out of it. They may miss National Honor Society. They miss all the cumulative honors that they would normally get in their junior or senior years if they stayed in the same school for 3 or 4 years."

To avoid these problems, some families postpone moving until their youngsters have finished high school, and others seek out a friend or relative in the old community with whom the youngster can live until his or her high school years are completed. Often, however, no alternative is completely satisfactory.

One mother lamented that her daughter, who had been "a super little girl" in her old community, suddenly fell in with "a bad group of kids" in her new school and got into a series of battles with school and local authorities after moving at age 13. Often, the stresses of an unwelcome move, coupled with a desire to be popular, prompt some youngsters to act in negative ways in order to call attention to themselves.

For all these problems, however, youngsters—particularly those who have never moved before or who find their own situation unpleasant—look on moving as an exciting adventure. Many youngsters, even teenagers, are more resilient than their parents give them credit for and can roll with the punches. They make new friends easily, adjust to a new environment (and even a new accent) naturally, and become deeply involved in wholesome activities.

One 13-year-old, who had always disdained "rah-rah" activities in her old school, found that the key to popularity in her new community was to be a cheerleader. She shed her dirty jeans and sweatshirt for a blue-and-white cheerleader's outfit and become one of the most "gung-ho" girls in school. After a year of saving her babysitting money, she spent Christmas vacation with a friend in her old community. Upon her return she told her parents, "The kids back there are just not as interesting anymore."

Minimizing Relocation Problems

When faced with a decision about whether or not to accept a job that requires relocating your family, here is a list of things *not* to do:

- *Don't* make a decision—either way—without consulting at least your wife and preferably your wife and children.

- *Don't* assume that because the job is right for you, it is therefore right for your family. *Your* ambitions and *their* needs may not be identical— or even closely related.

- *Don't* discount their misgivings and concerns on the theory that they're not important or that "everything will work out for the best." Their feelings are important to the family's well-being and probably to your own ability to function at optimum effectiveness in the new job.

Here is a list of things to *do:*

- *Do* take the family into your confidence before you make a decision. Smoke out the feelings of each member as to what's good and what's bad about a possible change.

- *Do* recognize—and let your wife know you recognize—that the shift may require more sacrifices from her than from anyone else. Expecting her to be grateful or to overlook the problems because of the "larger benefits to be derived" is shortsighted and could cause lasting, and justifiable, resentment. This is especially true if a large share of the burden for arranging the move and settling into your new home will fall on her shoulders.

- *Do* spend time with your wife evaluating the offer from the family's point of view as well as your own. Also spend some time troubleshooting "what could go wrong" with plans for a smooth family transition and try to prevent and minimize the problems. Many of the experiences related in this chapter may help you anticipate problems and make plans accordingly.

Whether you want to make accepting or rejecting a tempting job offer your unilateral decision, or a family decision, is up to you. If you want to make it yourself, however, and want them to be happy with it, you must make clear "what's in it for the family" as well as for yourself.

One client of ours clearly outlined the pluses and minuses of a job offer to his wife and children and recorded the thinking of each member of the family on a notepad. He then made his decision to take the job in a distant city, went back to the family and explained why he had made the decision, and gave each member an opportunity to veto the move.

After an initial period of excitement, his wife and two children each began to have doubts about the benefits of the change. So he initiated what he calls "Stop and Talk Sessions," at which any member could call for a family meeting to discuss specific concerns. He also gave each member an opportunity to suggest criteria that should be used in deciding what community to live in and what to look for in a house.

Other steps suggested by executives and their wives to ease the transition include:

- Making plans to visit—or to receive visits from—friends in the old community.

- Resuming activities in the new community that have been an important source of satisfaction in the old.

- Accepting the fact that you may have to take the initiative to make new friends rather than wait for neighbors or business associates to seek you out.

- Joining groups that will facilitate making new friends. Churches, youth groups, civic activities, YMCA, Boy and Girl Scouts, and similar organizations can ease assimilation in a new community.

- Using business perks to the family's advantage—trying to include your wife and/or children in business travel plans occasionally, getting company passes to sports events for them, asking their advice about business decisions, or seeking their candid assessment of colleagues and customers.

- Setting aside time—no matter how busy you are in your new job—to attend to family obligations and concerns. One corporate wife who has moved frequently has nothing but praise for her husband's ability to juggle his time between job and family. "One reason I think our kids have been willing to move so much," she says, "is that he is a super Dad. No matter how busy he is, he finds time to spend with them. If he's on the road, he calls them. If they've had a tough exam, or been in a school play, he remembers and asks them about it. It's all a matter of caring and managing your priorities in a way that shows that you care."

No matter how you may rationalize it, *moving* is no fun. It's an aggravating and exhausting nuisance. But *the act of moving* can serve to bring a family closer together, if you approach it with sensitivity and patience.

"Separation, moving many times, they are really big problems," says the wife of one corporate "gypsy." "But if you're doing it together, and there is 'togetherness' within the family, it makes it all bearable. I just can't imagine doing it any other way."

Chapter 4
"What Should I Do First?"
(Strategizing Your Own Successful Beginning)

An executive recruiter of my acquaintance used to be continually asked by clients for whom he found jobs, "How should I handle myself on my first day of work?"

His advice consisted of two words: "Be yourself." This advice did little to reassure his clients. Executives, like anybody else, are capable of conducting themselves in a variety of ways, depending on the challenges they face and the climate of the company.

All new executives share a common mission—to begin building a record, and a reputation, as an effective leader—but how they conduct themselves to fulfill that mission depends on their specific objectives. A senior executive called in to bail out a company threatened with bankruptcy should obviously conduct himself very differently from one moving up a notch in an organization that is experiencing record sales and profits.

To clarify your 30-day objectives, ask yourself, "What do I want to *achieve, preserve,* and *avoid* as problems during my first month?"

Here's a sample list of such objectives, which may be helpful to you during your "settling in" period. It is not all-inclusive; yours may vary depending on the specific challenges you face.

During my first 30 days, I want to:

Achieve: **1.** A feeling by my boss, the senior management team, key board members, and key publics that I am the right choice—that I have the qualities this organization needs at this time

        2. A feeling by my management team that they want to work with me and for me

        3. An atmosphere in which everyone is motivated—and expected—to work at his fullest potential

4. An atmosphere that encourages ideas, initiative, and constructive criticism

5. Some tentative judgments about the capabilities, strengths, and weaknesses of my management team

6. An understanding of the current management process:
  a. How decisions are made
  b. Key decision points and who, in actuality, is involved in what kinds of decisions
  c. The strengths and weaknesses of this process

7. Some tentative judgments about the key issues and opportunities facing the organization

8. An understanding of the culture, expectations, myths, and sacred cows of the organization

9. Prompt and effective resolution of immediate issues requiring my personal approval

Preserve: **10.** Good relationships with my boss, key board members, the management team, and the key publics

11. My integrity and that of each member of the management team

12. (As appropriate) A feeling of continuity and evolutionary change rather than revolution

13. Ongoing programs and commitments

14. A commitment by my management team to doing what's best for the organization

Avoid: **15.** Giving managers cause to feel insecure or discouraged

16. Undermining the authority of managers (by, for example, "end-running" them to deal directly with their subordinates without their understanding and permission)

17. Causing a feeling of apathy or complacency by my managers and their staffs

18. Making decisions without first seeking the best management team input I can obtain to ascertain the facts

19. Wasted time and "wheel spinning"

The following objectives—or your variations of them—should prove helpful in meeting the common challenges that most senior executives face during their first month:

1. Setting the right climate

2. Establishing the right relationships:
  a. With the CEO and the board
  b. With your management team

c. With other publics you must deal with—employees, customers, trade, financial people and investment community, public officials, the press, etc.

3. Learning the ropes: identifying what's really going on *in* the organization and in crucial areas *external* to the company which most impact it (i.e., the marketplace, government legislation, etc.)

4. Dealing effectively with any issues requiring your urgent attention

5. Establishing a set of tentative priorities and budgeting your time

Let's look closer at each of these challenges to see how they can best be satisfied.

Setting the Right Climate

Your list of objectives (achieve/preserve/avoids) will help you determine and structure the kind of climate you want to establish. What remains is for you to communicate to the organization the climate and to show by your words and actions that you believe in it.

Most new senior executives will want to have a meeting with their key managers in the first week. Many of our clients hold a "working breakfast" at which they set forth their management principles and a provisional 30-day agenda. In addition, it is advisable to get people thinking about ways to improve the organization's effectiveness (moving in the right direction) and efficiency (getting there).

One of our clients made the following points with his management group on Monday morning of his second week, before entering into a discussion of specific agenda items:

1. "My job is to create an atmosphere in which each of you can do your jobs better."

2. "No one should regard me as a fount of wisdom; on the contrary, I've got a lot to learn from you. I am ready to begin the learning process today!"

3. "I look forward to meeting with each of you individually to get to know you better: your concerns, objectives, ideas, etc."

4. "I want you to continue moving ahead with your major programs but put yourself on my calendar to review them with me as soon as possible, so that I can better understand your operation."

5. "I will want a detailed briefing on *new* and proposed programs or projects so that I can better understand their implications before deciding whether or not to move ahead with them."

6. "You will find that I deal straightforwardly with you and everyone else. I expect the same from you. I want to know anything significant that's bothering you about the job, and I won't make any pretense about hiding what's on my mind."

7. "I operate on the principle that everyone is trustworthy and competent unless proven otherwise. While I can't guarantee that 6 months from today the composition of this management team will be identical, I will operate on the assumption that each of you belongs on it unless demonstrated otherwise."

8. "Any lack of integrity will be dealt with severely."

9. "I want you to participate fully in making improvements in the company, not only in terms of *what* we do but *how* we do it (the managing process). Accordingly, I will be asking each of you to consider what would help you do your own job better; what I should be doing to facilitate your success; and how the company can serve its major constituents (our customers, employees, etc.) better and more profitably."

This particular client had been parachuted in from another company to head a new group composed of several businesses that had formerly been autonomous. He went on to summarize his understanding of why the organizational change was made and to emphasize that it was now a fact of life and they must accept it. Thus, their challenge now was to identify and realize the potential synergies of the new group:

What are these potential synergies? I want you, this group, to develop them. Here are some ideas to start your thinking.

We all sell to the housewares trade, separately. We all advertise our products, separately. We all focus on consumers at home, separately. We all have separate administrative staffs. In all these areas, I want you to think about ways that we can pool our resources, cut costs, and increase our impact.

Here is something else to think about too. My impression is that the present organizational structure is built around distribution channels, which represent *our* needs, rather than around family eating habits, which represent *consumer* needs. If this is so, do we know what's really happening out there in the marketplace, or are we just producing to meet our internally generated goals, hoping it reflects marketplace reality?

At this point, he threw the discussion open for questions and comments. Several offered their ideas.

He then described his key objectives for the next 60 days:

1. To reach agreement on the issues that now exist
2. To crystallize our business objectives and gain approval of them by the senior management committee
3. To move quickly to implement the group management concept

4. To ensure that we all operate on the same wavelength

5. To achieve whatever improvements are necessary in working with corporate staff and other line operations

He again called for observations or questions. But this time, he confessed he wanted to take a quick pulse reading. "How do you feel about our discussion? What do you think we've accomplished or not accomplished here today? Has it been worthwhile?" he asked.

Typical comments were: "It's been more open than I expected"; "I didn't know what to expect but now I have a better feel for things"; and "I'm looking forward to reviewing my organization's programs with you and working together."

What had the meeting really accomplished? It had given the men a better feel for the new boss—what he wanted and how he operated. It had given him an initial reading on them. It had established that while he wanted them on his team, they would have to earn their right to remain there. And he had challenged them to help make the group a reality and a success by contributing their ideas.

There was a symbolic aspect to the breakfast meeting as well. The executive had called the meeting for 7:00 A.M. and adjourned it promptly at 8:00—the start of the company's normal business day. Before adjourning, he suggested they hold a series of 7:00 A.M. Monday breakfast meetings "to get to know one another better and not interfere with your scheduled work." By calling these meetings before working hours, he was subtly suggesting that he expected his managers to be available to meet early and perhaps to work late too—as indeed he does.

A magazine editor who set a very positive climate at his initial meeting with his staff did so by resorting to mankind's oldest icebreaker—humor. Taking over at a time when the publication was experiencing financial difficulties, he had himself introduced by his predecessor, who was being "kicked upstairs" to the publishing company's headquarters. The new executive thanked everyone for coming, and then said in as serious a tone as he could summon up, "I hope you people realize just what an awful fix we're in."

Instantly, faces fell as the staff worried that the straits might be even worse than they had been led to believe. The new editor paused for a moment to let his thought sink in. The shudder that went around the room was almost audible. Then, the executive added the kicker.

"What I'm referring to, of course, is the fact that we're sending to company headquarters the one man who knows all our secrets. We've been left alone all these years principally because no one at headquarters knew what it is that we do or how we do it. And naturally we have perpetuated this myth by reminding them at every opportunity just how difficult and thankless our jobs are. Now we have a man who knows better who's going to headquarters. A greater threat no organization on earth ever faced than a man going to company headquarters who understands its operation. God help us in the years ahead!"

The general laughter that followed this remark suggested that the new chief had won the group to his side. He went on to talk about the respect he'd always had for the competence of the staff and to say that he was greatly looking forward to working with them and jointly developing a strategy to overcome the very real problems that faced the organization.

The new head of a major division of a consumer goods company created a very different climate in his first 30 days. Without so much as even calling a staff meeting, he fired half the senior management group and reorganized the company the first day of his job, leaving a trail of blood in his wake. Within 2 weeks, he had introduced a major cost-reduction program and was well into an evaluation of the company's strategic posture in the marketplace.

His decisiveness won immediate plaudits with the CEO. Nonetheless, we believe this is a very high-risk strategy, to be avoided in all but the most extreme circumstances.

For one thing, in determining who to keep and to fire his first day on the job, this executive had to make judgments on the basis of what he'd heard, read, and seen as a competitor rather than from his own observations of how people performed given the constraints of the company environment. "Hell," said one corporate cynic, "for all he knows, he fired the wrong half."

Moreover, by acting precipitously, he risked demoralizing the people who remained and may have made it more difficult to win their cooperation and participation. In making changes before ascertaining the facts for himself, he was not planning with people but rather, in the case of some, plotting against them.

Establishing the Right Relationships

Your Relations with the CEO

There are two elements to establishing a good relationship with the CEO (or your superior, if you're hired at a level below direct reporting to the CEO): substance and style.

As to *substance:*

- What does he expect you to accomplish during what period of time?
- Why does he consider these crucial to the viability and growth of the company?
- What does he consider to be your "vital few" (or "vital many!" priorities?

- How is he going to measure your performance?
- Who are the people he believes should be involved in discussions of which issues?
- What decisions does he want to make himself?
- On which does he want you to get his input before you make them?
- What kinds of meetings does he himself want to attend or send a representative to? Receive feedback on?

As to *style:*

- What are the "dos and don'ts" to which you are expected to conform? (For example, are there certain customers you are expected to give personal attention to?)
- What kinds of written reports does he want to see, with what frequency? Does he expect them to be organized following a certain format?
- How often does he want to see you?
- Does he want to know how to reach you day and night?
- Would he like you to drop in on him occasionally or would he consider that an intrusion?

If you should find yourself in conflict with his method of dealing with issues or his list of priorities for you during your first month, try to ascertain *why* he feels as he does and marshal the facts that lead you to believe otherwise. Then approach him in a friendly way and mention that you're concerned about a possible difference of viewpoint.

If you feel strongly enough that your way is better, you might consider asking if he would be amenable to the suggestion that "for X period of time [concerning an issue or a way of working together], we try it this way and see if it works out. If not, I'll gladly go back to the other method."

You must strike a balance between keeping your superior informed of all important decisions (giving him a chance to provide input to them *before* they're finalized) and not burdening him anymore than necessary. How this balance is struck depends, of course, on the individual situation between the CEO and the new senior executive, and on your respective managing styles.

Your Relations with the Board of Directors

If you are a new CEO or COO, your effectiveness depends on many factors, but none is more important than the support you'll need to receive from the board of directors. Lower-level senior executives only occasionally meet with the board and then, of course, primarily to make recommendations, give updates, or outline plans. Whether your tenure depends on maintaining the support of your boss or the board of directors, however, don't expect a blank check from your superiors when you accept your assignment—even if you've been told you'll have virtual carte blanche to do what you deem best.

The executive vice president of a chemical company was told he had "complete authority to decide what to do on matters of organization and people." Following his own judgment, he elected to make no personnel changes initially, preferring to get to know each member of the team individually. It didn't even take 1 month to realize that his CEO wanted, first and foremost, "action" (the *kind* of action was secondary). Our client successfully resisted the pressure by stressing to the CEO the adverse consequences on organizational morale and marketplace momentum of taking action without giving each manager a fair opportunity to demonstrate his abilities.

A young executive who was made vice president of marketing and production of an important steel company suddenly found himself with more carte blanche than he knew what to do with. The man who was both chairman and president was too busy involving himself in government relations and attending international conferences to have an active interest in the internal workings of the company. So it was left to our client to oversee corporate operations.

This executive's situation, however, was exceptional. Generally, new executives find that in practice they have less authority than they had been led to believe they would have in their new assignment.

Though newly appointed senior executives might naturally conclude that their appointment represents a vote of confidence in themselves, our experience suggests that often they are chosen because they represent the best compromise among the conflicting demands of those board members or other senior executives who participated in the selection process. Accordingly, it is essential to arrive at a clear understanding with your boss (*before* you begin your new job, if possible) as to what your responsibilities and authority will be, and to what extent your powers might be circumscribed by relationships of the CEO, COO, or key board members with your subordinates. (Will they, for example, deal *through* you or seek to go *around* you to deal directly with certain of your managers?)

The sooner you translate the verbal understandings you have about roles and relationships, scope of authority, and appropriate channels of communication into a written summary modus operandi, the better you are able to judge how much room to maneuver you really have.

Your Relations with Your Management Team

No less important than establishing good relations with the CEO and the board is the necessity to get your management team on your wavelength. Sometimes, managers will welcome the appointment of a new chief, feeling

that change has been long overdue. More often, however, the newly appointed senior executive faces a variety of anxieties on the part of his managers, who don't know what to expect or how secure their jobs are.

Of only two things can you be sure in your new situation: Your managers
are eager to know what your appointment means to them in terms of their
own responsibilities, futures, and ways of doing business; and they will be
looking for ways to impress you with their own competency and programs.

Although this uncertainty and anxiety is apt to be greater when a new
senior executive is brought into an organization from the outside, the executive promoted from within faces problems of a similar nature, though of
a different order of magnitude. He must take care lest his early action
signals to the organization that (1) "We can relax now, he's one of us.
Good old Joe will protect us." Or (2) "My God, whatever got into him?
He's forgotten where he came from. The power's gone to his head."

On the premise that it is better to show confidence in people and hold
out high expectations for them (the hallmarks of a developmental style of
management) than it is to give them the feeling you don't trust them
or are looking over their shoulders (a reductive style of management),
we recommend that you try to make your subordinates feel they are key
members of your team. This gives them a sense of participation in forming your programs and policies—and a stake in your own success as the
new leader. It also begins to give you insight into their thinking and competence.

Unless you face problems so serious that immediate drastic surgery is
required, you might consider telling your team that, to the maximum extent
possible, you will make no changes or major decisions until you're confident
you understand the situation well enough to make the best decision, and
that, in any event, you will try to test any proposed course of action with
those most concerned to obtain their reactions. Nothing unsettles a management team more than a new "numero uno" who immediately begins making
changes without first ascertaining the facts.

Bostonians, whose pride in their ancient transit system is tempered by
a knowledge of its undependability, learned in 1978 what happens when
a new Transit Authority chairman makes changes before he's completely
mastered the job. The chairman retired more than 50 veteran officials within
little more than a year, filling the top slots with his own people. The system
ran with its accustomed mixture of efficiency and breakdowns until January
20, 1978, when it became paralyzed for days following a storm which
heaped almost 2 feet of snow on the area within 24 hours (and this was
nothing compared with the 3 to 4 feet of snow that fell 2 weeks later during
the infamous "Blizzard of '78" which shut down the entire city for 6 days!).

While some Bostonians sympathized with the Transit Authority, others
noted that the system had continued to run despite similar snowstorms in
1940 and 1969. What was the difference this time?

According to other transit watchers, the secret to keeping the system operating in heavy snow is to make the trains run with greater frequency than under normal conditions. In effect, the trains then operate as both passenger-carrying vehicles and track-clearing plows. But in 1978, the veterans who understood this double-duty role had either voluntarily or forcibly been retired.

Unlike the transit boss who put the old-timers out to pasture, the new president of a multinational corporation decided that he needed to keep his organization's long-termers on board. "No one," he told me, "can match their knowledge. Besides, what could be worse than for me to push some of these people into the arms of our competitors?" But he knew that several of these longtime managers had been slacking off. "They're pretty much coasting now, resting on their laurels," an aide told him. "Frankly, I think they need a good kick in the ass."

The client gave them what we call the "kick and confidence" treatment, telling them he would make no organizational or management changes until each had had an opportunity to demonstrate what he could do, but letting them know in no uncertain terms what was expected of them.

"Don't worry about having all the right answers," he said at an early staff meeting. "Just think about what you're committed to achieve and why, what resources you need to do the job. Give me a good solid plan, well troubleshot for holes, and once you and I agree to it, it's up to you to make the right things happen. If you do, we'll have no problems."

In addition to dealing with your staff as a group, you should, of course, spend time with each of your key people individually and *in confidence*. Try to find out what "bugs" them, how you can be a better resource to them, what are their career aspirations, and what ideas they have to make the organization more effective.

At these meetings, you should seek to establish an authentic one-on-one relationship with each of your senior people—to make them not only respect you but want to work for you. In doing so, you can begin laying a foundation for mutual confidence and high motivation that characterizes effective organizations.

At such meetings, be careful to avoid expressing opinions that you don't want others to know about. Rumor mills churn constantly when a new man comes on board. Be careful not to supply the grist that keeps them turning.

Your Relations with Key Publics—Customers, Vendors, Trade, Financial People, Public Officials, the Press

Obviously there is a limit to how many places the new executive can visit in his first 30 days. Your name will have circulated to these various publics before your first month has elapsed and you should give the impression—either by beginning a round of visits, phone calls, or letters—that you are anxious to meet all these key people and tap their insights.

Attending a trade meeting might be a good way to begin—less for what you will learn substantively (unless you don't know the industry) than for the opportunity it affords you to meet important customers and prospects, to get a feel for how the company presents itself vis-à-vis the competition and what people think of it, and to ask a few thoughtful questions. Before investing time at such a meeting, however, you should ask yourself what you want to *achieve, preserve,* and *avoid* by your attendance, and then tailor your participation accordingly.

It is also important to troubleshoot "What could go wrong?" at such a meeting and take action to prevent it from happening. One of the obvious risks in attending such an affair before you have mastered your challenges is that you may say the wrong thing—and not even realize it!

A few years ago, a man proposed for a new Cabinet post, with little experience in Washington, was appearing before a Senate committee considering his nomination. Wanting to display a spirit of cooperation with Congress, he waxed eloquent on his belief in keeping Congress fully informed of his activities and plans. One shrewd senator asked whether, in view of his belief in keeping Congress informed, he would be willing to submit his Department's budget to Congress at the same time he submitted it to the White House. That way, the senator explained, Congress would have the benefit of knowing what the Department really wanted, before administration budgeteers could make their own adjustments in line with the President's priorities.

Replied the nominee: "Why, of course. You should have the benefit of knowing what we feel we need to do the job."

It was the wrong answer, for though it made sense in the context of the hearing, the White House and Congress have been fighting for years over that very issue; only the candidate didn't know it.

Five minutes after pledging his cooperation, he was summoned to the phone and the chairman called a short recess. When the hearing reconvened, the hopeful Cabinet officer sheepishly explained that he had given a mistaken impression. He would, of course, cooperate with Congress in defending the administration's budget request for his Department, but, he added, presentation of the budget to Congress was, "of course," a right reserved for the White House, not the individual departments. (He later confided that a call from the White House had prompted his "clarification.")

The lesson is that it is well to be briefed on the likely "hot buttons" of any group before which a new executive is to appear. We suggest to our clients a game called "What Could Go Wrong?" Many of them spend time "dry running" with us to explore the possible adverse effects of such a visit (usually more numerous than they anticipated) and to take preventive actions accordingly.

Learning the Ropes: Identifying What's Really Going On *in* the Organization and *to* the Organization

If you have researched the company and the job before joining it, as suggested in an earlier chapter, you have a head start in learning the ropes.

But once you've joined, you may find yourself with a very different challenge. While you'll have access to information you could not have obtained from the outside, you may find that people are more fearful of leveling with you, since you are in a position to influence the course of events—and perhaps their futures as well. If it is true, as former U.S. Attorney General Elliott Richardson once said, that "where you stand depends on where you sit" (i.e., everyone in the organization has his own *perspective*), it is also true that everyone in an organization has his own objectives.

How do you get at the *unvarnished* truth? There are several possibilities:

1. In your talks with people around the organization, probe your staff, your peers, and your contacts in other parts of the organization for their "feel" for the organization's problems and concerns. Doing this will test both your ability to put people at ease and your resourcefulness as an interviewer.

   However, this can also be tremendously time-consuming. Moreover, you'll have no way of knowing if people are indeed leveling with you.

2. You can detail people on your staff to do this, or establish a task force, or call in a management consultant to seek out the information.

3. You can supplement either 1 or 2 with visits to suppliers, customers, competitors, and trade representatives whom you mine for information and perspective on your own company's needs.

4. You can hire an outside resource skilled in conducting the kind of confidential interviews both inside the organization and outside that can give you a 360-degree look at your company: its strengths, its weaknesses, the issues and opportunities it faces, the myths, holy cows, shibboleths; the way decisions are *really* made and problems really solved (or left unsolved); and the hopes, ambitions, and ideas of the people who know it best.

At the risk of seeming to toot our own horns (since we provide such a service), use of an outside resource to gain this perspective can save extensive time and effort on your part. It also sends a signal to all concerned that you are open to new ideas and anxious to find ways to better serve customer needs.

A food industry executive known for his inexhaustible energy and intense curiosity made it a point to visit 140 supermarkets around the country in his *first 6 weeks* on the job. He began checking with the marketplace what people within the company had told him. His conclusion? "It must be years since most of my managers have seen the inside of a supermarket!" His checks convinced him of the high sales potential of foods that appeal to dieters and working women, and he proceeded to explore ways of revamping his company's product portfolio.

A textile company executive, while still new to his job, visited 15 executives of six retail chains to get a better grasp of his new employer's products, promotion techniques, and distribution practices. His findings, embodied in a 10-page report submitted to the CEO, included a number of recommended improvements in each of these areas.

Here is a sample list of questions the new senior executive of a consumer company might develop to focus his information-gathering efforts during his first few weeks:

1. How do consumers feel about our products and our company?

2. Why do customers buy our products? For those who buy competitive products, why don't they buy ours?

3. Who are our prime targets?

4. How do we seek to reach them—through what mediums, at what total cost, with what kinds of messages?

5. Where do our profits come from? Which product lines?

6. Where do they *not* come from? Which product lines?

7. How much are we spending to reach the consumer: what is the unit cost of advertising and sales promotion spending per dollar of sales of each product line? How does this compare with our competitors?

8. Why is there such an *imbalance* comparing the answers to questions 5 and 6 with 7 (as invariably occurs)?

9. What are the sales, share of market, and profit trend lines for the last 5 years in each product line?

10. Where are our profits likely to come from 3 years from now? (How much from existing products, how much from new products?)

11. What's our success record for new-product development?

12. How does it compare with competitors?

13. Indeed, how do we measure success? And are these the most appropriate measures?

14. What are the primary reasons for new-product failure?

15. How good are our people? How creative? How do we measure "creativity"? How good a feel do they have for what's happening in the marketplace?

16. Do we lose many good people? Why? How does turnover here compare with elsewhere? Do other companies try to take our people because we're so well regarded? Where do our people go when they leave here?

17. Is the general atmosphere here one of challenge and cooperation? Of dog-eat-dog competitiveness? Of empire building, with chiefs who don't talk to each other? How empty is the office at 5:00 P.M.? Or are people so "workaholic" they're still working at 7:00 P.M.?

18. Is there an organizational commitment to "excellence"? Does anyone even use the term?

Dealing Effectively with Urgent Issues

From your first or second day on the job, you may be faced with the necessity to make business decisions. Many, of course, will be easy to make; but sometime within your first 30 days—perhaps more times than you wish—you'll be faced with the challenge of making what you may consider a premature judgment because of an emergency. An issue may come across your desk for your resolution *before* you feel you've mastered enough of the facts to give you confidence in taking *any* course of action.

When you feel yourself confronted with such an issue, ask yourself:

1. Why is any decision necessary? What would be the adverse consequences of doing nothing?

2. If a decision *is* necessary, must it be made now, or can it be safely deferred until I have time to acquire information I need?

3. If it must be made now, must it be resolved by me, or could it be handled more appropriately by a different function or level?

4. If it must be made now by me, which resources are in the best position to help me make it?

If you must indeed settle or resolve it, we recommend you follow the ExecuTrak® Systems' decision-making process outlined in Chapter 13, "Do I Have to Decide Today?" (Decision Making under Pressure). In essence, this process calls for determining exactly *what* has to be decided and what *criteria* any solution must fulfill, assigning *priorities* to the criteria, and *developing* and *weighing* a list of possible courses of action against the ranked criteria.

Most importantly, after you have arrived at a tentative decision, trouble-shoot it for possible adverse effects by asking "What could go wrong?" and refine the solution to prevent or minimize the adverse consequences. The result should be a solution that meets your needs better than any single solution you may have considered before.

Handling a crisis during the first 30 days represents a special kind of challenge to the newly appointed senior executive. New managers, anxious to prove their leadership, are often tempted to overreact to crisis.

A second danger during the initial period is to rely on the "superior wisdom" of technical experts rather than come to your own conclusions. The classic example of a new executive who relied on the judgments of others "more experienced" is the late President John Kennedy. His decision to remove air cover from the Bay of Pigs invasion of Cuba was later recognized as a major strategic blunder.

The wiser course is to ask why the experts believe as they do, and keep asking "Why?" to each answer they give until you have arrived at the basic rationale that underlies their recommendation. We also suggest subjecting their recommendation to our "What could go wrong?" test.

Another danger—not always recognized as such—is relying on experience or instinct to suggest the best solution. We are all the product of our experiences. Not unnaturally, when we find a new problem, our first instinct is to scan for what similar situations we have faced in the past and how we resolved them.

Some executives persist in believing that the best solution to many business problems is a thorough housecleaning. "If I get rid of the crew under whom these problems occurred, and hire a new crew (bring in my "trustees"), I can fix this mess." But "quick-fix" solutions are rarely adequate solutions. Unless you first probe for real cause, your corrective action may further compound the problem, lower morale, and hurt the company's reputation.

One multinational company became a client of ours only after it had replaced eight presidents in 9 years in a vain effort to "shape up" a money-losing foreign subsidiary. The ninth president authorized us to conduct extensive confidential interviews of company personnel and outsiders who knew the operations well. Our analysis identified a host of deep-seated problems (see Chapter 8), several of which had been aggravated by the frequent change in chiefs.

Budgeting Your Time

How you budget your time during your first 30 days is a function of the priorities you set and the demands forced upon you by events.

Rare is the new executive who doesn't feel himself overwhelmed during his first month by the challenges he faces and the multitude of details that so easily can occupy his attention. You may feel that for all the homework you have done before joining a company, you have only scratched the surface.

Consultant Peter Drucker counsels that executives should do "first things first and other things not at all." But though sound advice, it is hard to follow when you find yourself confronted with demands to handle 10 things at once.

The key, obviously, is to set your priorities. How you set them depends on what you want to accomplish in your first 30 days. This chapter merely suggests the bases you must touch within that period. How long you linger at each one, and what you do while you're "on base," only you can determine.

The place to begin is to ask yourself, "What do I want to *achieve, preserve,* and *avoid* during my first month?" with regard to your superiors, your managers, the various publics, learning the ropes, and dealing with urgent issues.

Chapter 5

"What Do You Mean, 'I'll Be Dead in a Month?'"

(How One New Executive Survived His "Baptism by Fire")

The phone on my hotel nightstand woke me with a deafening ring. I glanced at my travel clock before answering it: 5:55 A.M. I picked it up without lifting my head and wrestled it to my ear with a grumpy hello.

At the other end was the familiar voice of a client, Ben Wyman, executive vice president and chief financial officer of a company I'll call Associated Industries.

"Can you come up in a few minutes?" he asked.

"What's up?" I replied.

"Something I want to talk with you about. Nothing too serious," he replied.

"Sure," I said. He said he'd order breakfast at 6:30 for the two of us in his room.

As I showered and dressed, I racked my brain to think what might be on his mind. We were at a modern resort hotel with his worldwide financial officers for a 2-day seminar aimed at hooking them up all on the same wavelength and updating the financial control system of Associated—the largest company of its kind in the world.

A few minutes later, after the usual morning pleasantries, he filled me in: "Quite suddenly and unexpectedly, I've been offered an opportunity I don't feel I can pass up. I can't say much about it at the moment except that I will be the president of a major corporation, one of the most creative enterprises in the world."

Sensing my intense curiosity, he leaned toward me and—"in strict confidence"—named the company.

I could feel my eyes widen. His own smile suggested that he was delighted by my reaction.

"It will be a real challenge—the kind of thing I feel I've been building up for all my life," he said. "New responsibilities in a new field in a company that can have a major impact on the way people think and the things they believe in."

I congratulated him, and asked if he had any concerns about the new job. "Yes," he said. As he began to tick them off, I whipped out my scratch pad and began to take notes.

Ben's most immediate concern was the conference. "How's it going to look having brought these people here and having you help us to get all on the same wavelength, and then find that the guy who controls the frequency is calling it quits? Doesn't this whole exercise become wasted effort?"

"Not necessarily," I replied. "But the fact that you'll soon be leaving and that no one must know it yet only makes it all the more important that we take care not to build false expectations."

Accordingly, we determined that in addition to the business objectives of the conference itself, Ben should seek to satisfy three personal objectives:

- "Not set any false expectations about my remaining as boss."
- "Not say anything to arouse speculation that I won't remain their boss."
- "Achieve the results for the conference we have set for worldwide finance, but do so in a way that will make its operations independent of me and capable of functioning without my supervision."

After listing those three objectives, we began discussing ways in which they could be satisfied. Ben felt relieved that he was able to identify several courses of action that would minimize any negative operational impact from this sudden career decision.

We also briefly discussed what were likely to be his initial challenges at the new company. But he held off the detailed discussion on that subject until a week later, when we met in his office in Chicago for a working lunch.

Again, as he talked I scribbled notes, and when he'd finished talking (and I scribbling), I asked if he wasn't a bit dismayed by the dimensions of his new challenge. "You may be walking into a snake pit," I said.

He nodded and smiled. "That's right, which is why I especially need you—to make sure I don't."

His central challenge—indeed the reason he was hired—was, in his words, "to make a business out of a creative enterprise and to do so without destroying the creative process."

On the strength of its creativity, the longtime chairman and vice chairman of the company had built one of the nation's largest business empires. But they had never developed the management tools or financial controls necessary to harness that creative energy and direct it in pursuit of overall company priorities.

"If my long-range challenge is to make a business out of this creative enterprise," said Wyman, "then my medium-range challenge is to make a management team out of this collection of prima donnas I inherited."

"Medium range?" I queried. "Isn't that your initial task?"

"I wish it were," he said grimacing. "Unfortunately, some of those people wish I were dead and one of them has even told me so. Before I can do anything to make these people into a team, I have to convince them I am not here to eat them up or rob them of their power. I have to communicate with them and win them over."

We left things there because of the need to devote our attention to cleaning up loose ends at Associated Industries. I helped him strategize a successful exit and implement the steps we had discussed to minimize the operational impact of his leaving.

I next saw Ben less than a week after he'd been ensconced in a magnificant corner office on the top floor of one of Los Angeles' grandest skyscrapers. He outlined the issues on his plate, and confided that he was really worried about whether he would be able to win over the group presidents under him. He described the presidents—each of whom was used to running a semiautonomous enterprise—as "princes who resent me as a schoolboy interloper who knows nothing about the business."

The description was only slightly overdrawn. The "princes" were the highest-paid executives at their level in the industry. They had chauffeured limousines and a private plane at their disposal. Several were furnished in-town apartments. They were pampered—but they were immensely talented too, and their talent had helped build and maintain the company's industry leadership, and with it the profits that made that pampering possible.

As for my client, though he was not exactly a schoolboy, he was only in his late 30s, a full decade younger than the youngest of the presidents. He was brought in from outside with no knowledge of the substantive aspects of the business. Furthermore, more than one of the presidents had been vying for—and led to believe he would get—the job that ultimately went to Ben Wyman. Their resentment was acute.

Some executives I know shy away from using an outside resource, not because they don't need help but because they're afraid to admit they're not "all-knowing." Some also worry that colleagues will interpret their resort to outside assistance as a confession of weakness.

Ben had no such hangups. Possessed of a highly analytical mind and shrewd insight into human behavior, he sensed that, while his strengths were many, his inexperience in this industry was a serious weakness that might lead him to commit errors that others would seize upon to do him in. One of his lieutenants had refused to shake his hand when they were introduced. "You'll be dead in a month," the man snarled. In his determination to prove the man a liar, Ben asked me to help him develop a strategy to "win over the princes."

We began by establishing the following objectives:

1. Get deeper insight into each man and determine how best to work with him to capitalize on his strengths.

2. Enable each to understand me better and relate more openly and spontaneously with me.

3. Break down barriers and encourage a common vision and interaction among the group presidents.

4. Develop a practical, decision-making/communication process to get the group on a common wavelength to solve important corporate issues and reduce suboptimization of goals.

5. Lay a firm foundation for discussion and commitment to resolving the following key issues:
  a. Structural organization
  b. Charter as president in relationship to group presidents
  c. Financial controls and reporting procedures
  d. Perquisites
  e. Acquisitions and internal development

We discussed each individual, what Ben had learned about the man's reaction to his coming, his own initial impression at a "meet the troops" session, and some basic facts about the businesses that each ran. We strategized a phone call from Ben to each man, determining what the objectives of each call should be, what concerns the individual might have that he should be sensitive to, etc. As he made each call, I took notes on what I heard and what I thought the person at the other end of the line needed to hear to be reassured. I then gave him my feedback on the call. And he would go on to make the next one.

To the man who had refused to shake his hand, for example, Ben said, "You know you've got my vote. As far as I'm concerned, you're the best man to run the division. And everyone I've talked to, including Manny [the chairman], agrees. You don't have to lose any sleep thinking that I'm out to replace you, because you have my word that I'm in your corner. And I hope you're in mine." That quid pro quo was important.

At one session a few weeks later, Ben and I discussed how to transform the men's reluctant (by then) acquiescence into active support for his leadership. Using the techniques that I call "achieve, preserve, avoid" (see Chapter 4), we devised a strategy designed to meet these objectives, among others:

- Demonstrate how his appointment can help them achieve their objectives.
- Demonstrate why he was chosen over them.
- Leave no doubt about his fitness for the job.
- Win their commitment to him and to his vision for the company.

At the next meeting with his staff, he implemented the strategy by making the following comments:

I know that some of you are not crazy about my appointment. Some of you are deeply disappointed by it. I'm not going to worry myself sick over that. I have a job to do here and so do you. I'll judge you not by what you think of me but by how well you do your job. I expect to be judged by the same standard. . . .

Why was I chosen? Certainly not for my knowledge of the industry; we all know that. I was chosen because I have something that none of the other candidates for the job have: I have the confidence of the chairman.

What does that mean to you? Simply this: You and I together can get things done if we work in *partnership* that we cannot get done if we work alone. And what I mean by *partnership* is simple:

If any program you recommend stands the test of our probing at meetings like this, and wins my personal approval, then I'll take responsibility for bringing you the sanction of the board chairman. Once I have agreed to back your recommendation, each and every one of you can hold me accountable for convincing Manny to sanction it.

If, after I've been here a while, we find that you're able to convince me but I cannot convince him, then I'm not the man for this job and I'll resign. But as long as I'm here, let's work together in *partnership* and get the job done.

The idea of anyone guaranteeing to deliver the board chairman's approval was mind-boggling to the prima donnas of this enterprise. And the idea of anyone offering to resign was a demonstration of stature they had not seen in the palace before. By demonstrating that he was on their side—and would not only go to bat for them but pledge to hit home runs—he went a long way toward overcoming their hostility.

I continued to help Ben strategize his relations with his key people over a period of months. But the thrust of our work turned to the very real business challenges that he faced and his delicate relations with the chairman and vice chairman. They had been used to running things themselves for so long that, despite their desire to have him do the job he was hired to do, they couldn't keep from meddling.

We advise all our clients in a new position to get their management teams away for a few days of work and familiarization. I felt that such a session was particularly important for Ben and he heartily agreed. Generally, I chair (or cochair with the client) these work conferences, serving in several roles:

- As a buffer and catalyst (to "run interference" among potential adversaries and turn energies to constructive channels)

- As an integrative mechanism (to help the new man and his people become a team committed to the same goals and successful interaction)
- As a methodology resource (to help them reach basic decisions about corporate mission and directions, objectives, accountabilities, authority, roles and relationships)

In this instance, Ben felt it was important that he run the session alone and that I not attend.

"If I want to demonstrate my leadership ability to these men," he said, "I don't want to leave any doubts about being my own man, capable of standing on my own feet, facing them down if necessary, and worthy of their allegiance."

"Once I've got them with me, and we're tracking together, then you needn't remain 'invisible,' " he said.

I could understand his feeling, and though I helped him develop an agenda and strategy for the conference and undertook a round of confidential interviews of the key players on his team, it was agreed that *he* should run the conference himself, following guidelines that we developed together.

The interviews revealed the concerns, questions, issues, and opportunities—as no direct meeting with the boss could—that were of most concern to the men. In addition to providing insights for Ben, the interviews helped:

- Win their commitment to the project
- Establish a climate of high expectations for the conference
- Establish Ben as a "two-way guy," someone committed to working in partnership with his key people in meeting challenges
- Identify the issues and opportunities that should serve as a focus for efforts to improve company effectiveness

Moreover, because the interviews and conference were his idea, the project helped clearly establish Ben as the quarterback of a new "team effort."

To help produce an atmosphere conducive to good relations and a positive outlook, we strategized that the setting for the conference should be:

- Significantly more appealing than the usual resort and convention sites for conferences
- Sumptuous
- Away from telephones and day-to-day pressures
- In keeping with the importance of the event itself

It was decided that these criteria could best be fulfilled by holding the conference for 3½ days on a 90-foot yacht in Puget Sound. The significance of the challenge the men faced is summed up in the conference mission and objectives:

Mission:

To determine what should be the future mission, business strategy, and appropriate organization of the company.

Objectives:

1. Consolidate the forward thinking of the corporation to define or redefine:
    a. Our raison d'être:
        (1) Who we are; what is our business today?
        (2) What kind of a company should we be in the future? What kinds of businesses should we be in, and what should be the geographical scope of such operations?
    b. The most effective strategy to assure our survival, growth and profitability (defined as earnings per share).
    c. What kind of an organization is needed to run the kind of company we want?

2. Determine how the Senior Management Team can best work together in directing our future growth and profitability.

3. Refine the strategic planning and decision-making process to improve scanning and detecting internal development/acquisition/divestment/merger opportunities—with the necessary flexibility to be responsive to them.

4. Identify and determine how best to:
    a. Capitalize on the factors facilitating our strengths and achievements.
    b. Reduce significantly those constraints to our increased growth, development and profitability.

The details of the work done there goes beyond the scope of this chapter. Suffice it to say, Ben succeeded brilliantly in getting his people on his wavelength, forming them into a team, overcoming their concerns about his leadership, and setting new directions for the company.

Before he resigned 6 years later to accept a high government position, the company's earnings had risen for 24 consecutive quarters. A brokerage house reported, "The excellent record of the last few years coincides with key management changes. . . . [The] company is a prime example of the benefits of increased sophistication in management techniques."

Ben also increased his own remuneration in that period of 5 years from $225,000 initial salary to more than $800,000 in salary, bonus, and perquisites.

Chapter 6
"Am I In Today?"
(The Crucial Role of Your Administrative Assistant)

A friend of mine, who admits to being a workaholic, joined a new company and immediately set about finding an executive secretary. He interviewed 17 women for 1 hour each and winnowed his list down to 7.

He gave each of the seven a letter he had written. It included 31 errors, both grammatical and spelling. "See if you can improve this letter," he told each candidate. "It has some errors. I'd like to have it back accurately typed in 12 minutes."

One woman returned the letter with 44 errors. Three did a first-rate job, my friend said, and two others did well enough that he wanted to test their skills further. So he asked his wife, Lori, to interview all five "semifinalists," reasoning that because his job required him to travel extensively, his secretary would have to deal frequently, at least by telephone, with Lori.

To each of the five he gave a letter he had received from a college president asking him to speak at an assembly. Each was instructed to draft a response accepting the speaking engagement and including a "bio" (biography).

I'll let him explain what ensued: "One of the girls didn't know what a bio was. Another wrote an acceptance letter and enclosed *her* bio. A third, obviously endowed with great powers of imagination, concocted a mythical bio for me. Two girls, fortunately, took the initiative to obtain the announcement of my appointment with the company and adapted it to the needs of the situation.

"This narrowed the search to two finalists. I tried each of them for a day to see how we would mesh, and ending up choosing Cindy because, besides being very competent, the chemistry was right: she ticked when I ticked and tocked when I tocked."

Though time-consuming, my friend's process of selection was purposeful.

He had tested the applicants' intelligence, initiative, secretarial skills, and responsiveness to his needs. He had also assured a choice compatible with his wife. This step may seem unnecessary to many executives, but—in view of the problems that often arise between executive secretaries and executives' wives—it makes sense in some circumstances. Not only did my friend lay the foundation for a good working relationship with his secretary, he also gave his wife a feeling of participation in a key early decision. This, he reasoned, might help her over those inevitable times when his frequent absences made her resent his work.

In serving our clients, we have come to know many executive secretaries and administrative assistants. We have observed their work habits and their interactions with their boss, and have formed some conclusions about the factors that make for success and failure in their relationship.

To supplement our own experience, we conducted two surveys. One asked senior executives about the challenges of a new assignment and the role an executive secretary or administrative assistant can play in helping them meet those challenges. The other survey asked similar questions of a number of executive secretaries and administrative assistants. The information in this chapter is drawn from both our counseling practice and answers to the twin surveys.

A Definition

Let's define our terms. Strictly speaking, an *executive secretary* is exactly what the name implies—a secretary who serves an executive, i.e., who performs such conventional tasks as typing, taking dictation, keeping the boss's schedule, making his travel arrangements, screening callers, etc. Many executive secretaries perform a range of additional services such as coordinating staff meetings, answering routine correspondence and inquiries, serving as a sounding board to the boss, checking on the status of decision follow-through.

Generally speaking, an *administrative assistant* has added responsibilities. He or she may function as office manager, troubleshooter, investigator, and/or manager of special projects for the boss, and may be freed from routine office chores such as typing. But these distinctions are often blurred in practice. Increasingly, executives are "crowning" their executive secretaries as administrative assistants to upgrade their status and self-esteem.

In years past, administrative assistants were usually men; women either did not perform the same work or performed it without benefit of title. Now, under the pressure of antidiscrimination laws and the women's rights movement, these artificial barriers are crumbling, and administrative assistants are as likely to be women as they are to be men. One legacy of the old order: Though women can now be called "administrative assistants" (even if their work is that of a secretary), men are rarely called "secretaries" (or even "executive secretaries"), no matter what routine office chores they perform!

For purposes of simplicity, we shall talk here only of executive secretaries. But all comments apply equally to administrative assistants unless otherwise noted.

Mission of the Executive Secretary

Essentially, the job of the executive secretary is to optimize the effectiveness of the executive by freeing him as much as possible from work that doesn't require his personal attention. That mission includes such objectives as assuring the smooth running of the office and keeping him informed of information and organizational intelligence he needs to do his job. It may involve promoting a good image of the boss, both within and outside the organization. One executive secretary responded to our survey by saying her job is to "provide the executive with the necessary time, information and assistance to carry out his duties in the most efficient and professional manner possible." That about says it all—except for the comment of another executive secretary who wrote that her job is to "keep the boss out of trouble."

She went on to explain that keeping him out of trouble requires:

1. Having him at the right place at the right time
2. Making him available when his boss wants him
3. Assuring that he isn't "surprised, embarrassed or otherwise caught off guard by his boss or subordinates"
4. Assuring that everything going out of the office is accurate and complete
5. Assuring that nothing slips through the cracks

Any executive who's ever had an outstanding executive secretary can reel off the qualities that make her so. Our survey respondents listed a total of 35 such qualities, including tact, the ability to get along with people and be sensitive to their needs (particularly the needs of the boss), loyalty, confidentiality, trustworthiness, intelligence, dedication, willingness to make an "extra effort," ability to follow through on instructions, thoroughness, attention to detail, cost-consciousness, experience, knowledge of function, good judgment, dependability, ability to work under stress, integrity, enthusiasm, sense of humor, and—from one respondent—"the ability to make a good cup of coffee." (Others would dispute this last requirement!)

There are, of course, certain qualities to beware of in an executive secretary. One of the most dangerous is a loose mouth. Some secretaries delight in passing on (or originating) office gossip. It is often meant innocently: "Boy, is Mr. Jones in a foul mood today. I think he must be worried about keeping his job. And no wonder, the way his department's sales are going. . . ." But its impact can be devastating.

One executive we counsel says there are two kinds of people in organizations: gossip mongers and gossip stoppers. Any executive who values his confidences will be a gossip stopper. He should take steps to assure that his secretary is one too.

Key Roles of the Executive Secretary

Exactly how you use your executive secretary depends, of course, on your own situation, managing style, and what other secretarial or staff services are available. Our survey respondents listed these roles for an executive secretary: receptionist, typist, stenographer; schedule maker or keeper; maker of arrangements for travel, hotel, meetings, and working lunches; screener of information, phone calls, mail, requests for decisions, meetings, and speaking engagements; coordinator of office work flow and of decision follow-through; office supply manager; and source of organizational information and intelligence.

Our surveys show that executive secretaries tend not to consider their basic typing and stenographic skills their primary contribution, although many employers still do. Executive secretaries tend to see their most useful roles as assuring effective follow-through on commitments by the boss or his subordinates and screening calls, mail, and other information, including highlighting important memos and staff papers. One administrative assistant said her most valuable contribution lies in "bringing the boss back to reality; raising his spirits when he is low and dampening them slightly when he's flying too high—always with his best interest in mind."

In our experience, the executives who use their executive secretaries to best advantage give them supplementary roles to play—for example, as a sounding board for ideas ("What do you think would happen, Miss Williams, if I did such and such?"); as a devil's advocate; and sometimes as a source for recommendations, particularly on personnel matters. *All* the executives who responded to our survey and in our experience put a premium on executive secretaries who can handle assigned tasks with little or no supervision and who are resourceful in finding ways to relieve the boss of routine chores.

Because of her role as the boss's "gatekeeper," an executive secretary may not always be popular with managers. Many secretaries confess to feeling themselves caught between conflicting pressures—from the boss not to let people through the "gate" unless absolutely necessary, and from managers who complain they can't see the boss when they need to.

A senior government officer whose secretary was caught in the middle of just such a conflict called a meeting to find a solution. His situation was acute because he had 35 managers reporting directly to him from various parts of the country. If all of them could reach him whenever they wanted, he would never get any work done. Thus, he needed a way of distinguishing those calls he absolutely had to handle himself from those that others could take.

With our help, he and his staff officers devised a system that assured if any of his managers phoned his office during the first hour of the working day, a response would be forthcoming within 2 hours. The ground rules were that the caller had to give his executive secretary enough details to permit her to collect relevant information. The official handled the matter by phone himself, delegated it, or set up an appointment for the caller later in the day.

To screen calls further, the secretary, with her boss's permission, set up a three-question filter that proved a tremendous time-saver for him. The questions:

• What will happen if this is not handled by him personally?
• How serious will that be?
• What is the value added if he becomes involved?

By "straining" all calls through this three-stage filter, she was able to weed out 60 percent of the demands on his time.

Serving a Senior Executive in a New Assignment

An executive in a new assignment—particularly one parachuted in from outside the company—needs all the help he can get in negotiating the hazards of his first few months. An executive secretary can be particularly helpful to her boss when he's new to his job. In addition to the roles outlined above, her knowledge of the company culture, traditions, policies, procedures, personalities, idiosyncrasies, and biases of key people can acclimate him to his new surroundings and help him avoid making potentially embarrassing faux pas.

One executive says his executive secretary provided "assistance and understanding" during his initiation, while another says his secretary was most valuable in explaining "how the company works, where things are, and who are the key lower-level personnel." A third responded that his executive secretary's knowledge of "how to cut through procedures helped insulate me from routine bureaucracy and produced faster results than I ever could have otherwise."

The executive secretaries also stress this familiarization role. One secretary suggested that her greatest value to her new boss lay in giving him a "fix on what constitutes accepted standards and practice here." And another found that her biggest contribution was helping the boss manage his work-load.

Eleven executive secretaries (and administrative assistants) responded to a survey question that presented a list of challenges that often confront senior executives in new assignments and asked in which areas the executive secretary could make a "significant contribution to a new senior executive's success."

- Ten said "establishing more productive relations with the management team"
- Nine—"dealing with various publics (customers, trade, public officials, the press, financial community, etc.)"
- Nine—"helping him make the best use of his time"
- Seven—"establishing productive relations with the CEO or other superiors"
- Seven—"helping identify issues and opportunities"
- Seven—"determining how best to help him achieve his objectives and priorities"

Nailing Down Responsibilities

To establish a productive relationship with your executive secretary, it's advisable to have a heart-to-heart talk with her as soon as possible after you take over. Because you'll be working so closely together, you want to establish a clear understanding from the beginning concerning:

- What you expect of her (duties, responsibilities, hours, procedures, letter and memo formats and distribution, filing procedures, response time to your inquiries, etc.)
- How you will measure her performance (standards for evaluation, frequency of evaluation)

In addition, you will want to know anything about her personal situation that might affect her ability to perform the job (health, small children, other obligations, availability nights and weekends, etc.).

One of my assignments with the president and chief executive officer of one company was to help him and his executive secretary clarify her responsibilities and performance standards. Out of our two discussions came the list on page 63.

This list, to be sure, establishes very demanding performance criteria. Note, for example, the several "Noes" (e.g., no serious complaints, no

CHART 7-A   Executive Secretary to President and Chief Executive Officer

Primary Objective: Assure maximum discretionary time available to the president and CEO

Performance areas (Ranked in order of priority)	Performance criteria
1. Exercise appropriate judgment with regard to:	
a. Following up items arising from meetings	Appraisal by Messrs. W, X, Y, Z (subordinates) of Ms. L's contribution. No alienation of subordinates
b. Keeping Mr. K's calendar	Worry-free existence for Mr. K from scheduling standpoint
c. Mail flow	Decreased paper flow into Mr. K's office
	With regard to (a), (b), and (c), *no* serious complaint from anyone, inside or outside company, who deals with Mr. K
2. Ensure accurate record of management committee and other meetings	*No* serious disagreement between Mr. K and subordinates as to what has been agreed upon
3. Ensure effective follow-through of commitments resulting from above meetings, and keep abreast of current status of follow-up	Minimum inquiries by Mr. K as to progress
4. Convey appropriate attitude of the office of the president and CEO	Successful test of management committee's perception of this attitude as determined by adjectives they use in describing her in the course of confidential talks with John Arnold
5. Ensure effective operation of the president and CEO's office and most effective scheduling of Mr. K's time	*No* snafus
6. Ensure appropriate image of president and CEO's office to outside world	Successful test of key outside contacts' perception (as determined by confidential talks with John Arnold)
7. Act as appropriate sounding board for subordinates	Decrease in traffic to Mr. K on matters of lesser importance
	No management committee member feels uncomfortable in testing out ideas on her
8. Act as sounding board for Mr. K	Increase in number of times Mr. K sounds her out

63

serious disagreements, no snafus in operation or time scheduling). In fact, the CEO originally was willing to allow more flexibility in the standards. But the executive secretary insisted she should be held strictly accountable for producing maximum results. "The better I do, the more time you have to do your job," she told her boss.

She may have been right. Part of the agreement she made with her boss was that if she could achieve these difficult objectives, her base salary would increase from $14,000 to $18,000 at the end of the year. Indeed, within a year, she was raised to $20,000 and 2 years later earns a base salary in the mid $20,000s. She is one of the most highly paid executive secretaries in the North American city where she works.

Why is she paid so much? "Because she's worth every penny of it, that's why," her boss told me when I asked that question (knowing full well what the response would be). Both the executive secretary and the CEO agree that she would not have been able to free up as much of his time and deserve anywhere near her current salary if she had not undergone the *discipline* of the above analysis and established such tough performance criteria.

Those "Go-fer" Chores

Executive secretaries often complain that they are asked to do chores that should be performed by an office boy or someone else with lower skills and lower salary. "It's ridiculous to have me buying birthday presents for his wife . . .", "You'd think I was a waitress the way he uses me to get everybody coffee . . ." we sometimes hear them complain.

Some executive secretaries grumble that they waste up to an hour a day trying to get through to busy airline or hotel switchboards—a job that can be better handled by a travel agency, at no cost to the company. "It makes no sense to have me hanging on the end of a phone when I could be doing what I'm paid to do," one executive secretary complained to us. (The experience of our *own* office bears this out!)

Another complaint is a frequent shift of priorities. "I'll be busy doing something that he needs 'right away,' when all of a sudden he'll descend on me with a batch of scribbled notes and say, 'I have to have this in the next mail so drop what you're doing and get on it.' It's maddening how he pays so much attention to managing his own time effectively, but has so little regard for mine."

How to Help Your Executive Secretary Become More Productive

If you ask any executive secretary how you can help her work more effectively, the chances are she'll have a ready supply of suggestions—if she believes you are sincerely interested and will not get overly defensive.

Most of her suggestions will involve allowing her to plan her time better and keeping her better informed—not only of what you're doing and want her to do, but *why*.

Seek out her opinion or her knowledge when it provides a perspective that might be valuable. Many secretaries are excellent sources of organizational intelligence—much better sources than fellow executives, who may be too absorbed in their work to notice many of the interpersonal stresses and strains that characterize organizational life. One executive who actively seeks out his secretary's knowledge of behind-the-scenes activity, explains frankly: "I'd rather hear from her what's going on than be surprised when my top man tells me."

In addition, we often find that executive secretaries are anxious to shoulder more responsibility than they are given. Some executives try to make their executive secretary part of the management team. She might, for example, be included in management committee staff meetings so that she can keep a record of the decisions made and the action plans formed, and even more importantly, she can assure better follow-through because she knows *who's* responsible for doing *what* by *when*. This role also enables her to serve as a better sounding board to the boss.

One executive secretary offered this opinion: "The more an executive secretary understands her boss's function, the better job she can do for him." Advises another: "Keep the executive secretary informed of current goals, issues, opportunities, action plans, etc. That way, he or she will know at all times what the priorities are and set their own priorities accordingly."

To summarize, keep her informed as much as possible, keep her challenged, use her to the limit of her ability, let her know what you expect of her, give her continual feedback on how she's doing, and avoid the temptation to take her for granted.

Some executive secretaries feel that they could do a better job of scheduling the boss's time than he can himself. "Executives rarely have a true concept of the amount of time that will be 'swallowed up' by meetings," says one executive secretary. "My boss will say, 'Harry's going to be up to see me but it'll only take 5 minutes,' when I know full well it will take a half hour and will keep other people cooling their heels in the reception room. If I kept his schedule, he would be on time more often."

Their answers to our survey suggest that executives agree with many of these points. In addition, they stress the need for initiative. "I'll bet right now my secretary can tell me things she could be doing to save me having to do myself, if she thought about them. The problem is, she's not 'tuned in' to thinking that way." To which we offer this comment: If the executive secretary isn't "thinking that way," maybe it's at least partly because her boss hasn't made her feel it's important to do so.

Like her boss, the good executive secretary knows how to use her own time to best advantage. She delegates authority that she doesn't have to exercise herself. She works from a set of priorities and continually monitors her workload against it. She is on the lookout for ways to help her boss, to save him time, to cut down on the number of concerns he must deal with. She is sensitive to his needs and tries to anticipate them, if at all possible. She not only feels *but is treated as* a valued member of a winning team, with commensurate rewards and recognition.

A Final Thought

It seems likely that in the next few years, many secretaries are going to undergo some consciousness-raising. In many organizations, secretaries occupy the lowest position on the white-collar totem pole. They are dead-ended, low paid, unorganized, subservient, and called by a name that increasingly seems to suggest disparagement: "Girl" (as in "I'll have one of the girls do it").

But, as Bob Dylan says, the times may be "a-changing." Though the women's rights movement has by and large bypassed the secretarial pool, guerrilla fighters are operating even there. Says the secretary to the president of one huge United States conglomerate:

"There's a big push on now for assertiveness training for women. They're trying to make women become corporate men in skirts. That's exchanging one kind of slavery for another, not freeing us to be ourselves. We make the mistake of measuring liberation by our freedom to burn our bras.

"The goal shouldn't be to make us feverishly ambitious sycophants like so many career-oriented men. The point is to speak up for humanizing the organization. When enough of us are willing to do that, we may see some real changes."

Chapter 7
"What Do I Really Want to Achieve?"
(The Crucial Role of an Outside Resource)

Unquestionably, management consultants *as a group* have a bad name. The popular conception of the consultant was summed up by Robert Townsend, author of the best selling book *Up the Organization* and the man who put Avis Rent-A-Car in the black, when he said:

"A consultant is someone who borrows your watch to tell you what time it is, then sends you a bill."

But even Bob Townsend recognizes that there are virtues to working with an outside resource. To be sure, there are charlatans among consultants as among any other group of professionals. It has always been a puzzle to me that consultants don't do more to offset the black eye which too many have given the profession. But doing that requires, in the first instance, an agreed-upon definition of what exactly constitutes a "management consultant." And on that, there may be as many definitions as there are consultants.

Consultants come in all sizes—from the large international companies with hundreds of professionals to the one-man practitioner. The Manhattan telephone directory lists 3½ pages of consultants. Their names appear in the Yellow Pages between "Malted Milk" and "Manhole Covers"—hardly a dignified setting for people who profess to be able to tell the captains of industry how to better manage their affairs!

For our purposes, the most worthwhile distinction is between those who offer a specialized or technical service (such as finance and accounting, electronic data processing, engineering) and those who bring a generalized approach to management problems that is adaptable to many different kinds of businesses and management issues. Thus the basic distinction is between specialists and generalists.

This chapter will discuss the proper role of the generalist in helping the new senior executive meet his challenges, inasmuch as this is the kind of service that my firm knows most intimately and to which business readers can most easily relate their own special needs in a variety of businesses and industries.

What a Counselor Can/Can't Do for You

A counselor is a consultant who works in an advisory capacity at the senior level. It is a mistake to think that he can *solve* management problems. Only management can do that. Rather, he is an outside, objective resource whose experience, perspective, analytical ability, and—most importantly—systematic approach to looking at new situations can guide the newly appointed executive in solving his own problems.

This process involves upgrading the executive's—and his management team's—skills at issue analysis and decision making, and applying these skills to such varied tasks as upgrading business strategy, revamping the organizational structure, accelerating diversification, optimizing advertising and sales promotion spending, and overcoming interdepartmental rivalries. Specifically, the counselor serves senior management in one or more of the following capacities:

1. As confidant and sounding board

2. As fact finder and communications link

3. As management team catalyst

4. As implementation monitor and strategic resource

Confidant and Sounding Board

Many senior executives in new assignments find it helpful to discuss—on a regular basis—their problems, ideas, concerns, plans, and options with a knowledgeable outsider, someone with whom they feel comfortable and can talk in complete confidence.

A good sounding board is not only a listener. He's a mind stretcher. By asking the right questions, he can help you develop new insights into *what you are doing and why;* he can guide you in determining *what you should be doing and how.* He can also help you sort out priorities, better manage your time, improve your key relationships, and anticipate and/or prevent problems.

Why an outside sounding board? Because all the insiders in whom you might be tempted to confide represent, in a sense, unknown qualities. Each speaks from his own particular perspective within the organization, his own agenda, and perhaps his own organizational biases and allegiances. Furthermore, confiding in any one individual in the organization often raises anxieties among other insiders, who worry about what kind of information on their own performance the organizational confidant may be filtering through his special "pipeline to the top."

On the other hand, the outside confidant with no organizational ax to grind doesn't represent a comparable threat, and his status as a concerned observer gives him a fresh perspective that veteran insiders lack.

Fact Finder and Communications Link

Fundamental to the task of the executive is the need for information— accurate, objective, up-to-date information on which to base his decisions. Much of the information he will need is his through the miracle of data processing and other management information services. But organizations are organisms that operate by a set of implicit rules and assumptions; even the best of them are victims of myths, sacred cows, and shibboleths that often prevent executives from identifying and resolving the basic issues and opportunities that confront them.

To obtain *this* information, it is often useful for an outside resource to conduct confidential in-depth interviews of persons with significant perspectives on the company or department. Your managers will probably speak more frankly to an outsider who does not hold their future in his hands than they will to you, who do. In addition, such a resource, if trained in the skills of interviewing and at putting people at ease in a setting where confidentiality of source is assured, can tap the collective wisdom of people in other parts of the company.

These interviews can also include knowledgeable customers, competitors, and people in the trade, the financial community, and government agencies, all of whom might hedge their opinions if they were talking directly with the executive or his inside representative (for fear of causing hard feelings, etc.). In addition to giving you the benefit of their insights, the process demonstrates to them that the company is "on the move" and becoming revitalized.

This information is distilled and presented to the executive and, at his discretion, disseminated to his organization in the form of a frank and detailed feedback report. Besides giving you a more accurate assessment of issues and opportunities than you—or even a member of your staff— can obtain, this process saves you valuable time in that you can be doing your job while the counselor conducts anywhere from 15 to 80 interviews. (In one instance, our company conducted 126 interviews for a new executive and distilled the findings down to a succinct report that became the basis of a subsequent plan of action, developed by him *and his team*.)

Management Team Catalyst

In a series of intensive senior management work sessions, the executive and his team use the feedback report as a basis for determining the priority issues and opportunities to be addressed. The counselor leads the group's analysis, probes, questions, distills, summarizes, and keeps the discussion on track. Their decision making culminates in the development of an action plan, with accountabilities assigned and performance criteria established to assure its execution. This process, which is essentially participatory and consensual, with the superior making the final decision, gives each member of the management team a stake in the success of the action plan. It welds them into a team. It also provides a unique opportunity for the new executive to size up the individual capabilities of each member—and for them to size him up too.

Implementation Monitor and Strategic Resource

The counselor retains an ongoing relationship with the new executive for a period of months (or however long the executive finds it fruitful) to check the progress of the plan against the timetables that were established and to help the new executive and his team overcome any obstacles to its success. He is available to advise on adaptations or modifications that events subsequent to the conference might require. In addition, in his continuing advisory role, the counselor helps the client think through emerging challenges and develop strategies to meet them.

My own basic approach to this task is to ask elementary questions: What are you doing? Why are you doing it? What objectives are you trying to satisfy? How else might it be done? What could go wrong?

We also find it useful periodically to study a client's calendar to determine how he uses his time. Very often, I find that his time commitments bear little relationship to those tasks he has designated as his primary objectives. When I call this discrepancy to a client's attention, he is invariably shocked (although he may confess to having had an "uneasy feeling all along").

A counselor can play no more useful role than to force a client to question his own assumptions and to bring his own time management and human resource utilization into better conformity with his business objectives.

What to Look For—And *Look Out* For— in Hiring a Counselor

To a counselor, no asset is more important than his reputation. To you, his reputation is less important than his references. Pay more attention to his track record than his credentials. How many papers he's published, what schools he attended, the degrees he secured, the professional associations he belongs to—these standards are *next to worthless* in assessing whether he can do the job you want done.

What you want to know is, what *results* did he achieve for other clients? What *value added* do they believe he represents? What did he do for them that they couldn't do for themselves? What was the bottom-line impact of his contribution? Were the results measurable in ROI, cost-effectiveness, etc.?

Demand to have names and phone numbers of recent clients. You or a valued member of your staff should talk with them personally and ask the above questions along with some of a more general nature: How satisfied were you with the service? How responsive was he to your overall needs? What, if anything, didn't he do well?

Then, of course, you must evaluate the answers to determine how relevant is the consultant's *experience* and *approach* to the kind of challenges that you face.

Some specific points to check for:

- Does the consultant take responsibility for helping you implement decisions or does his work end with a recommendation?

   Few recommendations are self-implementing. If the counselor doesn't take continuing responsibility, the recommendation may end up gathering dust on a shelf.

- Are the consultants for whom you have references the persons you'll actually be working with?

   If not, the references probably aren't worth much. Some firms use executives to sell a contract and "peons" to work it. You don't want to provide on-the-job training to inexperienced consultants, so insist on meeting and getting to know the people who will actually be doing the counseling; check out both them *and* their employer before signing a contract. (Or you'll end up paying for their education!)

- How much of your time and the time of your managers does the counselor actually need?

   Some consultants routinely assign a three- or four-member team to "camp on your doorstep" or "live in" with your managers for several months to study your operation. While some clients find this attention comforting, it adds astronomically to fees and is usually unnecessary. Like any group of guests who "don't mean to impose," live-in consultants will occupy hour after hour of your managers' time, asking questions, requesting facts and figures—all of which takes valuable time away from running the business.

Other pointers:

- Beware of "one-solution" consultants.

  I know several consultants who specialize in "reorganization." No matter what your needs are, if you hire them you can be sure they'll propose an overhaul of your structure. Some businessmen who've been burned by "professional reorganizers" consider the word "consultant" synonymous with "blood bath."

- Specify the project.

  As carefully as you can, delineate what the project *is* and what it *is not*; the responsibilities, time commitments, and results promised by the consultant; the time frame in which the project is to be conducted. Gain agreement on how the consultant's *own* performance is to be measured. Get all this in writing, of course.

If these requirements are met, you've probably set the groundwork for a fruitful relationship.

Some businessmen are skeptical of consultants who offer their services across a wide span of business issues in which they profess no technical competence. Our own firm, for example, helps executives come to terms with substantive business problems (e.g., long-range strategy and business planning; share of market and profitability; acquisition and divestiture goals) as well as human, operational, and organizational problems.

How can a consultant offer help in so many unrelated areas? The answer is that while the *information content* of these fields may be unrelated, the *methodology* needed to resolve them is similar.

The basic techniques of issue analysis, decision making, and opportunity detection are the same, whether the challenge is to determine how to send a rocket to the moon (an issue I helped NASA troubleshoot) or to determine what to do about an associate who isn't pulling his own weight (an issue we have helped numerous clients resolve).

Not all new executives, of course, need an outside resource, whether he be sounding board, fact finder, catalyst, strategy adviser, or whatever. We often give new executives the following list to help them clarify their needs:

Objectives of Sounding Board/Catalyst/Troubleshooter Role With Newly Appointed Senior Executives

1. Help you anticipate and avoid intraorganizational and interpersonal problems that can undermine your potential influence, contribution, and recognition.

2. Help you determine and implement the best ways to shape and manage your relationship with the president, chairman, board of directors, and key operating and staff senior executives to develop "win-win" rather than "win-lose" or suboptimal relationships.

3. Speed up the usual "learning" and "shakedown" time it takes to win their understanding, support, and commitment to your goals and plans.

4. Help you determine how to make the best use of your time and reduce unnecessary time drains.

5. Help you think through and determine how to crystallize the best thinking of your senior team on such issues as:
   a. The organization's identity, direction, objectives, and strategies.
   b. The most appropriate kind of organization to profitably grow its business and develop its people.
   c. Authority, autonomy, and role relationships.
   d. How best to strengthen the management team.
   e. The most appropriate decision-making mode, including determination of *what* information you need *when* and *how.*
   f. How best to develop organizational skills in managing necessary change.
   g. Forward planning, including how best to diversify and/or grow by acquisition or internal development (strategic and operating planning).

6. Develop a vehicle or structure to serve as an *integrative mechanism* with your senior management team to help assure:
   a. Rapid development of a *common vision.*
   b. Detection, efficient analysis, and resolution of the gut issues (in contrast with symptomatic problems) and opportunities.
   c. Evolution of an effective management process.

On page 74 is an agenda I developed for an early meeting with the vice president of operations of a large manufacturing company. The 4-hour session occurred just 3 weeks after he joined the company, following a successful career with one of its major competitors.

For any division or company to be successful, of course, it must have more than an enlightened leader. It must have a management team fully committed to the same objectives and in possession of the requisite skills to achieve them. A skilled counselor can help you win this commitment and impart the needed problem-solving skills.

These benefits, however, are not always self-evident. Some senior executives in new assignments fear that their subordinates will regard them as weak if they seek outside counsel. How does the executive know, for example, that his team won't see his "dependence" on outside advice as proof that "the emperor has no clothes"—that he's not equal to his new challenges? Alternatively, some managers fear that the boss's counselor may function as a spy, obtaining intelligence about them and feeding it to his client.

These problems can easily be overcome if you and your managers understand that the counselor is vitally concerned with your interaction—with putting you and them on the same wavelength, developing a common vision

---

Agenda for Meeting With Mr. John Sherman
20 April 1978

Hyatt-Regency

Mission and objectives of today's discussion: By 4:15 P.M. we want to have:

1. Identified key events, decisions, changes, and issues that have occurred since you joined that may have a significant impact on your performance and relationships with key people and organizations.

2. Completed an initial assessment of your relationships with key persons and organizations upon whom you either depend for effective performance or approval, or whose actions could significantly impact your own performance.

3. Determine the key decisions you have to make within the next 30 days.

4. Identified the key demands on your time during the next 2 to 4 weeks.

In light of the above:

5. Positioned the ExecuTrak® System to accelerate achievement of the objectives we reviewed together at our last meeting.

6. Determined the best plan and tentative schedule to help ensure effective resolution of the key issues and achievement of your vital objectives.

7. "Problem-solved" any particularly pressing issues.

8. Developed the tentative agenda for our next meeting.

9. Troubleshot the intervening period.

10. Discussed any personal concerns (e.g., family relocation, health, etc.) you may have at this time.

---

of the challenges to be met, and creating plans to meet them. In addition, by stressing that his involvement gives the managers an unparalleled opportunity to participate in setting the future direction of the company or department, the counselor gives them an important incentive to *want* to work with him.

One client gave the following explanation to his management team to gain support for the role my company would play during the new man's "breaking-in" period:

"I've often found it helpful in the past to get the senior management group off-site for several days early in the game to review where we're going and how we're getting there. Such a meeting also gives us a chance to determine what are the issues that this group as a whole should be concerned with, what issues are the responsibility of each of us individually, and how can *I* help *you* do your own jobs better?

"At this kind of meeting, I think it would be most helpful to involve a professional, objective third party with considerable experience in matters of this nature."

He then introduced my firm's name and background and went on to explain that the role of my company would be to:

1. Conduct penetrating and strictly confidential interviews with each of you, with selected persons from other parts of the corporation and outside organizations who know us well.

2. Distill these insights, perceptions, and judgments in a feedback report, setting out the issues and opportunities that face us. The report is in the nature of an overview protecting the confidences of each participant. Because this distillation represents information and opinion from so many diverse elements of our company and industry, it gives us a 360-degree perspective on our situation while saving valuable time.

3. Present the findings, conclusions, and recommendations to the team, and let us test them, shooting down any that aren't valid. Working with those that can't be shot down, you and I then establish an agenda to be worked at this off-site conference for several days.

4. The counselor structures and serves as a catalyst at the conference to maximize the face-to-face time of the group in working the issues we have all identified from the report.

5. The counselor evaluates the results and performs follow-through counseling to make sure the project continues on track after the plan is implemented.

"I want you to understand," he added, "that this consultant is not my agent or spy, but an *integrative mechanism* whose job is to help us work harmoniously together, see our challenges more clearly and improve the managing skills we need to meet them."

I must stress the importance of involving the management team in both determining *what* changes are to come and *how* these changes will be managed. This involvement assures an element essential to the success of any program of organizational change: a commitment to its success by the people who must make it happen.

The wisdom of involving people in a search for solutions not only assures that the solutions chosen will meet the organization's needs better than one "handed down from above"; it also increases significantly the prospect that the recommendation will be carried out. Many consultants fail because they present a recommendation that is considered appropriate by *no one but themselves.* Unless the recommendation has the conviction of management behind it, it will probably be implemented halfheartedly, *if at all.*

This raises the whole question of consultant accountability. You hold your managers accountable for results. You should hold your consultant similarly accountable—not simply for presenting a report or a recommendation or completing an assignment by a certain date, *but for reaching specific mutually agreed-upon objectives.*

We encourage clients to hold us to specific goals. It helps us keep our eye on the target, assures that both we and the client are on the same wavelength, and provides a much-needed standard by which both we and the client can judge our performance.

Here's an example of a performance contract for consultants. It was designed by the client and ourselves before we undertook an assignment to advise an international project team that was seeking to both upgrade the performance of a European subsidiary and improve its working relationships with the parent (a United States–based multinational corporation) and regional headquarters in Europe.

In this instance, there were five principals who needed to be satisfied with our work: the president of the parent multinational corporation; the president of the European region; the president of the subsidiary; and the project team chairman and vice chairman. The task of drafting performance standards was complicated by the fact that, as advisers, we were not ourselves expected to produce quantifiable results (e.g., an increase in the subsidiary's return on investment or share of market), but only to facilitate the work of the project team, which was charged with doing so.

Performance Measurement Standards—"Project Team" Assistance

John Arnold ExecuTrak® Systems will have contributed "significant value added" when:

Third quarter:

1. Strategizing, structuring, and implementation of the project design is approved and implemented without derailment (i.e., cancellation of the implementation team; resignation of the Chairman or subsidiary President; postponement of the initial conference, etc.).
2. Counsel provided by us is assessed by the Chairman and the Vice-Chairman as "superior."
3. Based on their contact with us, subsidiary President and the Regional Headquarters President trust us, have confidence in us, and value our contribution as "excellent" or "superior."
4. The preparatory conference in Paris is evaluated by the Chairman, Vice-Chairman, and subsidiary President as having been "effective" in terms of results achieved in each of these areas:

a. Identification and troubleshooting of concerns
b. Effective interaction of members
c. Agreement of all members on role and value of Project Team

5. Our interview/Survey Feedback Report is evaluated as "superior" and carrying "significant potential value added" by Chairman and Vice-Chairman and by subsidiary President.

6. The initial Work Conference is appraised as "successful" in terms of:
a. The climate built
b. The Action Plan developed
c. The enthusiasm and commitment achieved
   as evaluated by the *written critique* of each Conference participant.

7. The Chairman completes third-quarter project management successfully as measured by the parent corporation President's appraisal of his performance.

Fourth quarter:

8. All principals at year-end agree that, without the consultant, the project would have been considerably more difficult to implement and achieve, and was well worth the sizable investment.

9. At year-end or early [next year] the Chairman's leadership is appraised as "excellent" or "superior" by the three principals whose support is crucial to the plan's success (Presidents of parent corporation, European region and subsidiary).

10. Both Chairman and subsidiary President give ExecuTrak® "superior" references to potential new North American and European clients, either on their own initiative or in response to inquiries.

Another measure of our contribution was reflected in the fact that, *within 3 months of our work with him,* the team project chairman was made executive vice president for European operations.

The ultimate test of a consultant's effectiveness is the same as that of an organization's effectiveness: its effect on the bottom line. Thus, a tribute I prize very highly is that of a new senior executive who was parachuted into an organization and who used us in all of the capacities outlined in this chapter.

His evaluation of our performance was described this way in a memo to the corporation's chief executive and operating officer:

"The cost/benefit ratio has been excellent by any measure. I am confident that this project has speeded up the process of identifying problems, clearing up our organizational structure, and getting my management team working together with clear goals and objectives by a minimum of 4 to 6 months. If you were to credit this project for only 5% of our first quarter profit projections, *it has paid for itself in less than one month."*

Chapter 8
"Whom Can I Depend On?"

(Revitalizing the Organization)

Frequently, an executive is parachuted into an organization to help revitalize the organization. Generally, organizations become candidates for revitalization only when their business begins to lag. Thus the new executive's charge becomes twofold: to revitalize the organization and to turn the business around. Organizational revitalization often—but not always—becomes the means to achieve the end of turning the business around.

A new executive faces several temptations in such situations. They include:

1. Cleaning house, sweeping out the "old order" and bringing in a new regime, personally loyal to the new boss (usually colleagues from his last assignment)

2. Imposing on the organization new policies, practices, and procedures (usually those the new boss employed on his last assignment)

3. Embarking on a crash cost-cutting campaign, paring expenses to the bone, sometimes to the point of profit-managing ("short-terming") the company

4. Some combination of the above

These strategies, though widely practiced, are, in our experience, short-sighted.

Cleaning house risks sweeping out the good managers with the bad—and administering a dose of shock treatment to the whole organization from which it may recover only with great difficulty.

Imposing practices on a new organization because they worked at another organization can be dangerous. It's a little like prescribing a certain medication for a patient with a stomachache without determining if the patient is suffering from indigestion or appendicitis.

Cost cutting and profit management generally produce early, positive bottom-line results that impress superiors. But if they produce short-term

79

benefits at the expense of long-term profits, they may ultimately prove self-defeating.

All these strategies have their place in the business-doctor's medicine kit. But—as with medical doctors—they should not be administered in the absence of a thorough examination to diagnose the real organizational ailments. It's not simply a case of "it's better to be safe than sorry." No executive wants to have the responsibility of telling the stockholders: "The operation was a success, but the business died!"

New Strategies

More sensible, we believe, is the kind of approach employed by the new president of a group of operating companies in Latin America that were owned by a multinational packaging corporation headquartered in New York. Bill Davis, as we'll call this president, followed a radically different course from those outlined above. Essentially, his approach had four elements. They are applicable to almost any situation an executive in a new assignment might face:

1. Identifying the issues: Finding out what's *really* going on in the organization—and why.
2. Getting local management "buy-in" on the problems uncovered; making the managers feel a sense of responsibility for the outcome, a feeling that the problems are *theirs* to solve, not only Bill's.
3. Resolving the issues with a view to doing what's best for the business, not what's best for any particular managing function or department.
4. By steps 1, 2, and 3, winning the understanding, support, trust, and commitment of the managers—something none of his predecessors had ever achieved.

The results of Davis's strategy were as dramatic as any that can be claimed by the proponents of the above turnaround formulas. Moreover, his strategy produced more lasting benefits, as we shall see.

The multinational corporation was a giant pulp and paper company whose Latin American investments—some acquired a decade before, some built since the acquisition—had never been in the black. In an attempt to make them profitable, corporate management had installed, and then fired, eight presidents in 9 years! The home office rationalized each failure by saying that everyone they sent down contracted "island fever."

In addition to the parade of presidents, numerous task forces and corporate staff (including the headquarters controller, personnel chief, and specialists in production efficiency and organizational development) had tried their hand over the years at "fixing the problem." Yet things continued to deteriorate.

It is, therefore, not surprising that when Bill Davis arrived at the sleepy Latin American town that was headquarters for the box plants, paper mills, and sales force that made up the bulk of the Latin American region, he was treated with little more than a shrug of the shoulders. "The common reaction," he told us several weeks later, "is 'Here we go again; another gringo is being sent down by corporate to shape us up. Ho-hum. This, too, shall pass!' "

After Bill described the situation, I asked him what he concluded from his people's reaction. He thought a moment and said, "I think they're trying to tell us something. They don't see this as their company at all. They view home-office executives as overlords, who come down on expense accounts to enjoy the weather and spout ideas that make unnecessary work for them. They see themselves, in corporate's eyes, as little more than 'dumb natives.' "

"Is it possible then," I asked, "that you put your finger on the real problem? No one is listening to them and the problems that they face so they don't feel any responsibility for the results the home office is complaining about?"

"I think that's it exactly," Bill declared, his eyes lighting up as the idea in his own mind became crystallized.

Out of our discussions evolved the outlines of a project that would involve the local managers in identifying the issues that *they* believed were adversely affecting the business. It would be their project, not New York's. We would listen to their diagnosis and really try to hear them, then feed back to them what we'd learned before proceeding further.

If the managers "bought-in" to the results of our feedback, we would then help them develop their own course of treatment, while serving as a catalyst and methodology resource to help them implement the plans they made.   •

This was a totally new and different approach, and Bill's reaction was immediate and enthusiastic: "It should work," he said. "And really, it's a lot less drastic than what New York has been doing all these years. We've tried telling them what's wrong, and we've seen that it doesn't work. If we try listening to what they think is wrong, how much worse off can we be? We might be a lot closer to the mark because they, after all, know their situation and their problems a lot better than we do."

But he added an important caveat: "The whole thing has got to come across as believable in their eyes. It can't be just another corporate scheme to make them shape up—or to 'get the goods' on them!"

The problems had been building for years. Nine years after the acquisitions were made, this division was losing $100,000 a year on sales of $25 million. In addition to the frictions between the home office and the field, relations were also strained between the box plants and the paper mills that serviced them. The plants, each of which was located in a different country, blamed the paper mills for poor-quality paper; the mills charged that the box plants made unreasonable demands on them.

In an attempt to bring some order out of the chaos, New York had created a central divisional office in Latin America. Bill Davis had concluded, however, that this additional layer of management duplicated some support services available from the home office and exacerbated the frictions between New York and the local operations. Moreover, he reasoned, since each plant produced for a different country and was subject to different laws and different local conditions, detailed centralized direction was counterproductive.

Accordingly, one of his first acts was to decentralize controls in favor of a concentrated cost-reduction and engineering approach at the individual plants. He stripped the central organization of all people except himself and a controller. Each plant was given responsibility for utilizing its equipment to the fullest and reducing its manpower where necessary. In addition to trimming overhead, the move had an important psychological benefit: It demonstrated to the managers that responsibility for their performance rested squarely on their shoulders.

But defusing tensions between the home office and the field and producing lasting bottom-line results could not be so easily mastered. That called for a new approach to identifying and resolving the basic issues of the business. That approach had three phases: diagnosis (interviews and management surveys); treatment (work conference), and evaluation (follow-through and reinforcement of plans and initial results).

Phase 1: Diagnosis

On my first trip to the region, I spent a day privately with Bill Davis, helping him identify his mission, key objectives, time priorities, and the key issues on his plate. He then introduced me to the group that had been tapped for participation in the project. It included 22 men, among whom were the managers of the individual plants and the mills, regional sales reps, and executives of New York regional headquarters. Of the 22 men in the project, 12 claimed Spanish as their mother tongue, 5 English, 2 French, 2 German, and 1 Slovakian. One member, the New York–based director of finance and planning, held an M.B.A. degree. Fourteen others had a high school education or less.

Because of the many previous attempts to achieve a turnaround, announcement of the project was greeted with the expected "Here we go again" response. But this feeling had considerably abated by the time phase 1 was completed.

Helping to build credibility for the project was the fact that we told all the interviewees that our feedback report would clearly distinguish between the perceptions of New York headquarters' respondents and the perceptions of the managers in Latin America. This made both groups anxious to get their views "on the table" (albeit anonymously)—the headquarters people portraying the local managers as "natives with island fever" and the managers themselves citing examples of significant initiatives to prove they were indeed capable of running their own affairs.

Thus, despite the initial reservations of many of the men, the confidential interviews (of company personnel and selected outsiders) succeeded in eliciting frank opinions and previously unrecognized insights.

The fact that we spoke some Spanish and had knowledge of the paper industry may also have helped smooth our path with some of the men. But we purposely refrained from falling into the trap of suggesting substantive solutions to any problems, fearing that the advice of yet another group of "gringos" might suggest to local management that we were "just a shill for New York."

In addition to the interviews, we administered our copyrighted Change-Management Climate Survey to get a reading on the basic management processes at work. This survey indicates where managers stand on a scale from "problem-reactive" to "opportunity-focused." It also illuminates whatever explicit problem-solving, decision-making, and planning systems they use, and provides insight into the effectiveness or ineffectiveness of internal communications.

To the top managers, we also administered a Personnel Inventory Survey, which helped us form preliminary judgments about their basic management characteristics (e.g., to what extent were they motivated by such goals as achievement, affiliation, or influence?).

A computer analysis of the interview and questionnaire responses—first fed back to Bill and then to the group—documented the obvious and revealed some previously unacknowledged sources of frustration. Among the obvious: Morale was low and confidence in the division's future lacking. Among the not-so-obvious was the discovery that the home office required 42 *monthly* financial reports from the division. No wonder the managers believed that the more New York tried to help them, the more it wrapped them in red tape!

The analysis documented a stack of issues heaped on Bill Davis's new plate, including poor cashflow, a fuel-oil shortage, excessive and potentially obsolete inventory, overdependence on a limited product line, a heavy load of accounts receivable, and a balky communist labor union.

The computer analysis helped Bill categorize, evaluate, and set priorities on the various issues, and also served to structure the intensive work conference that was to follow.

Phase 2: Treatment

The work conference was held in the mountains of one of the countries where a box plant was located, away from the pressures of the office and the telephone. It included both day and evening sessions for 6 days, with one night off to attend a local festival. Participants were brought in from operating plants and mills, the regional sales organization, and New York headquarters. Some were known antagonists. Some agreed to attend only after telling Bill Davis they thought the session would be a waste of time.

The conference turned out to be anything but a waste of time. After some initial climate setting and a simulation designed to instill a "win-win" orientation in the group, we outlined a suggested system for analyzing problems, to separate out symptoms and identify their root causes. We next outlined a system for management committee decision making. The group accepted both systems after some discussion. Bill then asked which of the issues outlined in the feedback report was most critical to the future of the business. The consensus was the poor cashflow situation.

Under our guidance, the group proceeded to search for the cause of—and the solution to—the poor cashflow situation. The questions were tough and the answers frank. What was the main reason for the poor cashflow? The largest box-plant customer had been receiving 120-day terms. Why did he receive such generous terms? Because he was the largest customer. Would his business be lost if the terms were shortened? Absolutely. Could the price be raised to minimize the adverse impact of his terms? No, an aggressive competitor stood ready to move in.

Well, why does this customer *need* extended terms? Because he's underfinanced and has to carry a large inventory to satisfy *his* customers. If his cash position were improved, could his terms be shortened? Probably. What would be the optimum solution from the point of view of the division? To shorten his terms *and* raise the price. Is there any way *he* could benefit from shortening his terms and raising the price? Sounds unlikely. Is it conceivable that if his cash position were improved enough through the division's initiative, prices could be raised and he still would benefit? Yes, it's conceivable. Has he explored bank financing to improve his cash position? Probably not. Do our finance people have any ideas about how he could obtain bank financing? Let's ask them.

The result was a plan—with contributions from sales, advertising, finance, design, manufacturing, and shipping—that did indeed raise the price and shorten the terms. It also benefited the customer. By taking out 12 notes of equal payment, he would obtain bank financing, the ability to take cash discounts, guaranteed supply, reduced inventory, same-week delivery on key items, packaging design assistance, and the inclusion of his products in a trade show.

The plan was presented to the customer by the involved plant manager and salesman. When he saw that his monthly payments would be no more than they were currently, he realized the company had considered his interests as well as its own. He accepted!

Our client received approximately $690,000 from its customer's bank immediately, without having to grant any discount. It passed along labor and material costs to the customer as they occurred. Because of its improved cash position, it was also in a position to sell the same customer additional items that he wanted, but which it previously could not supply.

Although the offer wasn't presented to the customer until after the conference was concluded, the entire decision and presentation plan was structured at the conference by one of the several teams set up to work specific issues.

The team process itself deserves some mention. Each team included representatives from the mills, the plants, sales, and New York. Each team would analyze the issue it had been assigned and present to the whole group its recommendation and an explanation of how it was arrived at. The team chairman would conclude his presentation by saying, "Okay, now shoot it down!"

The group would then troubleshoot the proposal to identify its vulnerable elements and suggest changes to remedy them. The result was not only a series of stronger proposals but a spirit of group camaraderie and mutual interdependence that had never been achieved before.

The development of this "win-win" plan for the key customer was like a shot of adrenaline for all the conference participants. Objectives that had formerly seemed unattainable suddenly were seen as possible. One team, for example, had been given the assignment of determining whether the division should bid on the linerboard requirements of a large shipping company. Its initial reaction was to dismiss the question as a waste of time. The competition, it was reasoned, had the account locked up. Besides, the division had never done any business with the shipping company.

Now, using the decision-making system to design a proposal that would represent a "win-win" solution for both the division and the shipping company, the team prepared an aggressive proposal. Bill Davis later reported: "A supercharged sales team pitched the company and returned with a $90 million contract, the largest in the history of all overseas operations."

Bill Davis's leadership was clearly established at the conference. The crucial moment occurred at a point early on the second of the 6 days when a crisis threatened to derail the proceedings. But Bill Davis's shrewd handling of the situation knitted the group closer together and went a long way toward establishing him as a leader the men could trust.

For months, rumors had been circulating that one of the paper mills was going to be sold. When the rumors surfaced at the conference, the men became distracted from the work we were doing. It was clear that the rumors demanded an immediate affirmation or denial.

I was leading the group at the time, and noticed Bill Davis scribbling some notes on a sheet of paper in front of him. Five or six pairs of eyes were staring suspiciously at him. After a few minutes, he interrupted me to ask for a short recess. "An issue has come up that I ought to address and I want to meet with some of this group right now in another room," he said.

Twenty minutes later he and the others returned. He read us the objectives he had scribbled on paper before getting together the involved people. Essentially, Bill wanted to put to rest rumors of the pending sale of the mill and demonstrate to the men his own desire to be completely open with them, to head off any need to rely on rumors to obtain information in the future. His objectives, as he read them to us, had served as the focal point of the team's discussion:

1. I intend to be completely honest and open with you regarding the question of selling the mill.

2. A possible sale *is* under discussion. But *no* decision has been reached.

3. I respect the progress that you have made to reduce costs at the mill.

4. But the key economic and supply problems appear to be beyond the control of the mill.

5. I'm open to suggestions from any and all quarters for making the mill economically viable.

6. In determining the future of the mill, the corporation's responsibility to its stockholders will, of necessity, be the overriding consideration.

7. If a decision is made to sell the mill, all employees will be treated not only fairly but generously. I personally will go to bat for you and for them.

8. In the future, managers will not have to rely on rumors to find out what's going on. You'll be informed on a regular basis. I'll see to that.

9. If at any time, any manager feels that I'm holding back on you, I want to know about it. My style is to deal forthrightly with people as I want you to deal forthrightly with me.

10. I'll continue to be as open and forthright on this issue as I will on any other. You can count on it.

While his statement did not relieve all the anxieties in the room, it perceptively raised the group's spirits. It was as though someone had said to division management for the first time, "Look, let's be honest with each other. There's a legitimate problem here and it's not going to be solved by fighting each other, but rather by searching for solutions together."

A footnote: The mill was eventually sold, but the men were kept informed of each step along the way. The mill manager elected to move elsewhere. And the settlements with employees were seen by them by fair and generous. None of the men had reason to believe that Bill had held back on them. Other results of Bill's conference were:

- A new shipping system that permitted a cut in materials inventory from an 8-month supply to a 2-month supply
- A tightening up of internal accounting that allowed reduction in the number of financial reports to New York from 42 per month to 8
- A reduction in indirect overhead expenses to the level of 3 years previously, even though volume had almost doubled
- A strategy for salvaging $270,000 in bad newsprint debts that called for obtaining a customer's approval to deliver just enough stock to keep his newspaper in business, with stock guaranteed for delivery, under certain circumstances, just hours before the presses were ready to roll.

In addition, a search for ways to minimize a staggering increase in fuel-oil costs prompted a decision to try a new approach to bid solicitation. Fuel oil was the basic raw material that fired the mills. They were totally dependent on it. For many years, a public-bid solicitation brought offers that suggested collusion among the suppliers. Each year a different company would offer a low bid; the bids of its competitors were never in the same ballpark. Yet each new year's low bid was higher than the low bid of the previous year.

Within 2 weeks after the conference, Bill Davis received the last bids from the seven "competing" petroleum companies. They showed price increases ranging from 150 percent to 325 percent over the previous year. Such price increases would have a disastrous effect on the bottom line and perhaps force divestiture or liquidation of the operations. Bill decided to "take on" the oil companies and not give in to his initial feeling that "we're at their mercy, the bastards." Using the same decision "troubleshooting" techniques that had resulted in landing the $90 million contract, he:

- Contacted other major industries in areas where his plants were located and formed a "purchasers' cartel" to counter the "producers' cartel" that was suspected of rigging prices
- Contacted the local governments and asked their help in combating collusive bidding practices
- Approached other potential sources of supply and solicited bids on behalf of the cooperating consuming companies

These efforts enabled him to successfully negotiate a fuel contract with one of the seven petroleum companies and hold oil costs virtually on a par with those of the previous year, and considerably below the prices being paid by New York for its continental United States operations to some of the same companies.

Phase 3: Evaluation

To assure that the conference was not a "one-shot" affair, a follow-up session was held 2 months later to evaluate the results and reinforce application of the methods. A happy ending was that just 4 months later, the profit plan was being met for the first time!

At the end of the year, return on investment had soared to 16 percent. Year-end dividend was equal to the initial capital investment in the area. The men proved themselves capable of running their business at a level of profit that more than fulfilled the expectations of the home office.

Bill Davis wrote the following assessment, in reviewing the project for a paper-industry trade magazine:

"We developed a common language and a common vision that enabled us to talk and think effectively about problems and projects. We focused on those problems and projects, not on each other. In the process, we developed trust and managing tools, which allowed decisions to be made at the lowest possible level."

The message that the men put into place as a result of the conference proved effective in dealing with a variety of new business situations. For example, one project, identified at the conference but left for later resolution, was the need to improve the ability of the division to serve customers during a strike. One union struck annually, regardless of need. Customers, in fear of running out of boxes, would apply pressure for a settlement.

Their concern was eventually relieved by staggering negotiations in the different countries. This not only allowed continuing production—thus no interruption of the flow of goods to customers—but it provided the division with a stronger negotiating position with each union. It also served to improve relations among the sister companies by increasing their interdependence.

Conclusion

There is nothing mysterious about the methods Bill Davis used to revitalize his organization and bring about a true business turnaround. The same techniques are available to any new executive parachuted into an organization who believes in systematically working with the management team to identify and resolve his problems and recognize and exploit his opportunities.

Chapter 9
"What Business Am I In?"
(Updating Your Mission and Charter)

There once was a company in Bridgeport, Connecticut, called the Frisbee Pie Company. It sold its pies in 10-inch metal pie tins that almost looked like discs. Students at Yale University in New Haven used to eat the pies. Then they would play catch with the discs.

The pies are no longer made because the Frisbee Pie Company went out of business. But other companies saw a market in the discs. They took the discs, changed their composition from metal to plastic, rounded the edges, and tossed the nation—and the world—a new game: frisbee.

The Frisbee Pie Company saw its business, as many companies do, in terms of products (in its case, pies), rather than in terms of customer needs and wants. What its customers needed and wanted more than pies (which, after all, could be obtained from any number of competitors) were discs to play catch with! Because the Frisbee Company didn't recognize the opportunity, it lost its chance to produce them.

Lots of businesses make the same mistake. They define their business so narrowly as to exclude major opportunities for growth. Hollywood missed capitalizing on the advent of radio and television because it defined its mission in terms of "motion pictures" rather than "entertainment." Railroads in the United States went into decline partly because they saw their mission in terms of supplying fixed rail services rather than caring for the needs of travelers (i.e., multimode transportation, restaurants, hotels, etc.). Levi Strauss & Company, originator of the blue jean, correctly foresaw society's growing informality as a way to move denim from work clothes to middle-class respectability. But it was the New York couturiers who realized—and cashed in on—the fashion potential of the trend.

The lesson is this: As a business defines itself, so does it limit or expand its opportunities.

One of the great sources of satisfaction in our own practice is being able to help companies remove the blinders that tradition and convention impose on their perspective, and make them aware of the untapped potential that exists in the marketplace and in their own organizations.

One model for the wisdom of a company reexamining its mission is the success story in recent years of Dow Jones & Company, publishers of *The Wall Street Journal, Barron's Financial Weekly,* and the Dow Jones Business News Service. The 1969–1970 recession plunged the *Journal,* which represented 95 percent of company net income, into its severest advertising decline in 25 years. Company earnings dropped more than 20 percent. So Dow Jones began looking for ways to make itself less vulnerable to the business cycle.

Dow Jones redefined its mission and transformed itself from a *"business news* company" to a *"communications* company." Armed with its new mission, it began a diversification program that has since made it a media conglomerate, with holdings that include a chain of small-town daily newspapers, a book publishing company, a general consumer magazine, interests in two newsprint mills, a weekly business magazine published in Hong Kong, a computerized news-retrieval service, and an Asian edition of the *Wall Street Journal.* It also offers an advertising-sales organization in the United States and overseas that represents its own and 22 foreign publications in 47 countries. The company is now described by a publishing analyst at Kidder, Peabody, & Company, as "a major cash-flow generating machine."[1]

Says Chairman and President Warren Phillips, chief architect of the company's diversification: "We don't exclude anything within communications. We would look at anything in the field of providing information" as falling within the company's mission.

As an executive in a new assignment, early in your tenure you should grapple with the challenge of rethinking—and perhaps redefining—your company's or function's mission or charter. If you do this collectively with your management team, you will have a head start in establishing a common wavelength and committing your managers to common goals.

Chartering

In this chapter, you will find guidelines to follow in redefining your organization's mission and charter. In addition, you will see how to translate those general statements of purpose into the establishment of the key performance areas that determine the success of your business. This process, which we call *chartering,* has three essential elements:

[1] Quoted in *Business Week,* Nov. 13, 1978.

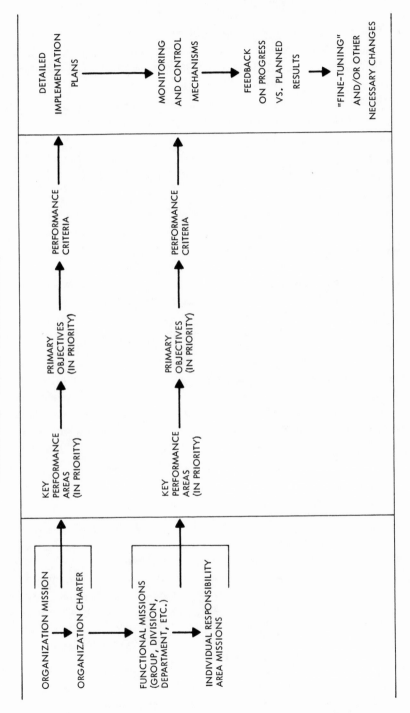

- Phase 1: The *"why"*—Define your mission and charter.
- Phase 2: The *"what"*—Identify the key performance areas and specific objectives for each department or function of the organization necessary to fulfill the mission and charter.
- Phase 3: The *"how"*—Draft the specific plans by which you will attain the objectives to fulfill the mission and charter.

In this chapter, you will see examples of phases 1 and 2. With a grasp of the essentials of the "why" and the "what," you should be able to establish your own "how"—specific plans tailored to the needs and requirements of your own organization or company.

Phase 1: The "Why"

Let's define our terms. The *mission* statement is a simple one-sentence description of the organization's reason for being. It answers the questions "Why are we here?" and "What business(es) are we in?"

A clear and concise mission statement demonstrates and communicates the organization's direction. It also provides a framework for establishing organizational goals and priorities. Further, it serves as an important motivator for managers and employees, giving them a sense of purpose and direction.

The *charter* is an expanded mission statement. It expresses the philosophy and overall objectives of the organization while "staking out its turf." It thus serves as the organization's hunting license, distinguishing it from all others.

The Mission Statement

Identifying your organizational mission requires defining your business not in terms of your own production, distribution channels, or sale of products, but in terms that satisfy consumer *wants* and *needs.*

Ice cream makers and vendors missed getting in on the ground floor of a revolution in consumer tastes several years ago when the yogurt craze hit the United States. The ice cream people defined their business in terms of a particular and static business—ice cream—when they should have been exploring ways of "satisfying consumer desires for frozen desserts that give people a cool feeling" (to improvise one broader definition of a mission that they might have considered). That definition might have prompted them not only to seek growth in frozen yogurts, but also to explore some of the advances in menthol and other breath-freshening agents that have been pioneered by candy companies, cigarette companies, and toothpaste manufacturers in the last decade.

Similarly, for years luggage makers produced heavy, durable suitcases without much evident concern for the difficulties travelers had in carrying them. The handles dug into your hands if you had to transport them any long distance. The luggage makers were more concerned with holding possessions than carrying them. Product innovation was largely cosmetic or limited to providing straps, dividers, and compartments to minimize crushing a traveler's belongings.

Those may indeed have been the important consumer points of difference in an age when people traveled by steamship or train and consigned their cases to porters as they began their journey. When steamships, trains, and porters all began to disappear, and people began increasingly to carry their own luggage, two developments occurred. First, a technological revolution made it possible to develop lighter and lighter luggage. Second, a shift to air travel, and the attendant difficulties and long delays in checking and claiming baggage at airports, produced a market for bags that could be carried by the traveler aboard the aircraft and either stashed under a seat or hung in a closet (i.e., the omnipresent airflight bags).

But while lightweight luggage was important to travelers, so was another quality, which manufacturers were late in discovering: maneuverability. Many travelers were less concerned with weight than with maneuverability— as Samsonite eventually realized in taking the plunge to introduce a line of luggage on wheels. Wheels are now revolutionizing the luggage industry—years after salesmen began putting them on sample cases to lighten their load! If a smart luggage maker years ago had recognized this consumer need, he might have designed a mission statement that read as follows:

> To meet the needs of travelers for maneuverable, easily transported *packaging* of belongings.

Note that the above definition is not restricted to suitcases or luggage. These are products, ways of satisfying a consumer need. The need itself is what counts—in this case, packaging. If luggage makers had indeed seen their mission more broadly, they might have noticed years ago the increasing numbers of travelers with packs on their backs, canvas carrying bags, and even plastic shopping bags—all ways of packaging belongings to which they might have responded earlier.

The lesson is that a good mission statement must be stated broadly and in terms of consumer needs, not specific products. At the same time, in writing a mission statement, you must avoid the temptation to define your business so vaguely that you are "all things to all people." Here, for example, is a statement one of our clients drafted several years ago (and which we subsequently helped refine):

To operate the company to its maximum potential for the benefit of shareholders, commensurate with fulfilling responsibilities to customers, employees, government, and society.

That statement has the advantage of not locking the company into any narrow product categories. However, it doesn't answer the question posed by the title of this chapter: "What business are you in?" It neither defines the business nor provides purpose and direction. What, after all, is "maximum potential?" What are its "responsibilities to shareholders" and the others? What goals or priorities flow from the mission? The statement provides no clues. It's a classic example of a "motherhood" statement.

A better fix on its business was made by a client that defined its mission as:

Expand our existing consumer franchise in tobacco while developing profitable, compatible products and/or businesses.

A diversified consumer products client defined a *two*fold mission:

1. To strengthen our position as a leading direct marketer to the consumer of leisure products and services, primarily in the categories of prerecorded music, sound, and related products, hobbies and crafts, and books and other products.
2. To achieve a significant market position in the manufacture, distribution, and/or retailing of hobby and craft products and services through conventional and/or direct marketing channels.

These mission statements give the tobacco company and the leisure products company a clear, concise *identity* and *purpose* to serve as a basis and thrust for planning and growth.

The Charter

A charter, like a mission, is a statement of what an organization is or wants to become. But it also expresses what the organization stands for, the principles and philosophy that will guide it. Here is the recently defined charter of a major food industry client:

The [company] consists of a group of interrelated and interdependent businesses filling consumer needs on a worldwide basis in the areas of:

1. Food prepared and consumed in the home, and food carried away from the home.
2. Food-related products and services in the home.
3. Other home-oriented products and services utilizing the strengths of the [company].

These consumer needs will be filled primarily by brand products and services, using whatever technological and distribution systems are required.

In executing the mission defined by this charter, we intend to stress quality in all respects—our people, our products and services, and our business conduct.

In explaining its charter, the client noted: "The focus of the charter is on the consumer in the home and the fulfillment of the needs of that consumer. Our mission is to do a superior job relative to our competition in defining the needs that exist at the consumer level and in developing products and services to fill those needs at a profit."

The charter of the tobacco client cited above committed the company to a specific share of market and operating profits over a 5-year period. It also expressed the company's commitments to be responsive to consumer needs, to set standards of excellence, and to be fair to all employees.

Some executives disparage charters as mere "window dressing." Certainly, if a charter statement does nothing but represent a public relations facade, it is of limited value. If, however, the charter is expressed as a *constitution* for the company, from which the marching orders flow, it performs an essential *direction* and *priority-setting* purpose.

In summary, the important steps in developing a mission and charter are:

1. Make them broad but directional.
2. Define the business base in ways that permit capitalizing on trends and changing conditions.
3. Define the business in terms of consumer or customer *needs* and *wants—not* company convenience or specific products or services.
4. Make them "living documents" that infuse *all* efforts of the organization.

Phase 2: The "What"

What does your organization *have to* accomplish to fulfill its mission and charter? There are four stages to the "what":

1. Define the *key performance areas* of the business—the factors that determine success or failure.
2. Identify the *primary objectives* for each key performance area.
3. Rank in order of priority the key performance areas and the objectives within each.
4. Identify the *performance criteria*—the standards—by which progress will be measured. These must clearly set forth *what* must be accomplished by *when, where,* and *to what extent.*

Why bother specifying these four steps? There's no question it's a time-consuming chore, and, let's face it, there are more thrilling challenges in the world than identifying key performance areas, objectives, priorities, and performance criteria. So why not just forget about it?

The reason is this: There are two kinds of organizations—those in which all functions operate in ways that contribute clearly to the overall purpose and objectives, and those in which the functions operate without systematic direction.

The choice is yours. Lots of organizations—businesses, government agencies, nonprofit and volunteer groups—have "made it" (however you may define that term) by hunch, by luck, and "by golly." But no organization is likely to survive for long (let alone prosper) if it is rudderless, especially if it faces either public or stockholder scrutiny or—more formidable yet—smart competition. The world is changing too fast for that.

Key Performance Areas

What are the *key factors* that determine the success or failure of your mission? These, of course, will vary from one industry, and even from one business, to another. But there are certain common elements.

From a checklist we developed for use by newly appointed senior executives, a consumer products client set forth his business's key performance areas as follows:

1. Profit
2. Planning
3. Volume growth
4. Trade relations
5. Consumer impact
6. "People" growth
7. Product quality
8. Acquisitions
9. Communications with parent corporation
10. New-product development

Note the differences between those key performance areas and these, which were established by a pulp and paper client:

1. Finance
2. Contract negotiations
3. Integration with another company (a firm that had recently acquired it)

4. Market standing

5. Management succession/organizational development

6. Government relations

7. Financial-community relations

8. Board of directors

9. Customer satisfaction

10. Compensation

11. Safety

12. Environment

Other key performance areas that might be relevant to your own first-year challenges include:

1. Management process improvement

2. Organizational structure

3. Internal development

4. Diversification

5. Public responsibility/public relations

6. Professional development

After you have identified the key performance areas of your business, rank or prioritize them according to importance. To determine relative importance, ask yourself, "Which is most apt to be the significant determiner of success in the given time next (year)?" The answer merits first priority. "Which is most apt to be second most significant?" etc.

Primary Objectives, Priorities, and Performance Criteria

It's easy to establish goals or objectives in each key performance area. The challenge is to set goals that are realistic, results-focused, and measurable.

Some companies set goals and make them measurable but neglect the important intermediate step: setting priorities, which is the key to allocating resources. To set priorities on objectives within each key performance area, ask, "Which is the most necessary to achieve?"

In the absence of setting priorities, companies often find out the hard way that they are devoting more effort to minor objectives than to those which are critical to their success. The rise of discount supermarkets, for example, suggests that conventional "full-price" supermarkets were placing too high a priority on providing consumers with attractive store surroundings, personalized bagging services, and other "frills," which were less important to cost-conscious food shoppers than lower prices.

On page 99 are examples of objectives and performance criteria established by one client, the marketing department of a major steel company. The company, using us as a catalyst to help the new executive vice president and his 15 VP's and department heads upgrade marketing effectiveness, made the listed breakdown of its business goals.

Just as organizations need to define their missions, key performance areas, objectives, priorities, and performance criteria, so do *individual* functions within those organizations. To fully meet their responsibilities, a newly appointed senior executive and each of his managers should specify their objectives in ways that implement the overall organizational mission and objectives most effectively.

Most management-by-objectives programs counsel managers to develop their individual missions and objectives in collaboration with their direct superior. This, it is said, assures that the subordinate will be fully committed to the mission and objectives established. We've seen overwhelming evidence that this approach does not go far enough.

While our clients' experiences confirm that an organization does indeed function better when each person helps determine his own responsibilities, their experiences suggest that it functions *even better* when each manager also has an opportunity to review his mission and objectives with others on the management team and to obtain the benefit of their thinking, criticism, and troubleshooting. The benefits of using the team as a sounding board in clarifying responsibilities include the following.

First, this provides coordination, assuring that no responsibilities essential to the smooth functioning of the organization fall through the cracks because no one is assigned them. If I'm doing A and you're doing C, team discussion properly focused will smoke out the need to assign someone to B.

Second, it assures mutually supportive objectives and priorities, eliminating overlapping or conflicting responsibilities. If my responsibilities require me to do X, and I can't do X unless you do Y, then Y has to be on your list of priorities as well as mine or I can't do my job.

Finally, it gives the whole team a common commitment to the division of responsibilities agreed to. All understand them and support them.

Thus, the team process for defining functional responsibilities is based on the premise that discussion and mutual accommodation—a process of give and take—will produce a clearer, stronger, and more effective definition of responsibilities than merely to have a manager work one on one with his superior. Moreover, this approach has the added advantage of allowing each member of the team to view the organization's challenges from a common perspective, rather than from his own narrow functional perspective. Each member knows how all the pieces of the puzzle fit together—and why.

To assure maximum coordination, many of our clients go further. They

Objectives and Performance Criteria

Key performance areas	Priority	Objective	Performance criteria
A. Profitability	1	a. To achieve a return on investment of	_____ by December 31, 1980.
		b. To achieve an earnings per share of	_____ by December 31, 1980.
		c. To reach a minimum share of market of	_____ % on _____ products by December 31, 1980.
B. Sales	2	a. Achieve sales of no less than	_____ tons of _____, and _____ tons of _____ at budgeted price of not less than _____ and _____ respectively by December 31, 1980.
		b. Achieve penetration of new and/or existing markets in specific geographic areas of no less than	1. _____ % for region A 2. _____ % for regions B and C 3. _____ % for all other regions by December 31, 1980.
C. Planning	3	a. Achieve a variation in forecasting accuracy of not more than	1. Short term (3 months)—5% 2. Medium term (1 year)—7% 3. Long term (5 years)—20% of actual sales for *any* product line.
		b. Ensure that product development is consistent with identified present and projected market needs as measured by	1. _____ % potential market share for product line A; _____ % for product line B; etc. within _____ months respectively. 2. No surprises.
D. Customer satisfaction	4	a. Receive no more than	a. 1% of orders in customer complaints about *any* aspect of our service or products in any 12-month period.
		b. Ensure any customer who complains about anything is notified within	b. Not more than 2 working days after our receipt of his complaint explaining what action is being taken.
		c. Ensure that the proper department is notified within	c. One working day of our receipt of a customer complaint
		d. Ensure that corrective action is taken	d. On every single complaint.
		e. Ensure agreement by management committee	e. No later than September 1, 1979, on mechanisms to limit customer-service complaints to no more than _____ (number) of (X) type of complaints; to no more than _____ (number) of (Y) type of complaints.

99

use the ExecuTrak® Coordination Matrix, which specifies the role of each function in the major types of organizational decisions.

One of our newly appointed senior executives outlined a 13-step marketing-sales process. Each function had clearly defined responsibilities for each step (i.e., as initiator, concurrence, approval authority, etc.). For example, the product manager was designated initiator for market analysis and plan, with concurrence required from commercial research and sales, subject to approval of the vice president of marketing.

The chartering procedure for individual functions is identical to that of organizations. On page 101 are excerpts from the objectives established by one client, the vice president of operations of a commodity business.

This objective-setting discipline enables newly promoted executives to create new objectives and performance criteria where none previously existed. For example, the president and chief executive officer of a company that merged with another committed himself to the following goal in the key performance area of "mergers":

Objective:

To ensure successful merger of the sales companies of [his organization] and [the other organization] as measured by:

1. Losing no more than one manager whom we wish to retain at the level of regional sales manager or above in the next 12 months,

2. Losing *no* contracts with any of our 10 principal customers for reasons other than competitive pricing, and

3. No more than one decision per quarter requiring the CEO's arbitration between the two sales departments.

In the key performance area of "human resources," a sales manager set these targets:

Objectives:

• To ensure the establishment of primary objectives and performance criteria for every sales position within my purview as measured by approval by the Vice President—Sales, no later than March 31, 1979.

• To ensure development of a "career path program" for sales personnel, as measured by approval of such a program by the Vice President—Sales, no later than June 30, 1979.

• To ensure no lack of adequately trained personnel for each position, as measured by an evaluation of each person's performance against approved criteria by December 31, 1979.

Fiscal 1980 Primary Objectives and Performance Criteria for Vice President (Division X) Operations

Mission: To ensure that (Division X) Operations satisfies market needs for _____ and _____ in support of the corporate mission as measured by achieving the following:

Key performance areas	Priority	Primary objectives	Performance criteria
A. Profitability	1	Achieve aggregate product-line profit of $	No less than $_____ million before tax and corporate allocations.
B. Customer satisfaction	2	a. Improve customer satisfaction as measured by	a. No less than _____ % of all product shipments meeting quality and shipment time specifications on a monthly basis beginning January 1, 1979.
		b. Strengthen relationships with key national accounts	b. As measured by increased sales to no less than 4 of 6 key accounts in the 12-month period.
C. Organizational structure	4	Achieve complete organizational realignment with all incumbents functioning in new positions, as measured by	Board approval of realignment by January 1, 1979, and all positions filled and functioning by July 1, 1979.
D. Management performance, development, and depth	7	Achieve approval of Employee Training and Development Plan to have replacements identified and ready to occupy a minimum of _____ key management positions within the next 5 years, as measured by	Board approval of plan by October 1, 1979.
E. Environment	8	Ensure that all operations comply with new governmental restrictions, as measured by	*Not* one governmental citation for noncompliance.

Summary

Every organization should have a clear, concise, and purposeful statement of mission. Every organization should also translate that mission into objectives, priorities, and measurable criteria for each function. Having counseled literally dozens of companies in chartering, I can honestly say that we know of no company with a strong sense of purpose and direction that hasn't identified its mission in some disciplined manner.

Chartering relates the entire organization to one central unifying purpose. It gives everyone in the organization a sense of purpose and challenge. It enables senior management to allocate resources, to obtain early warning of deviations and shortcomings, and to evaluate the contribution of key business components and individual managers.

In sum, translating your business goals into measurable criteria significantly increases the likelihood that *what you want to happen will indeed occur.* In an age of uncertainty, it is a powerful force for controlling your organization's destiny—and your own!

Chapter 10
"Where Should We Be?"
(Planning with People)

First there was planning. Then came long-range planning (now commonly referred to as "old planning"). This gave way to strategic planning. Herewith, we introduce our own contribution to the state of this evolving art: strategic *team* planning. "What is *that?*" you ask.

Strategic *team* planning is a way to broaden the traditional planning process within a corporation, group, or division to allow maximum feasible participation of all relevant managers, professionals, and even employees, in the design of a plan. For a senior executive in a new assignment, *team* planning has three advantages over conventional forms of planning.

First, it draws ideas and insights from a broader pool of talent than is normally tapped in the formulation of a plan. Thus, it increases the likelihood that a wider range of promising options facing the company will be considered.

Second, because the planning process becomes a collaborative undertaking—involving the boss, his subordinates, and (for some particulars) one or more levels of *their* subordinates—it becomes a focal point and organizing vehicle for putting the organization on a common wavelength committed to common goals.

Finally, because of widespread involvement, planning is transformed from an "esoteric exercise"—removed from day-to-day responsibilities—into a part of the fabric of the organization. Each department and function feels a stake, and responsibility for, its portion of the plan.

Strategic planning is a concept that came into general use in the 1960s as a way of attempting to systematically determine how best to allocate resources over time. Unlike "old planning," it *begins* with a determination of the destination to be reached at the end of the planning period, most often 3 to 5 years.

Old planning tended to project into the future the historical direction of the company and establish benchmarks to measure progress against plans. Its starting point was "where we are."

Strategic planning, on the other hand, requires a conscious management decision early in the planning process of "where we want to be" at the end of the planning period. The actual plan becomes a road map to take the company "from here to there." Strategic planning requires managers to answer the questions "Where do our best opportunities lie?" and "How can we exploit them?"

Many companies leaped on the strategic-planning bandwagon in the 1960s and early 1970s. This was a time when economic growth was fairly steady and the future offered reasonable assurance of conforming to the planning assumptions that had governed the immediate past.

In 1974, however, the Arab oil embargo triggered twin inflationary and recessionary spirals, throwing many company strategic plans into a cocked hat. In the years since, strategic planning has been refined to provide greater flexibility in the face of economic uncertainty. Many plans today include both a primary strategy and a backup (contingency) strategy to follow in case the assumptions on which the plan is based should prove invalid.

With these refinements, the steps in the strategic planning process, in simplified form, are these:

1. *Determine where you want to be* at the end of the planning period. This typically includes a decision on financial goals (return on investment, return on assets, share of market, etc.) and other objectives, such as "to be number one (or number two) in X industry"; "to grow in ways that make us less vulnerable to the business cycle"; "to become less dependent on (a few) key accounts," etc.

2. *Determine where you are* with regard to company strengths, weaknesses, and capabilities in relation to the environment (government, consumer or customer trends, technical advancements, competitive activities, etc.).

3. *Identify the gap* to be filled (the difference between 2 and 1 above).

4. *Evaluate options* to get to your chosen destination, including an assessment of the outlook for present businesses under probable conditions, and again under negative conditions; and new businesses (whether bought or built).

5. *Choose the best option(s).*

6. *Develop an action plan* to get from here to there.

Strategic plans can be produced in a number of different ways. Many companies turn to an outside management consultant to design their plan. Others commission internal planning departments to do the job, either on their own or in conjunction with an outside resource. Both of these approaches can have significant flaws, however.

Studies by outsiders typically fail to reflect the reality of internal pressures and constraints. These pressures may be day-to-day responsibilities and/or political sensitivities of leading company executives. Moreover, some consultants specialize in recommending pet solutions. A consultant whose experience lies in acquisitions, for example, may favor this route to company growth at the expense of others that might be more promising.

If outsider plans tend to inaccurately reflect internal reality, insider plans often do not contain an objective analysis of company strengths and weaknesses. In addition, internal planners often do not have a good enough grasp of external opportunities to consider all the options available, or they may dismiss some as unthinkable (e.g., "We really don't want to consider profit-managing this company, do we?"). What is needed is a process that can overcome "management myopia" in looking *outward* and the imperfect understanding of company culture of those looking *inward.*

In addition, because both insider and outsider plans tend to be developed without wide participation within the company, they often fail to enlist the commitment and "buy-in" of those who will be responsible for carrying it out. The result is often a plan ineffectively implemented.

The strategic team planning process used by our clients seeks to combine the broader perspective of an outside counselor with the insights and detailed knowledge of the business possessed only by insiders. It also attempts to solicit the widest possible participation within the company.

A Strategic Team Planning Project

The following is an example of how a newly promoted chief executive used this process in his company. He established a strategic team planning project with three overall objectives:

1. To help the company determine its direction and goals for the next 5 years
2. To develop a detailed plan to achieve them
3. To transform the management committee from a collection of independent—and frequently feuding—baronies into a smooth-functioning team under his leadership

Significantly, the direction the company ultimately established was suggested by a third-level manager, whose ideas might never have been solicited under more conventional forms of planning.

In this case history, all names—company, industry, and individuals—are disguised, for obvious reasons. Suffice it to say that the company is a household name in the consumer goods industry, and this example illustrates the process used by newly appointed executive clients in a variety of industries.

Jim Kramer, recently installed president of Kroften Products, Inc., and his executive vice president, Lloyd Hastings, came to our offices with the following story:

The company was in dire straits: The smallest of five companies in the industry, Kroften's volume and market share had been declining for more than 20 years; it had run through four presidents in the previous 5 years; the business press was sizzling with rumors of the company's possible sale by the parent corporation, which seemed to regard Kroften as more of an embarrassment than a profit generator, though the business did indeed generate high profits year after year.

To make matters worse, the government was seeking to discourage the public from consuming the industry's products; consequently market growth was at a standstill and trending down. Any new business for Kroften would have to come at the expense of competitors. But the competitors, being larger and more profitable, could afford to outspend Kroften in advertising and sales promotion.

Kramer went on to explain that Kroften had precious little credibility at the corporate level. "We have been chasing numbers from year to year," he remarked. "Each year, we predict we will halt our decline and we come up with an annual plan to do so. As time goes by, we realize we can't meet the targets we've set. We begin loading distribution channels, cutting advertising, and taking other short-term measures that will buy us another year. Our basic problem is that we've been asking ourselves, 'What do we have to do to keep Corporate off our backs?' instead of asking ourselves, 'What will it really take to turn around our business?' I guess my predecessors were afraid to ask that question."

In addition to its marketplace and corporate problems, the company faced serious internal strains. Kramer, who had been elevated to the presidency from vice president of sales when his predecessor was fired, had made little progress in establishing his own leadership of the company. It was not simply a matter of not knowing what direction offered the best hope for Kroften's future. Several departments were hardly on speaking terms with one another.

Henry Thomassen, head of operations, presented a special problem in this regard. A 35-year veteran of the company, Thomassen was a member of the parent corporation's board of directors and a leading figure in local community affairs.

"He technically outranks me," noted Kramer. "In fact, he's on the board of directors, even though my boss and I are not! And he is suspicious of any attempts to find out what's going on in his department. How the hell do you run an operation where you have an independent empire like that?"

He concluded his cheerless remarks by saying, "Frankly, if you people don't feel we have a chance, then please tell us and we'll forget it. There are times when it seems that the best thing for us to do would be to throw in the towel. But if you think there are ways we can turn ourselves around, then I would like to hear a proposal from you. I sure don't want to be known as the man who let Kroften go down the drain."

"Why are you interested in developing a strategic team plan?" I asked. Kramer smiled and winked at Lloyd Hastings.

"My boss [the group president], asked me the very same question when I told him I was coming up here to see you. What he said was, 'Kramer, how can you think about putting together a 5-year program when you don't know if you can stay in business for the next year?' I'll give you the same answer I gave him.

"If we can set our sights on a 5-year target that will really turn this company around, next year will take care of itself."

Kramer was willing to gamble on the fact that if corporate headquarters could see a credible plan that would lead to greater profits within 2 or 3 years, it would be willing to let the company alone in the interim to reinvest its profits. It was a gamble that would be severely tested before our project was finished, but it made eminent sense.

The industry was a very profitable one, with a 20 percent to 25 percent return on investment. Though Kroften had never failed to produce profits for the corporation, profit contribution was shrinking. Moreover, its declining volume and market share made it increasingly difficult to maintain its products in national distribution. With costs rising, some influential figures at the corporate level were openly suggesting that the assets employed by Kroften could be used to better advantage elsewhere.

In short, either the company would have to undergo a strategic redirection or it would have to resign itself to being sold off.

But what kind of strategic redirection? That was the question Kramer set out to answer in coming to us.

We were neophytes in the industry represented by Kroften. But we had been novices when we went to work for our first clients in the food industry, the steel industry, the canning industry, the paper industry, the communications industry, and numerous others. I explained to our guests that while the facts and challenges differ from one industry to another, we have found that the techniques for resolving them are *identical.*

We explained our process to Kramer and Hastings, noting that we could not guarantee that the company would indeed remain in business if it followed our approach. If, however, there was a way from Kroften to achieve a turnaround, we could help the company recognize it and exploit it.

"That's your reputation," said Kramer.

Out of our discussion evolved a proposal to use the strategic team planning process as a means of both designing a turnaround strategy and revitalizing the organization. "I would also hope," said Kramer, "that we would approach the project in a way that really fires up everybody in the organization, including lower-level managers. We are facing a critical morale problem, and I'm afraid we're going to *continue* to lose good people to other companies if something isn't done soon."

Specifically, our role was to serve as diagnostician, methodology resource, and catalyst to help Kramer and his management committee identify "ambitous but achievable" 5-year goals, develop and evaluate alternative strategies to achieve them, draft a detailed implementation plan with responsibilities assigned and benchmarks established to assure that it would be effectively carried out, and position the plan for maximum support at the corporate level.

I have faced unfriendly audiences before, but never have I faced an audience that was as sullen as the 11 managers around the horseshoe table in the wood-paneled room of Kroften's headquarters on a torrid afternoon in August, when Kramer and Hastings introduced several members of my staff and me to the management committee. Kroften was an old, tradition-bound company, suspicious of outsiders. The thought that the company needed a consultant to help solve its problems was a bitter pill for these proud managers to swallow, particularly since the man who was "imposing" this outside resource on them had, so far, failed to win their allegiance.

I described our process, our backgrounds, and our proposal. I introduced the members of my staff, and tried to introduce a note of humor. But no smile cracked any face around the table. Several members sat bolt upright in their chairs, arms folded against their chests.

When I called for questions, there were none. Kramer and Hastings pledged their full support of the effort and urged the management committee to cooperate with us in every way possible.

I must confess that as we began our work the next day, I had my doubts that we would receive much cooperation.

I suppose it was the professionalism of our staff that won them over. As we conducted confidential interviews to identify the strengths and weaknesses of the organization, to help tap the insights and ideas of each manager, the men began to open up. Perhaps they realized that this was their first true opportunity to have a say in the future of the company—and to be heard by someone who had no "ax to grind."

By the time we had finished conducting our interviews, we had passed muster on the internal company grapevine, and the managers had begun to feel a stake in the outcome of the project. I realized the change most dramatically 6 weeks later when we presented to the management committee the feedback report outlining the issues, opportunities, and other findings of the first phase of the project. Commented one of the members: "We have seen the enemy—and he is really us."

Phase 1. Identify Ambitious But Achievable
5-year Goals

Kramer agreed with us that it is wishful thinking to set a company's mission
and long-term goals without first making a thorough analysis of its strengths,
weaknesses, capabilities, and constraints, and attempting to identify the external or environmental changes that will affect the company during the planning period. At Kroften, compiling this information took a number of forms:

- 104 confidential interviews to determine the company's competitive
  strengths and weaknesses, market trends, lifestyle changes, and possible
  opportunity areas for future evaluation. Interviews were increased from
  the original 60 because of the valuable information and *enthusiasm* generated in the company by our penetrating approach. Interviewees included
  68 managers, from company president to union president; 12 persons
  from corporate headquarters, including the corporate president and his
  chief financial officer; and 24 outsiders, including former company executives, financial analysts, advertising agency representatives, distributors,
  suppliers, and editors of trade journals.

- A compilation of industry trend data, company profit and volume, and
  market share trends.

- An analysis of the company's existing product portfolio, using the now-
  standard measures of growth generation and cash generation to identify
  "stars," "hopers," "cash cows," and "dogs."

- An evaluation of the relationship between marketing expenditures and
  share levels, comparing company performance with the performance of
  competitors.

- A comparative analysis of manufacturing costs, efficiencies, and product
  quality defects for the industry.

This information, outlined in the feedback report, became the subject
of an initial 4½-day intensive management committee work conference held
at an off-site location under the leadership of President Kramer.

The feedback report became the vehicle for confronting a number of
potentially embarrassing issues that no member of the management committee had felt bold enough to raise before. These included lack of teamwork,
low morale, unclear definition of responsibilities, interference from the parent corporation, haphazard planning—and doubts about the leadership ability of Jim Kramer.

On the question of his leadership, Kramer took the criticism in stride,
expressing gratitude that the issue was now "out in the open where we
can deal with it."

"Now that I know the depths of this feeling," he said, "I can go about
trying to change that perception. If I can't exercise the kind of leadership

that this company requires, then I don't belong in this job." Several of the members individually praised Kramer for his courageousness and his lack of defensiveness.

The feedback report also unearthed some misperceptions among company managers. For example, it had long been believed that manufacturing costs were out of proportion to the industry as a whole. Our comparative study of manufacturing costs showed that Kroften's manufacturing costs were within industry norms, and that product quality—also thought to be a pressing problem—was not significantly different from that of its competitors.

In addition, our report established some favorable points about the company's current position that had been largely overlooked: It had outstanding, but idle, capabilities in research areas that could be capitalized on to give Kroften a competitive advantage.

Finally, our analysis showed that the company's portfolio was overly skewed toward declining product categories and that the company had no entries in one of the fastest-growing segments of the market—despite impressive company research capabilities in this area.

On the basis of past performance, industry trends, and information provided by corporate headquarters regarding profit expectations of the company's subsidiaries, the management committee established tentative year-by-year goals regarding profit and market share for the 5-year planning period. It also formed interdepartmental task forces to research questions and bring back reports for a *second* conference a month later. On the basis of the information to be researched, the second conference would be devoted to developing and evaluating alternative strategies to refine and achieve the goals decided upon.

Since the first conference had been largely devoted to assessing the company's current position ("Where are we?"), the second conference would be designed to explore "Where do we want to go?" The research reports would cover major trends and developments in the next 3 to 5 years regarding:

- Economic conditions
- Competitor goals and strategies
- Market trends
- Population changes, geographic shifts, consumer lifestyle trends, and new segmentation possibilities
- Law and government policy
- Labor-management relations
- Raw material supplies and costs
- Opportunities for increased productivity and efficiency
- Research abilities and technological changes

- Alternative marketing and distribution strategies
- Other ways to use company resources—sales force, distribution network, research and manufacturing facilities

Under Kramer's direction, the group also designed a strategic planning flow chart, which appears on the next page.

The new president asked the members at the conclusion of the conference to write a brief, anonymous assessment of the initial conference. Typical evaluations were:

- "Positive spirit of working together with common objectives."
- "Better team spirit—attitude, ability to work together."
- "A firmer commitment to the success of the company."
- "A strong sense of direction toward establishing future goals for the company."
- "Better knowledge and understanding as to how to manage properly and effectively.[1]
- "A start has been made on establishing a true consumer franchise that can turn the business around."
- "We defined *who* are and *what* we want to do, which should lead to *how* we want to do it."
- "A commitment to direct and honest communications against the business instead of against particular personalities."
- "The start of a formal planning process to better identify long- and short-term goals, objectives, and priorities."

Phase 2. Develop and Evaluate Alternative Strategies to Achieve Goals

The second phase of the strategic team planning process is to design strategic options on the basis of the information developed from the task forces. At Kroften, the reports prepared by each task force were presented at conference no. 2.[2] Key opportunities identified by the task forces were prioritized by the management committee and essential information bearing

[1] This comment refers to an aspect of the project, which goes beyond the scope of this chapter, devoted to upgrading management skills in decision making, problem solving, the conduct of meetings, and communications.

[2] Between conference no. 1 and conference no. 2, Kramer asked us to conduct two 1-day seminars for 34 middle managers to familarize them with the strategic team planning process, solicit their ideas for the future direction of the company, explain what they could do to support the effort, and encourage them to feel a greater sense of involvement and responsibility for assuring a turnaround at Kroften. These sessions led to the establishment of a middle-management *coordinating committee* to foster interdepartmental cooperation in resolving problems that did not require attention at the management committee level.

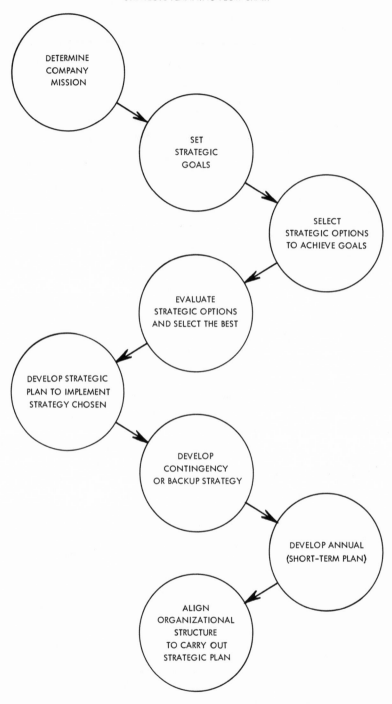

on the company's future was recast in the form of broad strategic options. Essentially, the options facing the company were identified as:

1. *Retrenchment,* including profit management, contracting out specific functions (e.g., manufacturing, product specialization, etc.)

2. *Status quo with changes* (organizational realignment, a major product breakthrough opportunity, etc.)

3. *Diversification,* including acquisition of related consumer goods companies that could use company resources to manufacture, market, distribute, or conduct product research for other parts of the corporation or for outside companies

One task force brought back an analysis of the relationship between levels of marketing expenditures and marketplace performance. It showed that a new product had not been introduced successfully by any company in the industry for the previous 5 years *for less than* $35 million a year. In order for Kroften to put that kind of money behind a new product, the company would have to confine its new-product activities to only one entry every 2 years, possibly even every 3 years.

That fact—coupled with the knowledge that marketing expenses were escalating dramatically year by year—cast the conference in gloom for a time, because the members realized that it might be impossible to sustain the level of activity that might be necessary to launch a new product successfully, even before the end of the 5-year planning period.

Moreover, it became clear that a true business turnaround would require reducing profit contributions to the parent corporation for a period of 1 and possibly even 2 years. And with Kroften already under fire for not producing enough profits, there was serious question whether the corporation would view this prospect favorably and give the company the time required to achieve the turnaround.

The group decided to design a *turnaround* plan with a view to what was best for the business—not merely what was best in the short run for the parent corporation—and try to demonstrate that it was in the corporation's best long-term interest as well. To do so, there would have to be enough "honey in the pot" at the end of the 5 years to justify the period that corporate headquarters would have to wait to get there.

But how, even if profits could be minimized for a year or two, could Kroften generate enough resources to effectively compete with larger companies that could outspend it? And how could the company continue to afford a national sales force when there were areas of the country where it could not maintain distribution on its present products because of its low share of market?

Groups have a way of generating a kind of internal momentum that throws off ideas *synergetically.* That is, a group collectively may inspire ideas that individual members could not reach on their own—*if* the group is using a *creative methodology* and a *catalyst* to keep them focused and imaginative.

Under Kramer's leadership and using our methodology, the management committee developed the following idea:

Since 80 percent of the company's sales were in 60 percent of the country, and the costs of maintaining the sales force in the remaining 40 percent of the country were not justified by sales in those areas, and since the company could not hope to compete effectively on a national level if the costs of marketing continued to escalate, why not explore ways of confining Kroften's marketing and sales efforts to the markets in which it had a strong consumer franchise, handling the other markets either through brokers or not at all?

The regional concept had surfaced several weeks earlier, when a third-level manager mentioned to one of our interviewers that he had researched a "regional strategy alternative" to continued national distribution. But it had never before received serious consideration within the company. Discussion of the option had been foreclosed by arguments that "no national company has ever successfully retrenched to a regional base" and "if consumers can't buy what they want when they travel, they won't buy it at all."

Now, however, it became clear that a regional strategy might enable Kroften to compete dollar for dollar with its larger competitors in the markets of its greatest strength, assuring that it could not be bested for lack of resources. It could concentrate its resources where they would do the most good—where the company could get the most "bang for its buck."

But which were these markets? How should they be identified? And how should they be serviced? What were reasonable volume share and market share expectations in these areas, and what would they be nationally? What would happen to the bottom line if the company were to move to a major market or regional strategy? Would Kroften risk losing its franchise because of competitive pressures, population mobility, trade resistance, chain retail-buying practices, or lack of corporate support?

The group concluded that it needed more information about the comparative risks and benefits of alternate regional and national strategies for the next 5 years.

It also decided to pursue possible new ways of employing its resources, such as offering its sales force to distribute the products of other consumer goods companies, undergoing product research for other companies in its areas of distinctive expertise, and even supplementing its own product line with new acquisitions in related businesses.

Conference no. 2 concluded with a tentative statement of the company's future business mission and charter and a refined set of strategic goals. It was agreed that the mission should be to "develop a consumer franchise to reverse the volume and share decline in 'X' business while providing a base for future growth." Kroften's objectives would include a minimum return on assets to the parent corporation of 15 percent a year in the *fifth* year of the plan. Year-to-year targets would be set at lower levels, the exact level to be decided according to the specific strategy adopted.

Kramer assigned the alternative strategies to task forces for future research, with recommendations to be presented at a third conference. The group also voted to expand the number of conference participants beyond the 11 management committee members to include 7 key subordinates.

Conference no. 3, which took place 3 weeks later, employed our decision-making process to help the expanded group funnel down their analysis to the best strategic plan option from the several presented.[3] On the basis of the strategic objectives established and the assumptions agreed to, a detailed computer analysis was run of the comparative national, regional, diversification, and other options. Based on the computer-developed data, Kramer and his 17 subordinates agreed that one particular *regional* plan was superior to any of the other alternative strategies.

Although the research failed to turn up an example of a company that had successfully moved from a national base to a regional base, it was also unable to establish any persuasive arguments why this could not be done. Indeed, the financial projections argued persuasively for this strategy.

The regional strategy offered less potential in the fifth year and thereafter than the strategy of remaining a national company, but the projections indicated that it should produce improved profit contribution to the corporation the second, third, and fourth years, while maintaining the company's market share at levels that would assure effective distribution. A national approach, on the other hand, would run heavy deficits in the second, third, and fourth years, even if more than one new product could be marketed nationally at competitive spending levels—which was doubtful.

Best of all, this strategy would permit Kroften to continue to compete head to head with its larger rivals in the areas where it chose to fight. Finally, if the new strategy were successful—or if a new-product breakthrough justified expanding its chosen business base—the company could grow market by market and emerge as a stronger national force than before, possibly by the fourth year.

The 18 members agreed unanimously to adopt this particular regional plan as the company's main strategic thrust for the 5-year period, and to work out details for review at an expanded management committee meeting 3 weeks later. As a backup or contingency strategy, it chose to work out

[3] For a description of the ExecuTrak® decision-making process, see John D. Arnold, *Make Up Your Mind* (New York: AMACOM, 1978).

details of continuing a national strategy based on the possible success of a projected major new-product introduction in the first year of the plan. To avoid moving to a regional strategy before the marketplace impact of the new product could be gauged, it was decided to remain national for the first year of the plan, while setting the groundwork for the regional shift beginning in the fourth quarter if the new-product introduction did not meet the volume and market share goals established for it.

Phase 3. Draft a Detailed Implementation Plan

Once the strategic goals, basic strategy, and backup contingency strategy have been set, the next step calls for establishing the nuts and bolts of the plan. Between conference no. 3 and conference no. 4, each department went to work detailing its part of the plan. Kramer named an internal project coordinator to work with the company financial vice president and individual departments in orchestrating the elements.

Marketing developed its 5-year scenario, spacing new-product introductions and adjusting advertising and sales promotion spending levels to conform to the year-to-year objectives. Sales worked out the details of tailoring its field force to the needs of a regional marketing system. Manufacturing worked up a 5-year capital expenditure program. Market research drafted a consumer research program that would serve as the spearhead for new-product development.

Each element of each department's program was charted on a master ExecuTrak® planning sheet that detailed costs, start-up and completion dates, how results would be measured and monitored, responsible individuals, and possible problems and preventive actions. Adjustments were made by the coordinator and financial vice president to eliminate conflicts (e.g., a new-product introduction in an area of the country being phased out by the sales department), and the final plan was assembled in a notebook. The book was reviewed by the expanded management committee at conference no. 4 and approved with minor refinements.

Phase 4. Position the Plan for Maximum Support

Proper plan positioning requires that you know your audience. Who are the people that need to be convinced? What will they be looking for? What do they want and expect from the company? What are their doubts, their likely objections, their biases, their "hot buttons"? What kinds of presentations impress them? What kinds bore them? What will they likely find most impressive about this plan? And how can it be strengthened? Where would they find the plan most vulnerable, and how can the vulnerability be overcome or reduced?

Kroften's plan had to leap three hurdles: the group president, whose favorite question—based on his conduct of annual plan presentations—was "What are you going to do different?"; the corporate president, who had an aversion to reading and to long presentations; and the corporate board of directors, who knew little of the internal workings of the company but would be skeptical of the company's ability to reach whatever goals Kroften established on the basis of its past performance.

The group president's question would be easily answered; this plan represented a dramatic departure from anything the company had done before. The corporate president's requirements could be met by a concise, visual presentation using overhead transparencies, including charts that vividly portrayed the different bottom-line results that could be projected from continuing nationally versus shifting to a regional strategy. The board of directors' skepticism would be a problem. To the extent that the corporate president shared these concerns, the presentation would have to demonstrate why this plan—as opposed to a series of annual plans whose goals the company had not previously met—could indeed be achieved.

These concerns dictated a two-pronged tactic. An explicit, persuasive rationale would have to be developed for shifting to a regional strategy— a *why* to give context and meaning to the *what* and *how* of the bare figures and facts of the plan itself. Moreover, the plan would have to be thoroughly troubleshot to determine all the things that could go wrong and what specific mechanisms would be built into the plan to remove or avoid these. This was done, with transparencies developed identifying the major potential problems and the actions that had or would be taken to treat each.

Three presentation dry runs were held with members of the management committee. Everyone's performance was critiqued and all transparencies evaluated for relevance, coherence, and conciseness. The final presentation was clocked at 1½ hours with up to another 1½ hours for questions and discussion.

Conclusion

The above scenario can be followed by any senior executive to develop a viable, opportunity-oriented strategic *team* plan while generating maximum support and commitment to its success. It is particularly beneficial for a newly appointed senior executive because it helps him solidify his team, establish the right directions early in his tenure, demonstrate his leadership to his superiors, and become thoroughly familiar with both the organization's inner workings and the marketplace challenges he must confront.

At Kroften, the strategic team planning project continues to pay dividends to Kramer and his managers. It welded a divided and uncertain management into a highly motivated team with clear direction. It provided a showcase to identify and elevate middle-management talent. It led to a major organizational realignment that tightened up the managing process, reduced overhead, and brought about significant gains in productivity. It spawned a sales-incentive program that improved the efficiency of sales calls and resulted in the company's surpassing its volume goal by 24 percent the first year.

The key to these benefits was a determination by the company's CEO to think through the company's mission, strategic goals, and strategies with his people rather than rely on a management consultant's recommendation or that of a corporate staff function; to accept and build upon frank and constructive criticism of his leadership and organization; and to undertake an innovative *team* planning process never before tried in the industry, a process that shows promise of rebuilding the company and providing the secure and profitable future it seeks.

Chapter 11
"Where Do All the Pieces Fit?"
(Creative Realignment)

Every new senior executive wants to put his distinctive stamp on an organization. Sooner or later, that may mean realigning the organization.

Many act sooner, rather than later, for a number of reasons: Reorganization is dramatic, decisive. It demonstrates that someone forceful is in charge. Short of issuing termination notices, nothing a new executive can do will have a more immediate effect on combating organizational complacency.

Finally, reorganization can buy the new executive precious time with his superiors. He can resist for perhaps several months the inexorable pressure for results, arguing plausibly, "We all have to settle into the new structure before you can see the progress."

Superficially attractive as these "benefits" might be, there are powerful arguments against immediate reorganization. A new structure is a little like a new suit of clothes. No matter how stylish it may be, it won't look good unless it fits. And you can't find the right organizational fit until you know, on the basis of firsthand experience, what, if anything, is seriously wrong with the old organizational fit.

Moreover, organizational structure is not, after all, an end in itself; it's a means to carry out your business objectives. The structure either facilitates or frustrates achievement of these objectives. A reorganization that is undertaken without regard to business objectives may end up doing more harm than good—buying you time *now* at the expense of results, both now and later.

Of course, you may want to make some small temporary structural refinements soon after beginning your new assignment. But that's different from reorganizing your company or departments.

One of our clients found upon joining a new company that he had 14 subordinates reporting directly to him. "I can't get any work done," he complained. His first temptation was to reorganize.

On the basis of some questions we posed to him, he concluded it would be better to make only interim changes. "I can make some changes now," he reasoned. "But it will be awhile before I can know with any assurance what the *right* changes are to make." He cut the number of direct reporting subordinates to 3: two executive vice presidents and the chief financial officer. The 11 others were temporarily assigned to one of the 3 for a period of 90 days.

This wasn't an ideal solution; temporary solutions rarely are. But it was the only way he could free up the time he needed to learn his job and think about where he wanted to lead the company.

Reorganization

When should you reorganize? How do you know that some type of realignment is needed? What's the best way to do it? What are the pitfalls to look out for? How do your people fit in? How do you get the support necessary to "make it work?"

These are important questions. The success of your business may depend on the answers, so let's explore each of them in turn.

When Should You Reorganize?

Except for temporary and emergency adjustment (to cope with sickness, resignations, or other special problems), you should probably make *no* organizational structural changes until you have:

1. Developed, with the support of your subordinates, a clear statement, approved by your superiors, of your business mission and objectives
2. Read the strengths and weaknesses of each of the key players
3. Solicited criteria for any organizational realignment from your own organization and your superiors (see below)

If you are coming into a job from the outside, it will probably take you *at least 90 days* to accomplish these three steps *wisely*. If you're moving up or laterally in an organization you know well, on the other hand, the process may take only 30 to 45 days.

How Do You Know When a Realignment Is Needed?

The answer to this question is critical. Many companies undertake reorganizations, it would appear, simply for the sake of reorganization, particularly North American companies. In Japan, where continuity is valued more than change, an executive who joins a company and reorganizes is considered to have taken a very drastic step. The more normal practice is to stick with the "tried and true" organizational structure unless there is an overriding reason to change it. And why not? Organizational *re*alignments, after all, are a cure for bad organizational *a*lignments. They should *not* be a cure for bad business strategies, bad product offerings, or the wrong people in key positions.

Yet how many companies reorganize for reasons that have nothing to do with structural problems! Accordingly, to determine whether a realignment is truly needed, the first step is to ask yourself—and others:

- "What *is* happening *for reasons of the present structure* that *shouldn't* be happening?"
- "What *isn't* happening *for reasons of the present structure* that *should* be happening?"

We are often called in by companies to help them answer precisely these questions. As a result of our probing and fact finding, they sometimes find that what they thought was a problem in the way the organization is structured is instead a problem in clarification of authority and accountability, or roles and relationships. That is, the problem may lie in uncertainties as to *who* has *what* decision-making, decision-execution authority and *how* the *process* should be managed. If that is the problem, the chances are it would continue under any new structure.

If, on the other hand, the kind of probing we suggest demonstrates the need for structural changes, the company can move forward with greater confidence. The organization also will be more apt to accept changes if the need for change has been *demonstrated* rather than perceived as the result of some new executive's whim.

What's the Best Way to Realign? What Are the Pitfalls to Look Out For?

Obviously, there is no one, all-purpose organizational structure. Some consultants have been known to favor certain organizational patterns and seek to impose them wherever they go; beware of those who offer solutions in search of problems. It is rare to find two companies in which the identical organizational structure is really optimal for each. Although companies may face similar problems, organizational structure and staffing solutions should be designed for distinctive needs and opportunities.

The experience of our clients suggests that the best way to realign is as follows:

1. Get guidance from someone with a proven track record in helping companies make—and implement—realignments.

2. Get inputs from everyone in the organization whose perspective would be helpful or whose commitment is important to making a new structure work.

3. Obtain inputs from key outsiders who know the company's problems, opportunities, and strengths and weaknesses well.

4. *Rigorously* weigh the effects of alternative structures on your key people— and ways of creatively using your key people under alternative structures.

5. Give as much attention to troubleshooting and positioning your changes for maximum support as you give to deciding what those changes will be. The best organizational structure in the world isn't worth the paper it's printed on if it can't command the support—*up* and *down* the line— from those needed to make it successful.

One of our clients, president of a large corporation, determined he was ready to reorganize after 6 months on the job. Rather than act unilaterally, he decided to challenge his management committee to take part in the process. At a regular weekly meeting of the group, he reviewed his reasons for believing a realignment was necessary, calling attention, for example, to the major changes the industry had undergone since the existing structure was established 15 years before.

"Obviously," he said, "what I ultimately decide is a judgment that I alone must make. But I think everyone in this room can help me make a better decision by giving me the benefit of your ideas as to what objectives any organizational realignment should seek to satisfy."

Using our methods of specifying criteria, the group produced 40 suggested objectives. Several of them duplicated objectives he had already developed with our assistance, but several others were new ones. He discarded a few of their suggestions as impractical (e.g. "Structure should be acceptable to every manager"), and produced for our next meeting with him a consolidated list of 34 criteria that he thought important to his determination of the best structure. They ranged from "Ensure best product in terms of quality and service" and "Ensure retention of all key customers" to "Avoid empire building," and "Minimize unwanted turnover of key personnel." The client also asked his boss to suggest criteria, as well as two of the company's most valued customers (who felt flattered to be asked).

Here are six areas—drawn from a lengthier Master List of Suggested Realignment Criteria we use with clients—in which you may want to consider establishing criteria for your reorganization:

1. Sales, share of market, and earnings
2. Decision making and planning

3. Operational administrative efficiency and control

4. Company reputation

5. Human resource utilization

6. Minimizing disruption during transition

Translating your realignment criteria into alternative structural arrangements can be either a mechanical process or a creative one. If you are exploring the options with an outside sounding board experienced in this process, it can be an invigorating and creative experience.

A cigarette manufacturer faced a particular problem in his production department that made him want to ensure greater accountability of all elements in operations as part of his reorganization. The more we discussed reorganization, the more it became clear to both the client and us that what was needed went beyond manufacturing or indeed even operations.

Given criteria for any realignment developed with the contributions of the top 17 executives and managers, and because the company was plagued with nagging quality problems, the chief executive and operating officers decided to make one person accountable for all facets of product quality, including research and development, raw material purchases, manufacturing, bottling, and distribution. Out of such discussion was born the concept of a "vice president for product assurance." The position—unique in our client's industry—is one of five that now reports directly to him under the new alignment. Before reorganization, this client had 9 vice presidents reporting directly to him, leaving little time to invest his own management talent where it could do the most good.

Normally, our clients will consider up to a dozen varying structures, some of which might vary only in degree from one another. With our help, a major food marketer developed three structural options with 10 variations in total, as shown in the accompanying table. On the basis of the criteria we helped the president and his team establish, and the priorities they assigned to each, we helped him evaluate each of these 10 options.

Option no. 10, "Reorganize marketing around menu segments," fared best, but it was deficient in a couple of important respects. We showed him how to overcome these deficiencies by incorporating elements of other options (as described in my book on managerial decision making[1]), which produced a new structural alignment tailored precisely to his needs, although different from any other structure in the industry.

"Creative realignment" is 180 degrees removed from the sheer mechanical "by the numbers" approach employed by some consultants. It likewise bears no relation to the "organizational bloodletting" that many companies

[1] John D. Arnold, *Make Up Your Mind* (New York: AMACOM, 1978).

Basic Organizational Alternatives

A. Retain current structure	B. Consolidate profit centers	C. Consolidate staff support functions
1. As is, absorbing change in composition of business.	6. Consolidate all these food divisions.	(Research and development, market research, new-product development, advertising/sales promotion, etc.)
2. As is, with key personnel changes.	7. Consolidate two of the three food divisions.	8. Consolidate marketing.
3. Consumer services absorbed by marketing services.		9. Leave marketing as is.
4. Consumer services absorbed by line organizations.		10. Reorganize marketing around menu segments (breakfast, snacks, main meals, desserts).
5. Line organizations as is; centralize key support at group level.		

engage in periodically—an exercise in needless self-flagellation and made even worse by some consultants, whose reports "legitimize" what the president unilaterally wants to see changed.

Creative realignment is a process for determining and implementing organizational change that is based on a thorough analysis of organizational needs, includes the input of those on whom its success depends, and seeks to generate even better alternatives from those basic alternatives previously identified. These alternatives are then rigorously evaluated and troubleshot.

Where Do Your People Fit In?

After you have tentatively outlined your basic new structure, you face the challenge of determining *who* to fit *where*—and who might not fit at all.

Some executives follow the path of least resistance in reorganizing: They build their structure around the skills of their people (e.g. "We need a marketing vice president; we have a good product manager, so let's make him marketing VP").

Your product manager may indeed be the best marketing VP you could name, but how do you know? If you operate (as most of our clients do) in a highly competitive environment, you need the best man—or woman— for each key position. The purpose of organizational realignment, after all, isn't to "play musical chairs" and accommodate people, but rather to help assure that you can achieve your primary business objectives. To the extent that the people you have in key positions can help you do that, and in the process grow professionally, you want to *retain* them. To the extent that you need new people to do that, you want to *obtain* them.

Either way, your evaluation process must begin by looking not at the *people* but at the *functions to be performed.* For each key function to be established by the realignment, you should develop its mission and objectives. Then, identify each position's skill requirements. After these steps are completed, you are ready to analyze the pluses and minuses of your key people and match them against the requirements of each position.

The diagram and list show how one client, combining two dissimilar functions to form a business/human resources planning and development function, defined the mission and skill requirements for a new vice-presidential position.

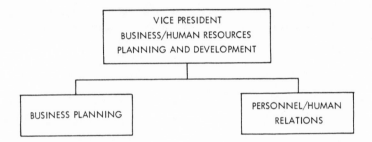

Mission:

1. Help assure effective implementation of 1979, 1980, and 1981–1983 plans

2. Monitor and counsel on development of all planning and performance review activities within company

3. Personnel/manpower/organizational planning and development

4. Special projects

Requirements:

1. Excellent organization and planning ability

2. Highly conceptual mind

3. Open-minded and perceptive

4. Excellent consulting skills

5. Business management/market orientation

6. Someone who can take over major operating responsibility in the future

Through our questioning, the client identified strengths, weaknesses, and potential concerns about each of the 11 senior managers and high-potential middle managers in the division. Then he matched each against the requirements of the six major functions that comprised the realignment structure he had tentatively chosen and chose the best manager for each position. He concluded that no one on his team had the "potential for distinction" required for this position, but he was able to fill it by promoting someone from the parent corporation.

Many executives, to save time, consider people only within their own disciplines. Our experience helping clients do creative realignment demonstrates that it often makes sense to consider ways in which managers' talents can be used *outside* of their own areas of specialization.

One client, using our guidance, took the most creative thinker in the sales department and made him one of two key subordinates to the marketing vice president, assigned to working with advertising agencies and key distributors to develop new marketing strategies. This happened to be a man whom he had *demoted* when he first became president, a man who subsequently demonstrated his resiliency and rose to the challenges. One year after his *promotion,* this man had so revitalized the distributor network with innovative and practical marketing strategies that he was made vice president of marketing.

Another client took a man with an impressive background in finance, operations, general management, and liaison with the board of directors, and made him head of a new corporate planning/acquisition/evaluation function. The man initially considered the move a demotion—until he recognized the pivotal role he could play in charting the company's future. This function is now the *priority* function in this rapidly growing client company.

Before finalizing your new structure and your choices for the major positions within it, it is well to check informally with people who have been around longer than yourself. One newly promoted executive planned to install a new operations vice president, whose responsibilities would include the materials handling department. His questioning revealed that the operations man had allegedly once gotten drunk and insulted the wife of the materials handling supervisor. The supervisor had vowed he would quit if he ever had to work for the offending manager.

When the client prepared to make the change, he visited the materials handling man, explained why he was making the move, and offered to transfer the man to a job of commensurate status if he didn't want to remain in materials handling. This man took the transfer and continued to perform well—after remarking to a friend that he would have quit if the matter had not been handled so skillfully. Without systematic troubleshooting, this pitfall would not have been identified and the company would have lost a valuable manager.

How Do You Win Support for Your Realignment?

If approval by your superiors is required, you will want to prepare—graphically, if possible—a summary of your rationale for making the decisions you have made, clearly demonstrating how the realignment serves the overall organizational mission better than the existing structure. There is generally no need to initiate a detailed discussion of all the alternatives. It might be worthwhile, though, to mention how many structures were considered before you chose this one, and to be prepared to discuss and show some of the others, if asked.

In preparing yourself for this presentation, it may be advisable to analyze the interests and potential "hot buttons" of each member of whatever committee it is that has to be convinced—whether it's the senior management committee, board of directors, or only one or two superiors. Then, tailor your presentation accordingly. Ask yourself: What portions of the changes are most likely to be questioned? On what grounds? By whom? How can you satisfy the objections? If you have to modify any part of it, which part should you modify, and how?

Obviously, you should be clear in your own mind as to how much of the plan you can afford to modify and how much must be accepted "as is" to achieve its intended effect. To go into a presentation with your superiors without having considered any "fallback position" is advisable only in situations where you are assured of approval—or are prepared to resign!

Marketing your realignment to the organization presents a different sort of challenge. Unless you are unconcerned about maintaining management motivation, you should plan your strategy here with utmost care. Again, an outside resource skilled in troubleshooting and positioning organizational changes can make a significant difference in developing a climate of acceptance for your changes.

The written announcement of the changes should be short and factual and should contain summary answers to the obvious questions your people will pose—the *why, what, when, where,* and *who* questions, as well as, "What does it mean to me? Where can I find out how I'll be affected?" Frame your announcement with a view not only to what the changes are, but—equally important—*who* will be reading it.

Especially where certain people are being passed over or demoted—or the announcement could be interpreted in this manner—be conscious of the impact the announcement may have on those who didn't get the position and their friends and families. Consider what impression you want to leave with customers, the trade, business press, and others who will learn of it. What you *don't* explain about the changes may be as important as what you *do* explain.

As a matter of courtesy, you should develop a realistic, time-phased plan to tell key people—subordinates, and maybe key customers and suppliers—what is going to happen. There is nothing more demoralizing to key people in an organization than to read in the newspaper, hear on the radio, or be told by others about major realignment changes that will affect them.

Although most newly appointed executives understand the need to prepare their presentations with concern for the sensitivities of each member of their team, some minimize the equally important element of *timing*. Ideally, members of your team should all be told—whether in a group or individually—on the same day. One of our clients made a list of 12 people he wanted to inform personally of a major organizational change, beginning with his executive vice president at 7:30 in the morning and continuing at 45-minute intervals throughout the day, ending at 4:30. He was exhausted at the end of that day, but his care assured that no one had to rely on rumors to find out what was going on.

Moreover, we helped this client strategize the order in which he should impart his plan. His instinct was to follow the chain of command, a move that, while understandable, was also fraught with problems because of the personalities and organizational relationships involved. For example, the marketing/sales vice president, who ranked third in the organizational structure and thus would be told in the morning, was a very close friend of two other managers who weren't scheduled to be told until afternoon. The three ate lunch together virtually every day they were in town. Thus, if "Mr. Marketing/Sales" was informed in the morning, Messrs. Market Research and New-Product Development would undoubtedly know it before the president got to them.

Couldn't Mr. Marketing/Sales be trusted? Under normal conditions, yes. But not this time. One of his luncheon-mates was to receive a major promotion under the major realignment; the other would be asked to resign. How could he be expected not to betray his feelings?

The solution chosen by the client was to tell the dismissed man first, the promoted man second, and Mr. Marketing/Sales last, despite the protocol implications.

Another executive also resolved to inform his key people of his reorganization on a certain day. Unaccountably, however, he "spilled the beans" prematurely to a key subordinate. Despite the aide's pledge of secrecy, by the time the president made his announcement 3 days later, it was already common knowledge throughout the organization, with the adverse consequences that had been anticipated if the announcement plan was not carefully implemented. Naturally, the aide denied that he was the source of the information. The president had only himself to blame.

Once your new structure has been approved and announced, you face the challenge of making it work. Here, it is vitally important that you again involve your people—*if you want it to work effectively.*

We have found in working with newly appointed executives that a realignment can become a galvanizing force for organizational revitalization. It also offers an opportunity for your managers to strengthen their management skill and interaction—and "gel" as a team under your leadership.

Here are the objectives of an "organizational realignment implementation" conference we conducted for key managers of a major forest products company. Its purpose was to "accelerate implementation of the realignment."

Objectives of [Company] Realignment Implementation Conference

1. Reduce narrow "divisional thinking."

2. Direct the energy of the new team to developing a sense of partnership and communicating "on the same wavelength."

3. Ensure that the *why, what,* and *how* of the reorganization are precisely understood and accepted.

4. Clearly establish the leadership, direction, governing philosophy, strategy, overall policies, and management style of the realignment.

5. Develop a common vision of the key issues, problems, potential obstacles, and opportunities created by the realignment.

6. Set the realignment mission, goals and objectives, and plans through the next fiscal year.

7. Nail down and win mutual commitment of each key function to the respective authority and accountability, roles and relationships, key performance areas, primary objectives, and types of performance criteria to be established.[2]

8. Develop a new company modus operandi.

9. Establish a follow-up results plan of *what* we're going to achieve, and *how* and *when* we're going to achieve it, to assure effective implementation of the conference and other realignment decisions.

Conclusion

In undertaking an organizational realignment, bear in mind that you are doing a lot more than shifting boxes on an organizational chart. You are seeking to *mobilize*—and *focus*—your resources more effectively.

Few decisions you make have a more far-reaching impact:

- On your managers' and other employees' performance effectiveness and career development

- On your customers and suppliers

- On the financial and investment community

- On the communities in which you operate

- On government agencies with whom you interact

- On the public image of your company

[2] See Chapter 9, "What Business Am I In?" for guidance on how to define, agree on, and mesh such responsibilities.

Just as an effective structure can enhance your organization's productivity, so can a structure that is too hastily determined—or negatively perceived—hurt the company's productivity and reputation, and your own leadership credibility.

This is one job where you may need more help than you realize!

Chapter 12
"Are They Part of Us?"
(Making Corporate Marriages Work)

As a senior executive in a new assignment, if you should plan to pursue your company's growth through acquisition, you may be interested in the following example of an all too common experience in the aftermath of corporate takeovers.

A major Fortune 500 petrochemical company purchases a smaller Fortune 500 company in an unrelated field. The headquarters and staff of the new subsidiary are told they will be allowed to complete a move of their corporate headquarters—begun before the merger—from, let's say, New York City to Phoenix. Now, a year later, the parent company begins a sweeping realignment of the subsidiary, which results in the firing or reassigning of scores of managers and other white-collar employees involved in the move.

Subsidiary executives and managers are caught by surprise. At least a half dozen of them say they have already sold their homes in the New York area and bought new ones in Phoenix, only to learn they have no job. The petrochemical company's employee relations manager emphasizes that the company will reimburse employees for costs incurred in preparing for transfers that have now been rescinded.

There is nothing unique about this story. It follows a pattern that increasingly accompanies corporate takeovers. That pattern goes as follows:

1. Initial takeover bid—often, but not necessarily, unfriendly—is carried out with little thought to the requirements of effective postacquisition management.

2. Assurances are given that there'll be *no major changes* without full consultation with the present management. Acquired executives are assured "We want to work with you," "You have nothing to fear," "We're all part of one team now," etc.

3. As "proof" of this high regard, the president of the acquired firm is told he will be reporting *directly* to the acquiring company president.

4. Within a period of weeks or months, virtually all the promises are forgotten; the reporting relationship is through a second—or even third or fourth—level liaison; morale in the acquired firm has plummeted; and the acquired managers describe their plight in terms of having been systematically looted, plundered, or—since marriages, corporate and otherwise, imply partnership—*raped.*

This scenario repeats itself in acquisition after acquisition. Yet few companies draw the obvious lesson: The better they prepare themselves for successful postacquisition integration, the better they will be able to achieve the benefits they sought by consummating the merger or acquisition. As obvious as this lesson is, *it is almost universally ignored.*

Techniques for Successful Postacquisition Integration

Leading business schools, private marketers of public seminars, investment bankers, and other consultants typically offer "complete" courses on merger and acquisition strategy with no focus on postmerger or postacquisition management. It is assumed that once the knot is tied, the couple lives happily ever after. It rarely happens that way, however—either in life or in business.

Luckily, there are techniques to assure effective postmarriage management. They have been successfully employed by dozens of companies. As an acquisition-minded executive, you must be concerned with finding ways to assure that the growth continues after the vows have been exchanged.

Research has shown that the success or failure of a company—as measured by such "hard" criteria as return on sales, return on assets, etc.—is largely determined by the strength of its management. More specifically, a company's performance is dependent on management's ability to operate within two rather distinct environments: the external environment of the marketplace and the internal environment of the company.

In the external environment, management must identify the factors that influence success (i.e., customers, competitors, suppliers, government regulations, etc.) and fashion a viable business strategy to capitalize on these. In the internal environment, management must organize the company's human and physical resources to effectively execute its business strategy and produce goods and services with maximum efficiency.

Frequently companies bent on finding acquisition candidates fail to probe how well the acquisition candidate manages these two environments. Similarly, they rarely concern themselves with how well the candidate's business philosophy and values, managing processes, and style realistically will fit with their own.

There is, of course, nothing that will prevent an acquiring company from taking a hard line toward its new subsidiary. A vice president of finance of an acquiring company reflected precisely this attitude when he told his counterparts at their first meeting: "Let's not forget that *we* own you and that *you* work for us—not the other way around."

Such an attitude is not only tactless and demotivating; worse, it is plainly self-defeating. The interest of the acquiring firm is best served *not* by imposing its philosophy, values, operating procedures, disciplines, etc., on its new acquisition, but by determining the best kind of "fit" to achieve business objectives and organizational synergies.

Case 1

"How do you determine what that new mission and optimum form of organization should be?" That was precisely the question asked me by the president of a worldwide commodity company which, in a surprise action, had acquired 51 percent of the stock of a major competitor. I'll call the acquiring company Herricks, and the acquired company Lawson, though these are not their real names. The way in which we structured a successful integration can serve as a model for companies willing to look beyond the next earnings-per-share report in devising acquisition strategies.

Essentially, our process is implemented in three phases:

Phase 1: Diagnosis This phase consists of an opportunity-detection and diagnostic process, drawing upon penetrating, comfortable, and strictly confidential interviews with managers of both companies to reveal the key issues and opportunities posed by the union, including administering one or more of our copyrighted survey instruments. These may include our Business Values Inventory, Environmental Factors Questionnaire, Change-Management-Climate Survey, and Decision Process Matrix.

The findings from these inquiries, which take the form of a feedback report, enable both parties to determine "the logic of the fit" and—if a decision is made to proceed with the acquisition—to develop at the outset a basis for trust, candor, and commitment of all parties to the success of the union. Our experience suggests that the basic beliefs, values, managing philosophy and styles, attitudes, and expectations of the acquired company's key managers will be crucial factors in ascertaining whether a "win-win" relationship can indeed be built and whether the potential synergies can indeed be realized. (In Europe, where "basic compatibility" has long been considered an important ingredient in acquisition considerations, companies are much more sophisticated in their understanding of these matters than in North America.)

Phase 2: Work conferences The second phase consists of one or more intensive, shirt-sleeved "common vision/ensuring success" work ses-

sions keyed to solving the issues and capitalizing on the opportunities identified in phase 1. Executives of *both* companies participate in these sessions,
which typically result in the group's establishing a joint statement of the
organizational mission, objectives, strategies, structure, authority and accountability, roles and relationships, performance criteria, decision and communication process, modus operandi, and action plans on specific issues.
We serve at these work conferences as both catalyst and methodology resource, focusing discussion and defusing tension.

Phase 3: Follow-through This phase consists of continuing service
(over whatever period of time the client thinks appropriate) as sounding
board to one or both sides, counselor, and troubleshooter:

- Develop a managing climate and style that best serves the goal of successful
  interaction

- Win the ownership and commitment of both parties to decisions reached
  and plans developed through phase 2's "working of the issues"

- Produce a viable modus operandi that shrinks the amount of time needed
  to achieve operating synergies while avoiding the "icebergs" that sink
  so many mergers and acquisitions

That Herricks acquired Lawson at all is ironic. Only a month previously,
it appeared that Lawson might make a bid to take over Herricks. Indeed,
the desirability of a bid for Herricks had emerged from a series of 56
interviews which my staff and I conducted with the 15 top executives of
Lawson and with key bankers, customers, government officials, and others
who knew well Herricks' strengths and weaknesses. Our feedback report
to Lawson's newly promoted president, John Thomas, outlined issues and
opportunities, including a strong belief that Lawson should try to take over
Herricks because of the obvious synergies that would be available to a
combined company.

Thomas, who himself favored the idea, told me he would bring it up
to his board of directors. I suggested helping him troubleshoot a presentation
to the board, but he said he did not think it would be necessary. That, in
retrospect, was his first mistake.

His second mistake was his judgment to go directly to the largest shareholder rather than strategize the best way to raise the subject with the
board. Without trying to anticipate why this shareholder might not see
the idea in his own best interest, Thomas approached him about a takeover
bid of Herricks. Only when the shareholder immediately reacted negatively
did John Thomas realize his tactical mistake: The shareholder was more
interested in getting his money *out* of the country, not putting more money
into an investment there.

Ironically, this was the same shareholder whose attention a few weeks later Herricks managed to capture in its successful bid to take over Lawson!

I learned of the Herricks takeover attempt the same time that my client John Thomas did. I was leading a conference of the top 15 executives at a mountain resort when—at 9:50 A.M. in a freak snowstorm—Thomas was suddenly called out to meet with a visitor. It was Herricks' president, who found this unusual way to announce that his company was making a tender offer for 51 percent of Lawson's stock. Before Herricks' tender offer was successful, two other companies entered the competition and upped the ante. But when the dust settled, Herricks had won out.

A few days after the tender offer was completed, I was interrupted in the course of an interview I was conducting on another project by a call from President Thomas.

"I just got a call from Herricks' chairman, George Tell," he said. "He wants to have dinner with me and my two key subordinates this evening in his city. He'll have his counterparts there too. He's asked me to reserve the next 2 days to discuss 'Where do we go from here?'" There was a pause, then he continued.

"I know this is awfully short notice, John, and you may have other appointments, but I would really appreciate it if you could join us for dinner and maybe the next 2 days so that—hopefully—I can arrange for you to serve as a catalyst. I'm afraid *they* have rather definite ideas on how we should be structured and managed, and I think it's important not only to the future of Lawson, but to the success of the integration effort, that the minority shareholder rights are protected too."

Three hours later, courtesy of a company plane, I was having dinner with the three top executives on each side in the most exclusive private club in Herricks' home city.

Thomas had seen me work as a catalyst seeking to reconcile divided opinion in his own company. Though I had not had the opportunity to explore the compatability of the partners before the match, I saw this as a test of whether or not I could turn what had some appearances of a "win-lose" contest into a "win-win" for all concerned.

There was an anxious moment when he introduced me, saying that I had been working with his company that day and he had insisted I come to the dinner because he thought my "perspective" might be helpful at the discussions tomorrow.

"I think John may be able to demonstrate some methods to help assure that the very important decisions we are about to make are in the best interests of both majority and minority shareholders."

To my relief, George Tell—a 6-foot 6-inch, very distinguished looking former senior Air Force officer, whom even his key assistants addressed as "Sir"—expressed no objections. Nevertheless, my enjoyment of the sumptuous dinner was diminished by the knowledge that I was seated between three very apprehensive-looking executives (from Lawson) and three very self-confident executives (from Herricks).

The next morning's session began on a friendly note, with both George Tell and John Thomas setting forth their hopes for the future success of the union, which made the combined operations the largest in their industry worldwide. However, I could feel the three executives of Lawson stiffen when Tell began outlining his team's plans for restructuring Lawson's sales force. Those plans included closing down the separate major sales offices that Lawson maintained in several North American cities, and consolidating all sales operations at Herricks' headquarters.

Obviously, there was no need for these two companies to maintain separate sales forces, since they both sold essentially the same product to the same kinds of customers. But Tell was operating from the unspoken assumption that because *his* company had bought Lawson, it should dictate the future forms the union would take.

At this point I interjected myself. I figured I had at most 10 minutes to win Tell's support for our process. I began talking:

"Let's pull back for a minute," I said, "and not talk about *what* is going to happen and *how* it should happen. Rather, let's think about what you want to *achieve* by this union, what you want to *preserve* by it, and what you want to *avoid* as problems by the union. The answers to these three questions will provide us with objectives or criteria by means of which you can better determine the truly most effective structure for the union. . . . "Isn't our goal here," I added, "not to determine what Herricks wants to see happen—or what Lawson wants to happen—but what, after consideration of the objectives to be served in the opinion of *all* of us, is found to be the *best* way to organize the company to assure a secure, stable, and highly prosperous marriage—one that will indeed be in the interests of both majority and minority shareholders?"

Tell, who had masterminded and engineered the takeover, had been standing the whole time I was talking. I knew he had a very short fuse. Was he about to blow up? I finished and nodded to him for approval. He uttered only one word and sat down: "Okay." He was willing to try the process.

Before the session adjourned, we had indeed outlined an organizational structure that both sides felt could build on the strengths of the two organizations. *It was different from either side's preconceived plans.* For example, each company would continue to operate as an entity with its own board of directors, with sales integrated under the former executive vice president of Herricks and all operations under the aegis of the president of Lawson. The sessions had explored and produced either answers or a *process* for answering such basic questions as:

1. What should our basic mission be?
2. What should be our commitment: to standardize our products?
3. What should our new image be? How do we project this to our customers worldwide? Why should it be good for each? For Herricks-Lawson? For each employee?
4. What should be the Herricks-Lawson view of the future?
5. What should be our expansion plans in North America and in the rest of the world?
6. How should we determine if we are accomplishing the mission? What should be the yardsticks and benchmarks?
7. Who determines corporate objectives of the merged companies?
8. What should be key authority, accountability, roles, and relationships?
9. In view of our current mixture between domestic and international, where should future sales be emphasized?
10. What should be the earnings-per-share goal of each owner of Herricks-Lawson?
11. What should pricing policy provide for, both long and short term?
12. What should be sales policy regarding contracts, brokers, etc?
13. How will our systems become integrated?
14. What is apt to be the reaction of competitors and how can we capitalize on this?
15. What should capital expenditure priorities be regarding new mills, acquisitions, modernization, etc?
16. How should we structure perquisites and benefits?
17. How far will we go to meet customer demand even if doing so costs Herricks-Lawson money?

Decisions that came out of this "common vision" conference helped mesh top management of both companies. But decisions on paper are worthless if not translated into practice in the field. Accordingly, we designed and implemented a series of projects for:

1. Herricks-Lawson finance task force to consolidate accounting, reporting, and control procedures in the two companies
2. An operations task force to rationalize the *priorities,* management *practices,* and *production facilities* of the two companies
3. A worldwide sales force *consolidation* project to rationalize the sales management structure of the two companies and get all members "on the same wavelength"

The "sales consolidation" conference represented a distinct challenge to integration hopes. Because the two companies had been competitors, the sales managers considered themselves natural antagonists. Now they were being told they needed to cooperate and *trust* each other. It called for a psychological about-face that could not be performed at the snap of the fingers.

Yet the necessity of such an about-face was of critical importance to the future of the organization. In the commodity in which these companies dealt, a single contract could be worth anywhere from $1 million to $50 million or more! The stakes at this conference were indeed high.

In our role as catalyst and methodology resource at the conference, here were my opening remarks:

I've seen a number of mergers and acquisitions occur at some of the larger corporations in this country. I've been able to participate, at some stage, in several of these. Regrettably, most of the time, we're called in only *after* problems develop—6 to 12 months, or even a couple of years after the merger or acquisition has been made. I can say in all honesty that Herricks-Lawson has taken a more thoughtful approach to determining how to produce optimum results than any other company in my personal experience. I think you men this evening are a testimonial to that. Each of you is here right at the outset of the relationship to help determine the direction, the identity, and the mission of new combined sales efforts. These decisions are not being made by a coterie of senior executives isolated on the umpteenth floor of a building. Rather, each of you will have the opportunity this week to have a hand in shaping the future of the company, and indeed your own future. . . .

During the next 3 days you're going to get to know one another quite well despite the size of this group. I think you'll find yourselves having an exciting time. We're certainly going to do our best to assure a stimulating, highly participative, and highly productive conference for everyone. There's going to be a minimum of lecturing by me and a helluva lot of hard work by you.

As Bob [Greenside, president of Herricks-Lawson sales] mentioned, it's going to require your trying to take off the blinders that each of us develops over the years from experience and habit. It's going to require asking questions, listening hard and well, perhaps reorienting your thinking; perhaps questioning values and beliefs you've had. It's going to require your trying not to think in terms of local problems or issues, but rather thinking in terms of broad principles for much of this conference, because the principles are going to determine and shape how local issues are solved and how opportunities are detected and moved on.

One of our roles is, in a sense, to be a whip to goad your thinking and also to keep you on track. I'd like each of you to keep yourselves and one another on track if you see someone getting on a tangent or getting a bit long-winded or beginning to look at something from a parochial viewpoint. In a nice way, raise a question about what are we trying to achieve by that part of the discussion.

If we do that, I think you'll walk out of here Thursday at 1 o'clock with much more of a *common vision* than perhaps you ever thought possible.

For tonight, each of you probably has some questions or concerns you'd like to get responded to or answered if possible this week. So a little later I'm going to ask you to divide up into teams, introduce yourself to one another in the team, and then list on chart paper the key questions on your minds, and we'll wind up the evening taking a quick look at what these questions are, and then Bob Greenside and I and some of the others will digest these and do the best we can to assure as many cogent answers as possible before you leave here Thursday.

Key objectives of the 3½-day session were to:

1. Get to know one another.

2. Begin "facing in the same direction"; get everyone on the same wavelength, with a common vision of:
   a. The *what,* the *why,* and the *how* of the consolidation.
   b. The potential synergies available to Herricks-Lawson, its own employees, and its customers.
   c. Develop a draft of a mission statement with primary objectives for the new worldwide sales organization.
   d. Develop a draft statement of the mission, key contribution areas, and primary objectives of the key customer account representatives.

3. Determine the best ways to follow up the formal written announcement to customers of the new company.
   f. Develop *skills* and a *plan* to ensure successful customer changeover (for example, from a Lawson account representative to Herricks) with strengthening and enhancement of both customer and business-prospect relationships.
   g. Ensure an atmosphere of excitement, of "We can make the right things happen!"

At the session devoted to developing a mission statement, we asked such questions as:

- Now that you are the biggest company in the world of your kind, what kind of responsibility does this bring with it?

- What kind of company should the sales company (technically a subsidiary) be?

- What do you want to create as your image in the marketplace? If this is the image you want, what should your corporate mission be?

After initial discussion, the 70-man group broke into teams, then reconvened to draft a mission statement as a result of their separate discussions. Similarly, we asked:

- Where's the synergy for the customer? (What are the advantages, if any, to the customer of this consolidation? What's in it—or what should be in it—for him?)
- How do we make these synergies happen?
- What are apt to be the customer's concerns about the consolidation?

Even before the sales conference had convened, we had attempted to focus the discussion and bring out the issues and opportunities by means of *confidential* interviews with sales managers from both companies. The feedback report we wrote based on their answers became the *vehicle* for initiating discussion and for assuring that we devoted the session to the actual issues and opportunities that they would confront in the new company's "reincarnation."

On page 141 is a diagram that we used to help plan and track our progress at the sales coordination meeting.

How did Herricks-Lawson benefit from all these integration efforts? Company executives credit the management and integration process with:

- Transforming an adversary takeover into a mutually beneficial relationship
- Creating an organizational structure geared to the achievement of optimum marketplace and operational synergies
- Speeding up the process of "productive interaction" by "at least 6 months"
- Avoiding the loss of even a single major customer worldwide
- Avoiding the loss of any top or upper-middle management executive on either side

One year later, as a result of the success of these efforts and his own performance, Bob Greenside was elevated from president of the sales subsidiary to president of the merged parent corporation.

Our own company benefited too. Following the initial project, we were engaged for five additional projects, working with different levels and functions of the organization.

Case 2

At another company, an executive recently parachuted in to head up a major business called us in to help iron out some problems with an acquisition made shortly before he joined the company. It was another case of *lack of postmarriage preparation.* After talking with the inherited management of the new acquisition, I wrote our client a memo summarizing the grievances

SALES MANAGEMENT
INTEGRATION MEETING AGENDA

1
- ACQUISITION
- MERGER
- INTEGRATION
- MARRIAGE
- APPREHENSION

2
WHY, WHAT, AND HOW LEADING TO THIS WEEK'S MEETING

3
- STRATEGY
- ORGANIZATION
- MANAGEMENT STRUCTURE AND RELATIONSHIPS
- PHILOSOPHY

4
IMAGE WE WANT TO BUILD IN MARKET
- MISSION AND KEY OBJECTIVES OF OUR COMPANY

5
MISSION AND KEY OBJECTIVES OF SALES REPRESENTATIVE

6
WHAT DOES THE SALES REPRESENTATIVE NEED TO KNOW TO ACHIEVE RESULTS

7
PLANNING HOW TO STRENGTHEN AND ENHANCE CUSTOMER RELATIONSHIPS

8
FOLLOWTHROUGH

SUCCESS

as managers might have done if they had been bold enough to speak their minds candidly to their new owner (which they were not). Here are excerpts:

> The Metcalf Company bought us within the past 9 months. While we expected to report to the president, we were told we would start off reporting to the executive vice president. But not for long. He shifted us to his deputy. Then, after a couple of weeks, we were introduced to a new manager, Coleman, whose background—believe it or not—is in a totally different business. Not only doesn't he know a damn thing about our products; he hasn't even started working for Metcalf yet!
>
> As you know, being a family business, we've always operated quite autonomously within the regions and made damn good money. But now we're being "Metcalfized." For example, they're forcing us to hook up with their computer system. To feed them the data they require of us in the forms that they want it takes us several man-months of work every month. It costs us 2½ times in overhead what our own system costs!
>
> We've also been informed within the past week that:
> 1. Our salaries will be cut in half.
> 2. Our cars will be taken away.
> 3. Several of the family (owners) are being forced to move.
> 4. Metcalf is trying to make a number of other changes *unilaterally* so that we conform to all of the "systems."
>
> There seems to be another reason for this also: One of our many new bosses apparently made a sales projection for us to meet the needs of *his* boss. This target is a "pipe dream." It has absolutely no relation to reality!
>
> In order to make those numbers, Metcalf has got to cut its operations to the bone anywhere they can. So overhead and salary and other perquisites are among the first to go. . . . What they're doing to save in salaries and perks will be more than offset by the damage they've already done to our company by changes which, to us anyway, just aren't rational, and by the insensitive way in which they "give us orders." At this point, we're frankly inclined to just "lean back on the oars" and "let Metcalf do its thing! . . . I personally made $5 million out of this sale; my brother, better than $15 million. . . . We're not going to let Metcalf bother us any more than we can help it. . . .
>
> I don't know who Metcalf is going to replace us with, but it is quite clear we don't fit in with their idea of how to run a company. If the other boys and I decide to "jump ship" within the next several months, Metcalf is going to be hard-pressed to get the earnings they are making all these changes for.

The irony of it all is that Metcalf was so busy looking for *new* acquisition candidates that it hadn't spent the time needed to learn how to manage the ones it had already acquired, let alone develop an "acquisition search/management/integration process" for future acquisitions!

Although the above "conversation" never occurred, when our client read it, he winced and said, "You've really registered. When you put it all together as you've done, John, it's a real horror story. Who would believe we've taken so many foolish actions out of context instead of developing a system in the first place?"

My purpose in sending the memo to the client was not only to help him think through what needed to be done to repair the damage made to this acquired company, but also to question what—if such views were ever conveyed to other acquisition candidates by managers of existing acquisitions—might be the effect on Metcalf's ambitious acquisition program? Furthermore, I pointed out, what does this kind of treatment say about Metcalf's commitment to the pursuit of "corporate excellence"?

To avoid such scenarios, we counsel our clients in:

1. Strengthening acquisition and integration skills, both in seeking and evaluating a company (especially the "human dimension") to help determine whether or not to make a particular acquisition, and developing a *process* to determine the best way to manage it (ensuring that, whether it's to be integrated or operated almost autonomously, it will be a "win-win" marriage)

2. Team building: developing a *common vision* of mission, objectives, strategy, structure, authority/accountability, roles/relationships, decision process, communication network, modus operandi, etc.

3. Developing *do-able* action plans with appropriate follow-through

We often play the role of an outside "cultural adviser" to an acquired firm's top executives, helping them to understand the conditions of the acquiring company, the cultural climate, the modus operandi, and the concerns, sacred cows, hot buttons, and expectations of the key people they must deal with.

Case 3

One conglomerate, which I'll call Socono Industries, turned to us for help after acquiring a smaller family-owned company, Ritchie Manufacturing, whose founder had sold out. The new president Socono installed to manage the acquisition recognized that things were not going smoothly. Our interviews with managers of both Socono and Ritchie revealed some rather amusing examples of nonintegration. One customer related the following anecdote:

Twenty-two months after the acquisition was completed, I received a visit from three representatives of Ritchie, which had become a division of Socono:

the vice president–general manager, the sales manager, and the account rep. All left their business cards. The vice president–general manager had been installed by Socono to run Ritchie: his card carried the name of Socono in bold letters. The divisional sales manager had come to Socono after long service in Ritchie. His card prominently identified him with Ritchie (though the Ritchie name was dropped with the company's sale to Socono!); only in much smaller letters did the name Socono appear on his card. As for the account rep, who was also a "Ritchie man," he was apparently refusing to acknowledge any change at all: his card was the one that the company had used for years, and only its name appeared! Yet all three men were supposedly working for Socono!

In all, our interviews among Socono and (former) Ritchie executives identified 34 shortcomings in the way the integration was handled. Among them:

1. "Four managers parachuted from the parent corporation on top of us without explanation."
2. Goals, objectives, and strategy were not clearly defined.
3. No clarification of mission, roles, responsibilities, or relationships.
4. Contradictory signals toward profit, return on investment, and other goals.
5. "Management by the numbers—telling us we had to achieve these goals and those goals without regard for our actual resources."
6. No explicit decisions of how the acquired company should operate— "just the assumption that we would follow their [acquiring company's] rules without telling us what they were."
7. Terrible "short-terming" (of the business) to wring profits to make *their* management look good.
8. Disapproval of requests (lose-lose) instead of how to ensure mutual benefit (win-win).
9. Decisions by fiat (no explanation).
10. Lack of an effective management information system.
11. Widespread job insecurity.
12. "Quality assurance not taken seriously since they took it for granted we made the best product in our brand categories."
13. "No performance appraisals or appreciation shown for our own talents."
14. "No attempt to capitalize on what we do especially well."

Summed up one of the disenchanted company's managers, "We're in a little Volkswagon going 80 miles an hour with the accelerator pedal all the way to the floor—with a huge Mack truck at our rear. It's only a matter of time before we blow a rod!"

In fact, what happened is what frequently happens in such situations: Several top managers felt themselves bypassed; they felt the acquiring company "wanted us out." Some resigned. I like to think our project may have saved the rest.

When the new president realized what a bad job had been done managing the acquisition, he fired the operations vice president, nailed down (with our help) authority, accountability, roles, and relationships of his position vis-à-vis corporate headquarters, and began a concerted effort to enlist incumbent managers in a major revitalization effort.

A "common vision/issue resolution" conference helped surface the problems and begin a *joint* effort to resolve them. But by the time things were straightened out—2 years later—valuable time had been lost and precious human resources had been squandered.

Conclusion

All the examples in this chapter are:

1. Real
2. Typical of problems that follow acquisitions, and often confront a newly appointed chief executive or operating officer, or group vice president
3. Easily avoidable by proper foresight and planning

What is needed is for newly appointed CEOs and COOs of acquisition-minded companies to realize that a corporate marriage is more than just an amalgamation of organizations. *It is a merger of people as well as philosophies and managing styles.* No less than a marriage between man and woman, it requires trust, consideration, commitment, and—above all—a recognition that the marriage is only healthy if the individual partners are healthy.

The pity of it is that merger- and acquisition-minded companies spend millions of dollars consumating a marriage. They don't lack for willing handmaidens, bridesmaids, or matchmakers in the form of investment bankers, accountants, tax attorneys, etc. But they expend *precious little energy* in grappling with perhaps the biggest barrier to effective integration: meshing men, and increasingly women, in ways that assure productive relationships.

In the long run, it is more crucial for a newly appointed chief executive or operating officer to "make a marriage work" than merely to "make a marriage."

Chapter 13
"Do I Have to Decide Today?"

(Calling the Tough Ones—Decision Making under Pressure)

No one likes crises. Everyone has to cope with them.

This chapter is devoted to explaining some techniques that our clients have found effective in dealing with crises, and some examples of how these techniques have been employed to resolve them.

We begin with a nightmare situation—the kind I hope you never have to encounter. John Townsend, vice president of operations of a large chemical company, had just announced a major reorganization. To oversee day-to-day operations and reduce the number of subordinates who report directly to him, Townsend named a veteran manager known for his intelligence, his energy, and his overall competence.

Red Winters, as we shall call the new number two man, was active in the industry's trade association and a leader in community activities. He seemed to enjoy a good reputation among his colleagues.

After clearing the changes with the CEO, Townsend announced the reorganization and his new appointment. Twenty-four hours later, the vice president received news that left him visibly shaken: His new second in command had been taking kickbacks from a major customer.

"It's been happening for years," Townsend explained. "I heard rumors of something like that, so I called him last week and asked if there was anything in his past with the company that he thought might embarrass him with the new job. He assured me there wasn't. Only after I made the announcement did he come to me again. I guess he had conscience pangs. An hour ago, he told me the story. It's all true. What a mess." Then he threw up his hands and sighed deeply.

What should he do? We have developed a decision-making process that permits a manager to focus all his feelings and facts, his concerns and values, on the search for the best solution to a problem. There are seven steps:

Step 1. *Smoke out the issues.*

Ask yourself: Is a decision really necessary? Why?

Step 2. *State the purpose of the decision.*

Ask yourself: What needs to be determined?

Step 3. *Set your criteria.*

Ask yourself: What do I want to achieve, preserve, and avoid as problems by whatever decision I make?

Step 4. *Establish your priorities.*

Ask yourself: Which are the criteria any solution *has to* satisfy to be effective (absolute objectives)? In addition, which criteria *should* it seek to satisfy (desirable objectives)?

Step 5. *Search for solutions.*

Ask yourself: What are all the ways these criteria can be met?

Step 6. *Test the alternatives.*

Ask yourself: Which alternative—or which combination of alternatives—best meets the criteria?

Step 7. *Troubleshoot the solution.*

Ask yourself: What could go wrong? How can the decision be improved to overcome or reduce any adverse impact?

In tight-time-pressure situations such as this one, some steps can be short-cut, as we shall see.

Applying this process to his own crisis, John Townsend negotiated step 1 in less than a minute. He reasoned that a decision was necessary because the revelations could cause serious embarrassment to the company if they went unpunished.

The answer to the question posed in step 2 would define the scope of the vice president's search for a solution. If, for example, he defined the purpose of his decision as "Determining *what to do* about Red Winters in view of the revelations," he would, in effect, keep open the possibility that Red could remain with the company. On the other hand, if he defined his purpose as "Determining the best way to terminate Red under the circumstances," then his eventual solution would revolve around ways of ending his employment.

After pausing a few moments and scribbling some words on scratch paper, Townsend formulated his purpose as "Determining the conditions under which Red Winters will leave the company, and the explanation that will be given, both internally and externally, for his departure."

Having determined his mission, John Townsend said he thought the best thing to do would be to call in Winters, notify him of why he was being asked to resign, and announce to the staff that there would be a "hold" in carrying out the reorganization, without giving any explanation.

"We can always think of some excuse later, after the immediate problem has been resolved," he said. "The important thing is to get that man out of here."

But would that indeed be the best course? I urged Townsend to devote 10 minutes to step 3, developing a list of things that a decision should achieve, preserve, and avoid as problems.

The heart of crisis decision making is setting the criteria that your solution must satisfy. You will find that the criteria themselves generate a better solution than you can improve. It took Townsend only 8 minutes to compile this list of decision criteria. My decision, he wrote, should:

Achieve:

1. Termination of Red Winters as soon as possible

2. Understanding of the real situation by all who need to know (president, selected board members, others?)

3. Ignorance of the real situation by all who don't need to know

4. A plausible explanation for R. W. not to take the new job—one that will hold up at least until he's safely out of the company

5. A feeling among those who do learn of the situation that the company did "the only thing it could"

6. A feeling among those that don't learn of it that nothing is awry

7. As little embarrassment to the company as possible

Preserve:

1. Smooth operation of R. W.'s division

2. A feeling among staff that the company and the operations department are under good leadership despite this "switch in signals"

3. The company's good reputation among customers in the trade, the press, and the public

4. Staff's understanding that the company does not tolerate wrongdoing and is committed to high principles of integrity

5. Orderly reorganization

6. My integrity

Avoid:

1. Arousing suspicions of wrongdoing by our handling of the situation

2. Further dealings with this customer

3. Other customers, press, etc., learning of real reason for R. W.'s leaving company

4. Any future kickback scandals

5. Giving R. W. anything that could be interpreted as a reward for his conduct (such as going-away party, gift, etc.)

6. Causing R. W. to undertake a destructive act:
   a. Toward himself or family
   b. Toward the company

7. Making it difficult for him to find another job

Obviously, all these criteria might not be compatible. Could any solution both achieve a feeling that nothing is awry and provide for R. W.'s termination as soon as possible? How could the company avoid arousing suspicions by its handling of the situation while denying R. W. the usual departure ritual such as a party or gift?

In normal circumstances, step 4 requires both distinguishing the absolute from the desirable objectives and numerically ranking the desirables. In tight-time-pressure situations, managers sometimes short-cut the process by omitting the second procedure. In thinking through this crisis, for example, Townsend identified the absolute requirements for his decision as:

Achieve:

1. Termination within 48 hours

2. Understanding by all who need to know

3. A plausible explanation—until R. W. is safely out of the company

4. A belief that the company did the right thing, and handled it flawlessly

Preserve:

5. The company's reputation

6. Its commitment to high integrity

7. Orderly reorganization

Avoid:

8. Anything that can be interpreted as a reward for R. W.

9. Acting in a way that causes R. W. to undertake a destructive act

Merely setting forth the criteria and priorities helped determine John Townsend's decision and the way it should be explained. Within 30 minutes, he had proceeded to implement the following four-part strategy:

- He requested and was granted an emergency meeting with the company president to explain the situation and the course of action he was about to take, and to ask for the president's support. He got it without reservations. The president volunteered to inform key board members and two other corporate officers with a need to know, the vice presidents of finance and public relations.

- Townsend then called in Winters and explained that Winters' conduct had left the company no choice but to terminate his employment immediately. He expressed his personal regret at this turn of events and said that he knew what a disappointment the decision must be to Winters and his family. To cushion the shock, he said the company would try to protect Winters' name by disclosing the actual situation to no one who didn't absolutely have to know about it. Others would be told that the strain of his own long hours had forced Winters to take a short vacation on the advice of his doctor. In return, Winters should realize that the company was doing him a favor in keeping the situation confidential and conduct himself accordingly.

- Next he called in his top managers, explained to them that on the advice of his doctors, Winters was taking a short vacation, and that the number two position would be left open for the time being. Meanwhile, the rest of the reorganization would proceed as scheduled. He asked if this turn of events would cause any unusual problems, and fielded a series of questions about the mechanics of the transition as they would be affected by Winters' absence. As to the state of Winters' health, Townsend said he could not go beyond the scanty information supplied by the doctor.

- Finally, he put out a memo to the staff explaining that medical problems had forced Winters to take a short rest, that the reorganization would proceed as scheduled, and that any unusual problems should be taken up with department heads.

Three weeks later, with no reference to Winters' situation, the company published a new code of conduct for employees. Knowledge of the true reason for Winters' departure never became general knowledge. The customer was cut off for failure to pay overdue bills.

Defining the Purpose and Criteria

In making decisions under pressure, never bypass the need to define your decision's purpose and set criteria. These steps are powerful focusing lenses in your search for a solution. They are important when you are solving a crisis alone, as was John Townsend. They serve an additional function when you're solving a crisis in groups, for they take the energy that often gets diverted into arguing for pet solutions and direct it to a collective search for the best solution.

In many group situations, the usual procedure is for the leader to give a description of the problem and then ask for suggested solutions. One person gives his off-the-cuff solution, another disagrees and offers a rival solution. Opinion gets polarized, and the process of decision making becomes a function of who has the greatest power and persuasive skills.

A more productive procedure, the one we use with our clients, focuses the initial discussion on defining the purpose—what, in fact, has to be decided; and the criteria—what objectives any solution must satisfy. Only when there is agreement on these two crucial steps does the group address the question of a solution. Not only does this process increase chances of consensus, it also assures that the solution reached grows out of the needs of the situation.

Here's how one group of managers used these decision-making tools to cope with a multimillion-dollar crisis precipitated by a surprise announcement from corporate headquarters.

Dave Emerson was divisional vice president of a U.S. auto maker's subsidiary in a foreign country. To preserve anonymity, we'll call the country Proudland, and the line of cars the story concerns, the Crimson. Crimsons were a major line of automobiles in Proudland until one morning when Dave received a phone call from corporate headquarters.

"I hope you're sitting down, Dave, because I've got some bad news for you. Just before the chairman and the president left on a European trip, they decided to stop production of the Crimson line in Proudland as soon as possible. It was strictly a business decision. We're wiring you the facts and figures that justify it. Sorry to have to tell you."

Within an hour, Dave had summoned his top staff and relayed the decision. The reaction was one of shock, dismay, and then resentment.

Recognizing the value in letting his managers vent their feelings, Dave asked for some reactions to the news. First came the hostile reactions: "Why don't they ask our opinion before taking drastic action?" "Why don't the Americans ever take into account conditions in our country?" "How could they do a stupid thing like that?" Then came the practical objectives: A new model was being readied for production. Commitments had already been made for a major advertising campaign. The dealer network had been carefully primed to market the Crimson.

"Okay," said Dave finally. "I think we have a picture of how we all feel. Now let's see what we should do about it. We know why a decision is necessary, but what's our purpose—what are we really trying to determine?"

One man suggested the purpose should be to "Do what corporate headquarters wants with the least adverse effect." Another suggested the group's mission should be to "Get corporate headquarters to reverse themselves." A third volunteered that the purpose of the decision should be to "Decide how to honor our commitments without hurting our dealers and suppliers or our public image." And a fourth defined the purpose as "Getting the

Americans to stop making decisions without regard for local factors."

Dave scribbled all the suggestions on chart paper, then asked the group to look at the suggestions and formulate a single statement of decision purpose. The group agreed that its purpose should be to "Determine how best to respond to the corporate directive halting production of the Crimson."

They then developed criteria based on the information teletyped from corporate headquarters, supplemented by their own knowledge of commitments made for the Crimson. Because they had stated their mission in wide-open fashion ("how to respond" rather than "how to comply" or "how to fight"), their alternative solutions covered a wide range, including: implementing the decision, seeking to modify it in favor of a gradual phase-out rather than an abrupt production halt, seeking to postpone its implementation, and fighting to reverse it.

As described by Dave:

> On the basis of our analysis, we could see that corporate headquarters had sound reasons for wanting to terminate the Crimson in Proudland. But the analysis also demonstrated that immediate termination would have very bad effects on our subsidiary's profit stance in the long run, on our work force, on service commitments to present Crimson owners, on our dealers, and on public opinion. There was also the possibility that immediate termination would leave a void in the marketplace that competitors would fill up, perhaps leaving us out in the cold for good.

> We felt that these factors had not been given sufficient weight by Detroit in calling for a production halt. It was clear that the best solution was to seek approval of a gradual phase-out rather than an immediate halt.

> But we couldn't get approval of a gradual phase-out from Detroit so long as the chairman and president were in Europe. They weren't due to return for another week.

> What should we do? If we were to postpone beginning to terminate until their return, we would be violating orders. If we were to begin terminating while awaiting their return, we would be carrying out the very action we were seeking to avoid.

> Because there was no one at headquarters who could overrule the chairman and president, and time was of the essence, we decided to contact the two men in Europe and plead our case.

The chairman and president are household names in the United States—people who are not used to having their positions challenged, and certainly not at midnight by long-distance telephone. But that is exactly what Dave did.

> Marshaling my arguments as cogently as I could, I placed a call to the two men in Europe, reaching them about midnight their time. They were surprised

at the phone call, but after their initial shock, they asked penetrating questions—including whether I was willing to lay my job on the line for my recommendation. I gulped and said that I was.

I explained step-by-step why a careful phase-out was the best solution, bringing to their attention circumstances they had not considered. When I was finished, the chairman asked a couple more questions, then said, "Okay, Dave, I can't shoot you down. We'll inform Detroit to put a hold on the decision until we get back. You phone my office and set up an appointment to see me next week. Bring along your analysis and we'll have our people check it out. Meanwhile, you better have done your homework."

Dave and his associates made their presentation to the two top officers the following week. On the basis of their analysis, the original corporate decision was modified in favor of the kind of phase-out recommended by the subsidiary.

"We developed our strategy and prepared our case in a day and a half," said Dave later. "I figure we cut down the normal process of coming to a decision of that magnitude by 5 calendar days at least, and perhaps 4 man-weeks of work. We would never have been able to work as efficiently if our people had not been trained in using the ExecuTrak® process."

Incidently, Dave's strong performance in Proudland—reflected by how he handled this tight-time-pressure crisis—earned him three promotions in short order. He is now on the rung just below the chairman and president as head of the company's largest division.

Searching Out the Facts

In dealing with both the kickback and Crimson crises, the decision makers had all the facts they needed at their disposal. Very often, however, before you can make the right decision, you must engage in a time-consuming search for the facts. Obviously, your decision is only as good as the facts upon which it is based. Thus, how you structure and organize your search for the facts is of utmost importance.

Only after you have the facts should you set your criteria and work through your solution. In the example that follows, we will see how a structured search for the best solution, based on a clear documentary record, provided the compass a new senior executive needed to successfully resist pressures from above for action that he considered unwarranted.

Two months after Dan Sanders joined an East Coast manufacturer of cosmetics, he encountered his first crisis. Reviewing sales and shipment figures for the month just ended, he was startled to find unusually large volumes reported. Checking the totals against projections, he calculated that September shipments constituted 30 percent of the year's targets. He made a few phone calls and concluded there was something wrong with the figures.

Sanders had been parachuted in over the heads of several longtime managers, some of whom resented his appointment. Only in the past couple of weeks had he sensed that people in the organization were beginning to feel at ease with him. He thought he was on his way to becoming accepted.

Now he was in a quandary: If the figures were indeed wrong and he made an issue of it, would he ever be accepted? On the other hand, if the figures were wrong and he didn't make an issue of it, was he really doing his job?

He hesitated only a moment, then dropped it on his boss, Greg Ryerson. "Greg," he said, "I think there's something fishy going on around here." He went on to explain how unlikely it was that 30 percent of the year's shipments had gone out in any one month. It was even more unlikely, he added, that 30 percent had been shipped in the month just ended, because heavy floods had shut down the shipping department for several days.

Ryerson expressed alarm at Sanders' report. "It looks to me like someone may have been doing some 'creative bookkeeping.'" He noted that under the company's bonus incentive plan, quarterly sales and shipment figures become the basis for calculating bonuses, and that September 30th coincided with the end of a quarterly bonus period.

"If anyone is fudging figures around here," concluded Ryerson, "I want to know about it. In fact, I want to know everything about it: who's doing it, how many there are, why they're doing it, how long its been going on."

He explained that company policies forbid doctoring shipment records, and that federal law, as monitored by the Securities and Exchange Commission, provides stiff penalties for doctoring sales figures by entering business booked after the end of one month in the previous month's total.

The crisis broke on a Thursday afternoon. Sanders had planned to leave the office early on Friday to return to his home near Boston and move his family to the new home they had purchased in a New York suburb. Back in his office, Sanders explained the situation to his administrative assistant and made plans to postpone the move for a week. He called his wife to break the news; it was not a call he relished making.

For the next 3 days Sanders worked almost around the clock seeking to determine the facts of the situation. He began by listing the questions Ryerson had said he wanted answered, then adding some of his own. He ended up with a list that we later refined to provide a fact-finding guide in many situations:

Twenty-Question Fact-Finding Guide

1. What happened?
2. Where did it happen?
3. When did it happen?
4. Has it happened before? How often?
5. If so, is there a pattern to it?
6. How has the company reacted in the past?
7. Who did it (perpetrators)?
8. Who authorized or ordered it and at what management level?
9. Who else condoned it or knew about it?
10. Did any of those involved report it?
11. Did those involved fully cooperate when discovered?
12. Did they do it to help themselves or the company?
13. Is it prohibited by law?
14. Is it prohibited by *written* company policy?
15. If so, did they know of such laws/policy?
16. Are there any mitigating circumstances?
17. In view of the above, how much of the blame properly belongs to:
    a. Perpetrators?
    b. Authorizers?
    c. The company "system and culture"?
    d. Other forces? (What are they?)
18. What's to prevent it from happening again?
19. Recommended punishment?
20. Recommended corrective/preventive action?

Sanders' investigation established the following facts: On the 29th of September the sales manager had notified the distribution department to fill 40 railway cars with cases for shipment the very next day. The customer's order had specified shipment by October 15th; thus there was no demonstrable business need for the order to go out on the last day of September.

On the morning of the 30th, the distribution manager notified the sales department that he couldn't ready 40 cars for shipment in one day. An argument ensued, and what happened next is in dispute.

According to the distribution manager, the sales manager told him he needed the shipments to make his quarterly sales quota. "You find a way to make them," the sales manager told him. During the course of the conversation, according to this version, the idea "came up" of indicating in the records that the shipments had indeed been made in September while the actual shipments would not go out until the beginning of October. Who suggested the idea cannot be determined. Nevertheless, it was agreed that this should be done, said the distribution manager, and he asked his assistants to do so.

According to the sales manager, he had no idea that any phony entries would be made in the records. "All I said was 'You find a way to make those shipments on the 30th.' Of course, I meant a legitimate way. There was no discussion whatsoever of doctoring any records," he said.

Contrary to what he had been told by the finance department, Sanders' inquiry also disclosed that the company had no written policies on monthly closeouts. Moreover, although the sales and distribution people interviewed denied ever doctoring records previously, several said that they had heard about "things like this happening before."

One old-timer confided: "It's a numbers game that people play from time to time. Either they've been told they have to meet their targets 'come hell or high water' or they are trying to boost their bonus. It's probably a little of both. That's the way the system works around here. No one ever raised a question about it before."

Ryerson, Sanders' boss, had been keeping CEO George Lipton informed of developments. Lipton expressed outrage when he first heard the news. "My God," he exclaimed, "we have a damn little Watergate on our hands." Now he told Ryerson he wanted to "see some heads roll." "This kind of conduct will not be tolerated," he said angrily.

Lipton was particularly concerned about a possible violation of federal law. The Securities and Exchange Commission requires that companies report monthly shipment figures by the fifth day after the close of business for the preceding month. If the figures reported are later found to be false, the SEC must be immediately notified of the fact. In addition, whenever a problem exists regarding the accuracy of officially reported figures, internal auditors must immediately report any discrepancies to outside auditors and at the same time to the auditing committee of the board of directors.

Working 18-hour days over the weekend, Sanders and his assistant, with the help of company auditors, corrected the false figures in time to avoid any problem of illegal reporting to the SEC.

"We're awful lucky," said Lipton when he heard that the errors had been corrected only hours before the September figures were due to be mailed off to Washington. "If this thing had gone 24 hours longer without being uncovered, we'd be eating humble pie right now."

Sanders and his assistant also put together a 75-page chronology and analysis of the incident, topped by a one-page summary. The report was based on the answers to their 20 questions. In abbreviated form, these were their conclusions:

1. What happened?
   October shipments were predated into September by apparent agreement of key distribution and sales personnel. The amount involved totaled $3.4 million.
2. Where did it happen?
   In the distribution department.

3. When did it happen?

On the 30th of September.

4. Has it happened before?

Yes, apparently, though no hard evidence.

How often?

Occasionally.

5. Is there a pattern to it?

Yes. Seems to coincide with end of quarterly sales reporting and quarterly bonus periods.

6. How has the company reacted in the past?

Hasn't come to management's attention before.

7. Who did it (perpetrators)?

Two people in distribution carried it out.

8. Who authorized or ordered it and at what management levels?

Manager of distribution, manager of sales, and their assistants.

9. Who condoned or knew about it?

Five other people in the two departments.

10. Did any of those involved report it?

No.

11. Did those involved fully cooperate when discovered?

Yes.

12. Did they do it to help selves or company?

Unclear. Sales—to help themselves and to meet quarterly sales quotas.
Distribution—to comply with orders of the company.

13. Is it prohibited by law?

Yes, if reported falsely, but it was corrected in time.

14. Is it prohibited by written company policy?

No. Company has no written policy.

15. If so, did they know of such laws/policy?

No indication they knew it might be illegal.

16. Are there any mitigating circumstances?

Yes. Sales and distribution departments cooperated in investigation; people involved are reputable people, long-time employees, good workers.

17. In view of the above, how much of the blame properly belongs to:

    a. Perpetrators?

        Little—they were only following orders.

    b. Authorizers?

        Some—they should have known doctoring figures was deceptive, improper.

    c. The company "system and culture"?

        A lot—Sales incentive system encourages/condones this behavior. Culture "looks the other way." Never been questioned before.

    d. Other forces? (What are they?)

        None.

18. What's to prevent it from happening again?
   Nothing unless we take appropriate action.

In answering questions 17 and 18, Sanders identified his decision purpose as "To determine the most appropriate corrective and preventive action to take to assure that such conduct does not occur again."
He specified the criteria his decision should satisfy as:

Achieve:

1. Punishment of the offenders

2. Punishment tailored to the degree of involvement of each offender

3. Assurance against any future attempt to doctor records

4. Clear understanding by staff of what are/are not proper practices, and consequences for violations

5. Removal of financial incentives to deceptive practices

6. A feeling by staff that course of action we take was "the right thing to do"

7. A feeling by CEO that course of action was "the right thing to do"

Preserve:

8. High motivation of staff

9. Company reputation for honesty, straight dealing

Avoid

10. Hasty, ill-considered action under pressure of CEO or chief financial officer

11. Letting any wrongdoer go unpunished

12. Scapegoating—picking on "small fry" while ignoring misdeeds of higher-ups

13. Blaming individuals for faults of "the system"

14. Adverse publicity

Armed with these criteria, Sanders went to Grey Ryerson, and together they considered each individual's complicity in the situation. They charted out a course of action that included the following elements:

Punishment

1. Six-month postponement of a raise the distribution manager had been expecting, along with a written warning that any future violation of company policy would lead to his summary dismissal.

2. Cancellation of a $9000 bonus that the sales manager had been told he would receive at year's end.

3. A written reprimand to the two people who carried out their orders. Unlike a warning, the reprimand would not constitute a step toward possible future dismissal, nor would it hold back their careers. (This course of action was based on the conclusion that the four were "acting in good faith" and had nothing to gain by their actions.)

4. Shifting from line to staff positions of two people who contributed to the deception on the grounds that they showed poor management judgment.

Corrective Preventive Action

5. A written policy statement communicated to all departments and made part of the company work rules and manual, explaining that doctoring records was grounds for dismissal.

6. Recommendation to draft a code of conduct for all employees spelling out proper and improper conduct in a variety of business situations.

7. Revisions in auditing practices that would require verification of shipment orders and could be used to quickly spot discrepancies.

8. A revision of the bonus incentive system to remove the potential advantage obtained from juggling order dates.

9. Meetings of sales and distribution department personnel to review the "mini-scandal," discuss their fiduciary responsibilities, and obtain ideas for formulating a company code of conduct.

In refusing to knuckle under to the demand to "make heads roll," Dan Sanders feared that he might be jeopardizing his own future. After all, he was new to the company, and he didn't want to be regarded as either stubborn or "mushy-headed." Moreover, he knew that the CEO was looking for decisive action and this was a situation that, on the surface, seemed tailor-made for decisive action.

On the other hand, having investigated thoroughly and concluded that the basic faults lay in the system and in practices that had been tolerated for years, Sanders could see no virtue in creating scapegoats. He also reasoned that in the long run, if his prescription was correct, the CEO would respect him all the more for having demonstrated early on that he was his "own man." Even so, he knew he was taking a chance by not choosing the easy way out.

At least he had the assurance that his own boss concurred in his analysis and his recommendations. In fact, Ryerson volunteered to take the report to the CEO himself and "try to sell it to him."

Before meeting with Lipton, Ryerson and Sanders spent some time troubleshooting Ryerson's presentation—asking what could go wrong, how the

CEO might try to shoot holes in their reasoning, and how they could bolster their arguments to answer any possible objections.

The strategy they chose began with an explanation that in formulating their recommendations they had taken into consideration a number of suggested courses of action, including a suggestion from "several persons" that those responsible for the deception be summarily dismissed. While grateful for the suggestion, they had concluded that the option of dismissal was not warranted by the circumstances and might, in fact, cause the company more harm than good. Among the reasons it was rejected:

1. Summary firings were unfair; they would persecute people for following practices that the company had tolerated for years.

2. Since the practices in question were not contrary to *written* company policy, aggrieved employees dismissed for their actions would undoubtedly sue for reinstatement.

3. The resultant publicity could do serious damage to the company's image and reputation.

4. The plaintiff would probably win such suits, thus further hurting the company.

5. Drastic action would have a serious impact on staff morale generally, since it would not be perceived as fair or just.

6. Since the records were corrected in time and no false numbers had been given to the Securities and Exchange Commission for the quarter just ended, there had been no violation of law.

In view of these considerations, Ryerson would say, Sanders and he had concluded that the wiser course was a combination of specifically targeted steps involving selected warnings, reprimands, transfers, indoctrination sessions, correctional policies, and preventive procedures.

Ryerson followed this script in his presentation, concluding his discussion by inviting the CEO to carefully study the 1-page executive summary and the 75-page report of the incident on which it was based.

"I think you'll find that the reason this happened isn't because of the people we have but because of the system we have," he observed. "I'm afraid things like this have happened before. What we need to do is assure that they can't happen again."

The next day, after taking the report home with him overnight, Lipton commended Ryerson on the report. He said that Sanders' handling of the investigation confirmed Ryerson's judgment in bringing him into the company over the heads of other managers. Ignoring the fact that he himself had wanted to "see heads roll," the CEO said: "I always admire a man who stays cool under pressure."

Conclusion

The techniques described in this chapter should help you develop the skills for making—and making stick—your decisions in crisis situations. As a senior executive in a new position or a new company, you will undoubtedly have plenty of opportunity to practice these skills.

Chapter 14
"Who Has a Better Idea?"
(New-Product Development)

The chief executive of a major health products company was deeply troubled. His firm was known on Wall Street as "the house of no research." It had been 3 years since the company had introduced a major new product. The few line extensions that had been introduced failed to meet their objectives. The board of directors was critical of him, and several heads of his marketing divisions were threatening to go elsewhere if he couldn't reverse the research division's fortunes.

In hopes of turning the situation around, he had parachuted in a topflight scientist to take over the presidency of the research division, which boasted 600 professionals in research facilities that spanned the globe. Now, 8 months later, there was still no sign of improvement. Several marketing division executives were calling for the new president's resignation.

The chief executive, Abe Colson, had learned at an industry association meeting of our work with one of his competitors a few years before, and called for an appointment. I assured him we would maintain absolute confidentiality of any new-product development plans and programs about which we learned in the course of any work that we did with his corporation.

Our first meeting was cordial, but his concern was evident. Dr. Colson was a stocky, articulate man with a reputation for decisive action and a good sense of humor, but neither I nor the two associates I brought with me to the meeting saw much evidence of his humor that day.

He got right down to business, outlining his concerns about the research division and its chief, Dr. Nicholas Troubat.

Troubat was a Frenchman, with a Gallic wit and a fiery temper, a bon vivant of impeccable academic credentials who had made a significant breakthrough in the health products field as a research scientist for a large European company 20 years previously. After a bruising court battle with his employer, he was awarded the patent rights to his discovery and founded his own company to capitalize on his research. The company prospered, and he sold out after a few years—to his former employer!—at a profit that assured that he could live, and die, a man of immense wealth.

Colson had known Troubat for years and had used him frequently as a consultant on specific company research problems. The two had become close personal friends. When Colson fired the "incompetent" research director he had inherited when he took over as CEO, he immediately called Troubat, who accepted the presidency somewhat reluctantly.

Now Colson was ready to conclude he had made a dreadful error in judgment. Troubat was demonstrating little sense of leadership of the division, and it did not appear that he was winning the support and confidence of his key people.

As evidence of his own frustration, Colson reeled off a series of questions to which he said he had vainly sought answers from Troubat:

> Why does it have to take 7 years or more to develop and get a product into market in this industry? Why are there more than 100 steps to the new-product development process in this company? Why is it that the division rarely meets its deadlines? Why do they always seem to be scrambling to meet emergencies? Why are they so defensive in talking about their priorities and budgets? Why do they resent anyone who questions what they're doing? Why are they constantly tied up in association meetings all over the country, and sometimes abroad? Why, if this company has over 700 products in the marketplace, do so few of them have a significant share of the market?

He concluded by saying, "Frankly, I'm ready to fire Troubat tomorrow if he's the basic problem. But I'm not sure anyone knows what the basic problem is. I hope you can find out and help correct it. We need dramatic results, and if he's not the man to produce them, then I'll find someone who is."

I told Colson that no president could produce dramatic results without winning the trust and support of the division's managers and other professionals. I questioned whether Troubat had.

I also said that, while the new president had obviously not made an auspicious beginning (to put it mildly), if he had the qualities that were necessary to lead the division, we could help to bring them out and, in the process, build the foundation for a successful turnaround.

After sounding out two of the CEO's associates about the research division's problems, we asked to have a room and the services of a typist for 90 minutes to put together a proposal. The proposal, which Colson approved 3 days later, had a deceptively simple sounding purpose: "To accelerate new-product development at _____ Corporation." The project's objectives:

1. To win the ownership, participation, and commitment of research division management to necessary change.
2. To identify and resolve the key issues that are causing suboptimal performance.
3. To clarify the mission, objectives, priorities, performance criteria, and roles and responsibilities of the division and its major components.
4. To develop a viable and streamlined managing and new-product development for the division.

It was to be an unusual challenge for us. Although we had worked for dozens of senior executives in numerous industries, we had always had our clients' support of the project at the outset. In this instance, at the time of our proposal was approved by Colson, the research division president was not even aware of the project. He was vacationing in another country and suffering from a very painful back problem.

Our first challenge would be to win Troubat's support for the objectives of the project and for the use of our resources as catalyst to help him do *his* job better.

It wouldn't be easy. At our first meeting, held in Colson's offices 2 weeks later, I had the uncomfortable feeling I was confronting a mad genuis. Although small—almost wizened—in appearance, Troubat was a truly intimidating man: always restless, invariably demanding, and with a thick French accent that masked an extraordinary command of the nuances of the English language. He could describe a ballet in words that could almost make you think you were there. And he could swear with a crudeness that would make a sailor blush. Although his famous temper rarely showed itself in corporate headquarters, at research division headquarters—several hundred miles away—he was known to engage in frequent shouting matches with scientists, engineers, and managers who displeased him. His booming voice (extraordinary for a man of such small stature) could be heard from one end of the floor to the other.

Troubat was coldly polite at this initial three-way meeting, but I had the distinct impression that he interpreted my presence as a sign that Colson had lost confidence in him.

I felt the full fury of his emotions a week later, when I met him alone at his research division offices in another state to begin implementing the project.

The office itself was modern, and elegant in its simplicity: a large wall-to-wall Finnish carpet, teak furniture and paneling with floor-to-ceiling bookcases, one wall lined with photographs of his degrees from leading universities in Europe and the United States, citations from major associations, and patents he had acquired.

After only a moment or two of initial pleasantries, he launched into a diatribe against the project and my own presence.

There's no goddamn way that Colson or anyone else is going to tell me how to run my research laboratories. The trouble with this whole stinking company is that it's run by marketeers, who would sell their souls to make a dollar, and don't give a good goddamn about improving health. We are working on developments that could produce a new generation of health products. If you think you're going to divert me from that goal to put schlock on the market to make the bottom line better next month or next quarter, you're sadly mistaken, Mr. Arnold.

When he had finished, I paused to let his words sink in. Then, trying to keep my voice as quiet and unemotional as possible, I began speaking:

Mr. Troubat, I understand completely how you must feel to have me here today. I'm sorry that the decision had to be made while you were out of the country, but, as you know, Dr. Colson felt sincerely that you needed some guidance, and he didn't want to wait. Now, you and I both know that we were hired by him. But *you're our client* now. *We work for you.* Our company is prepared to do whatever is necessary to help you succeed in proving to the marketing division that this can and will be the finest research division in the industry.

The success of this project means a good deal to us. Just as Dr. Colson heard about our success from another firm, the industry will learn if you end up leaving the company, and we are blamed for it. So we are committed to your success. To achieve that success, we've got to find a way to work with you. Equally important, you've got to find a way to work with us. If you and we don't find a way to work together, we'll both "go through the slats."

My talk must have relieved some of Troubat's anxieties, because he invited me to his home for dinner that evening. And although I wasn't entirely certain that I wouldn't be poisoned (given the Dr. Jekyll and Mr. Hyde quality of this complex man), I gladly risked whatever gastronomic fate awaited me when I saw the sumptuous meal that his corpulent butler-chef had prepared (he was a man of obviously independent means).

The meal was one of the finest I have ever enjoyed, abetted by three exquisite wines from his extensive wine cellar. We talked long into the night about his own scientific accomplishments, politics, music, art—everything but his current business problems.

I must have "passed muster," because the next morning he agreed to go ahead with the project, providing he had a strong voice in how we proceeded. He made it clear, however, that he was doing so "under duress."

We agreed that the project would have the following elements:

Phase 1: Diagnosis This would consist of:

1. Interviews with more than 60 executives and scientists, including 17 from the division, a dozen at corporate headquarters, managers in other countries when they visited the United States, as well as officials of government regulatory agencies and other outsiders who knew the organization well.

2. Administering several of our copyrighted diagnostic questionnaires. These included a Functional Interaction Matrix, which gauges the state of interdepartmental cooperation and pinpoints any obstacles; a Business Values Inventory, which tests any differences in perception between two interfacing organizations that may affect business performance (in this instance, the research division, corporate headquarters, and the marketing divisions); and our Change-Mangement-Climate Survey, to determine where and why administrative or management bottlenecks were occurring.

3. Two feedback sessions at which our findings would be shared:
   a. With himself and Dr. Colson.
   b. With himself and the management of the division.

Phase 2: Three work conferences The first would be devoted to analyzing and beginning to resolve the primary issues identified by the group's analysis of the feedback; the second, to establishing a management process to accelerate new-product development; and the third, to improving the managing skills and administrative practices of divisional managers. All three conferences would be aimed at creating a spirit of teamwork, assuming Dr. Troubat was indeed capable of winning the allegiance of the men.

Phase 3: Follow-through and results evaluation This would involve counseling by myself and several associates with Dr. Troubat and individual R&D managers to assure that plans stayed on track and achieved effective follow-through, and man-to-man work with Dr. Troubat and his liaison at corporate headquarters to resolve any remaining issues that hadn't been resolved at or between the conferences.

At our next meeting, Dr. Troubat approved with only minor modifications the extensive interview design that our firm developed, and we agreed on how *he* should explain to the research division's senior managers and scientists the reasons for the project, their roles in it, and the results to be achieved.

The senior management orientation meeting went off surprisingly well, considering Dr. Troubat had accepted the project "under duress." He began the meeting by introducing us and explaining that he had made up his mind to employ an external resource because *he* felt that an outside perspective was needed to help the division identify its strengths and weaknesses and determine how to rationalize the new-product development process to better meet the needs and demands of the marketplace and the corporation.

He went on to explain how our approach differed from that of management consultants or efficiency experts, who might make a study, hand the client a recommendation, and depart *with no accountability for results*. I was pleased to see that he stressed our role as a resource in identifying issues, problems, and opportunities, and in helping the management group analyze them and *make their own decisions*, while also helping the group to evolve and improve administrative processes. He stressed that we would make no substantive recommendations and not attempt to be "technical experts" who "tell us what to do."

He concluded by saying that we were there to *"help us help ourselves"* and asked the group's full cooperation in the project.

Our interviews probed such areas as:

1. What should the reason for being of the research division be?
2. How is the division perceived—both internally and by corporate headquarters, the marketing divisions, the government, and other outside groups?
3. What is its new-product development strategy?
4. How should it be different, if at all?
5. What are the division's distinctive resources and capabilities?
6. What are its weaknesses and constraints?
7. What are the sacred cows or myths about the division, both within the organization and outside?
8. What are their concerns about organization structure, politics, practices, decision making, and communications?

Six weeks later, the interviews completed, we submitted our feedback report. The diagnostic questionnaire and interviews portrayed a company in which:

1. There was considerable disagreement as to the appropriate role of the division and its place in the corporation.
2. Communication between the executive office and the research division, as well as between the marketing divisions and research, was described as "abominable."
3. There were no firm criteria that governed new-product selection or resource allocation, and no explicit procedures for determining when to turn the product spigot faster or slower—or off entirely—on some products.
4. Lack of policy direction, plus administrative and technical bottlenecks, were all hampering new-product development.
5. Product accountability and timetables were unclear and seldom enforced.

6. There was no systematic decision-making or planning process.

7. There was little teamwork among the departments of the research division.

8. Division morale was very low.

As one example of how the research division and marketing management often worked at cross-purposes, a scientist on the bench would get a call from marketing to run some immediate tests on a product and communicate the results to marketing as soon as possible. He would have to drop whatever he was doing to comply. Research management, however, would badger him for not working on research's priorities. The more fully he satisfied marketing, the further behind he fell in meeting his own divisional responsibilities.

The feedback also showed that while punishment was characterized as swift and severe, the division offered no incentive reward system. Finally, most respondents contended that it was the executive vice president, rather than the new president, who was the major management bottleneck in the division.

In arranging the first feedback session, Dr. Colson and Dr. Toubat said they would set aside 3 to 4 hours to discuss the report. I warned it would probably require 7 or 8 hours. In fact, it took 11!

It was a different Dr. Troubat who chaired the feedback session with his division managers 3 days later. He was patient, supportive, understanding, and almost enthusiastic. "Now we know what we're up against, boys!" he exclaimed. "Now we know how we're viewed and why so many corporate and marketing division people act as they do. It's up to us to prove to them we're the best goddamn research division in this whole industry— so let's get on with it!"

Our reluctant client had recognized the potential of the feedback for organizational self-improvement. After what must have been an intense internal struggle, he had decided to "lead the charge" rather than fight a rearguard action.

With our help, research division management evolved a set of criteria by which to evaluate the more than 80 issues they distilled from the feedback. They determined which should be tackled at the first of the three conferences and what information should be brought to the conference to aid their problem analysis and decision making.

At the time, I couldn't fully appreciate the impact of the feedback on Dr. Troubat, or the transformation he was just beginning to undergo. In his almost 10 months as president, he had apparently made no systematic attempt to analyze the new-product development process, let alone reform it. The challenge of managing seemed to bore him; hence he left it to his second-in-command, who was—the feedback disclosed—an inept manager.

Rather than run the division, Troubat much preferred to immerse himself in the minute details of each department. He would often be found prowling the research labs, bent over a table while the scientist whose chair he appropriated stood meekly at his side listening to a lecture on how to do his work.

Yet for all his obvious shortcomings, Troubat was a man capable of great growth and flexibility. He was shrewd enough to recongize that, along with the criticism, the feedback provided a perfect opportunity to "turn over a new leaf."

Accordingly, at the conference itself, instead of barking orders, he asked thoughtful, penetrating questions, listened intently, and sometimes deferred to subordinates when he found himself beginning to interrupt them from force of habit. By the end of the week, he had amazed every member of the 14-man group with his patience, his supportiveness, his openness, and, yes, his leadership!

As evidence of his leadership, he delivered a brilliant summation of the work of the conference on the last day, crystallizing the thinking of the entire group on "what had been accomplished and what remains to be accomplished." He also proposed (and the group immediately accepted) setting up five cross-functional task forces to address these critical issues in preparation for the second conference 6 weeks hence:

1. Streamlining and refining the new-product development process
2. Coordination with the marketing divisions and corporate headquarters
3. Revision of research policy board responsibilities and review of policies impacting product development
4. Assuring effective interaction of the three key R&D departments
5. Determining how best to realign the R&D organizational structure to meet the tentative divisional mission and objectives agreed to at the conference.

As is our practice at such conferences, before adjourning we ask each manager anonymously to appraise the conference's results. They were overwhelmingly favorable. Among the comments were the following:

1. "We've developed better ways of communicating between the executive office, marketing divisions, and ourselves."
2. "We identified problems and a methodology to resolve them."
3. "I have higher confidence that our recommendations and decisions have been well thought through and have a high probability of success."
4. "We've developed a win-win attitude toward the executive office and marketing division."

5. "We developed a set of proposals for processing new-product development information and the interaction of the three key departments."

6. "We've improved our research policy."

7. "We've established procedures for speeding new-product development approval."

8. "For the first time, we have a positive attitude regarding management planning and administration of the division."

The second and third conferences were even more substantive and exciting. They led to:

1. Adoption of a new-product development process and timetable that drastically reduced development time by allowing for certain tests to be conducted simultaneously rather than sequentially

2. Implementation of ExecuTrak® Systems' problem/opportunity inventory method of managing the division

3. Approval of a new organizational mission, primary objectives, and priorities

4. Adoption of a new organizational structure with accountabilities, authorities, roles, and responsibilities clearly spelled out and agreed to by each member

5. Approval of procedures clarifying responsibilities vis-à-vis the executive office, with safeguards established against marketing interference in the day-to-day details of the division.

All these changes had to be explained to and accepted by marketing and the executive offices of the corporation. I helped Troubat strategize a series of meetings with the appropriate executives to win approval for the decisions emanating from these conferences.

The Results

From the first interview to the final conference took 5 months. During the next 6 months, Dr. Troubat, having won the required approval, succeeded in revitalizing the entire organization. He installed a new structure, made appropriate staff changes (including the resignation of the executive vice president), instituted a new performance evaluation system that encouraged initiative and rewarded accomplishment, and integrated the corporate management information system and long-range planning functions into the ongoing work of the division.

Twenty-four months from my first meeting with Abe Colson, the chief executive, this was the record of the research division:

	A.	B.	C.
	12 months prior to project	12 months after initiation of project	Following 12 months
Number of new-product applications approved by government	0	3	4
Number of new-product applications filed with government and pending approval	0	0	2
Number of investigational new products "in the pipeline"	3	15	21
			(9 from col. B + 12 new ones)

Both Dr. Troubat and Dr. Colson believe the project proved a superior vehicle for turning around the direction of the research division. From a management viewpoint, it helped define the charter and role of the division in the corporation, helped boost morale, developed a far simpler and more effective new-product development process (including specific strategies for new compounds), established a more efficient organizational structure that eliminated serious bottlenecks, with clearer definition of accountabilities and authorities of all major departments and functions, and developed a career advancement and reward system through which people could grow through management and administration, not only through scientific "benchwork."

In the process the research division's management team had developed an explicit decision-making process and interdisciplinary new-product teams comprising marketing, research, and manufacturing; "pure" research had been separated from other research; a productivity improvement program had been instituted; and all meetings were being "ExecuTrak'd" for greater efficiency. In addition, using the momentum generated by the project, a new 7-year plan was virtually complete.

Most extraordinary of all was the transformation that had occurred in the managing style and practices of Dr. Troubat, who had shed his Dr. Jekyll–Mr. Hyde ways to become a much more relaxed, open, and professional manager.

Dr. Troubat recognized that his own experience did not equip him for managing the responsibilities of a complex research division. He had tried to compensate for his own managerial shortcomings by adopting a defensive and ultimately intimidating manner, rather than searching for the source of the problems. But when the project was forced upon him, he was shrewd enough to realize he could use it as a vehicle to identify and correct the problems and improve his own management practices and professional stature both in the corporation and in the industry.

From the initial adversary relationship between Dr. Troubat and myself there developed a very close, warm, and trusting relationship that continues to this day.

Needless to say, the company is no longer known as "the house of no research"!

Chapter 15

"But Will It Sell?"

(Increasing Marketing Effectiveness)

Probably no challenge you might face in a new assignment offers as much opportunity for significant results as marketing.

Your resources may be limited, but your opportunities for innovation are limitless. In every business situation we have encountered, executives willing to devote the time and use the discipline required have been able to significantly increase the effectiveness of their marketing.

More than in any other area of the business, in marketing you should begin your new assignment by asking, for every product or service within your purview: What are we doing? Why? With what results? What should we be doing differently?

Let's begin by defining our terms. Until recently, businessmen have thought of marketing as a means of "making people buy our products or services." The problem with that definition, of course is that—even with modern communications and the "revolution of rising expectations"—you simply cannot make people buy products or services they don't want to buy.

Accordingly, marketing, as we define it, is a three-step process:

- First, identifying the needs and wants of potential customers that are not being effectively met
- Second, producing products or services that meet those needs and wants
- Third, calling those products and services to the attention of potential customers in ways that will make them *your* customers

Looked at another way: People have certain wants and needs, in response to which you offer satisfactions or "satisfiers." Closing the gap between their needs and your satisfiers—that's the purpose of marketing.

This chapter takes one difficult marketing challenge and shows how a new executive turned chaos into order—and produced improved bottom-line profits for his corporation. This particular case was chosen because it is a rather extreme one. It illustrates many of the major marketing problems you might find in your new assignment. By learning its lessons, you will be able to understand the marketing challenges you may face and design appropriate responses to them.

Jake Bemis was parachuted into a cosmetics company that was losing market share to larger competitors in several critical product categories. The company had sales in excess of $500 million annually, but its needs were being subordinated by corporate headquarters to those of a rival division that had made a significant product innovation and was closing in on the number one competitor in its industry. One of the casualties of the company's second-class status in the corporate hierarchy was a sustained advertising and sales promotion program.

Although Jake's company had budgeted upwards of $88 million a year on advertising and sales promotion, its plans were periodically curtailed when the rival division needed additional funding for its own marketing campaigns. Consequently, executives complained that time and again they would gear up for an imaginative and sustained marketing campaign only to have to "pull in their horns" prematurely. Without the staying power of its competitors, the company was declining in market share and contribution to corporate profits.

This much Jake knew when he accepted the offer to become president. His subsequent research found—and our own analysis and interviews of people in the company, the trade, and competitors verified—that "stop-go" marketing campaigns were only one of his problems, however.

Others included a lack of definition and direction to the business and confusion among customers as to what it was really committed to; a sales force of questionable caliber and a size too small to make a significant impact; underlization of market research; lack of attention to analyzing profit contribution by product lines; and a style of decision making that was strictly "seat of the pants."

Jake had a reputation at his former company for wielding the ax to marginally profitable products and focusing investment firepower on products that would give the company the leading edge in the marketplace. But he was shrewd enough to recognize that to introduce such a policy here simply because it had worked elsewhere would be premature and counterproductive.

Jake reasoned that imposing such a change unilaterally would indelibly print on everybody in his new organization the belief that "the boss thinks his ideas are superior to any that we might have," and hence would in the long run prove demoralizing—even if it worked in the short run.

His problems included:

- **Product Trends:** Every product category in which the company competed was declining, with no reason to believe trend lines would reverse.
One product had more than 90 percent share of market in its product
category, but the category itself had been abandoned by most competitors
because of changing consumer trends. "It was like finding out that we
had 90 percent of the horseshoe market at a time when people stopped
buying horses," summed up one harried executive.

- **Product Contribution:** An analysis by product lines revealed that some
of the largest-volume products were actually losing money. On one product, the company was losing $5 per case in profit before taxes on *every*
case sold.

- **Product Goals:** One major product group was characterized by a growing year-to-year gap between profit plan and profit reality. The profit
plan Jake inherited for this product group called for a profit of $17
million; in the previous 3 years profit reality had shrunk from $15.2
million to $14.4 million. This year, the goal unaccountably had been
raised to $20 million, whereas Jake projected that—realistically—actual
profit contribution would dip to $14.1 million.

- **Sales Costs:** An analysis undertaken shortly before Jake arrived had
concluded that the company was spending roughly $70 per sales call.
A campaign was undertaken to reduce costs by limiting sales calls, thus
improving "sales efficiency." Not surprisingly, the result was lower sales!
Jake reasoned that the problem wasn't sales *efficiency* but sales *effectiveness.*
"The challenge," he concluded, "isn't to reduce sales calls but to generate
higher sales per call."

- **Planning:** The 5-year plan he inherited had just been completed prior
to his arrival, but the data that it was based on had been collected 5
months previously, on the basis of actual results achieved 3 to 6 months
before that! So the long-term plan was actually a product of results that
were almost a year old.

On Jake's initiative, we undertook confidential interviews of managers
within his own and another division of the company, corporate officers, a
select group of trade representatives, and even a competitor (who did not
know on behalf of which company we were inquiring). Jake, on his own,
spent 5 days probing seven major customers about company products and
marketing technique. On the basis of this research, we compiled for him
an analysis of company and competitive strengths and weaknesses in his
key product categories.

Along the way, we unearthed information about the internal company
culture that was acting as a barrier to innovation. This included feelings—
both within the company and in the trade—that the organization was "hide-

bound" in its marketing policies and procedures, had kept people "straight-jacketed," discouraged risk taking, and was slow to respond to new opportunities.

There was also the usual conflict between line and staff, with staff people at corporate marketing services believing that marketing men were medio-cre, uncreative, and "too tied to the past," and line people reporting that marketing services was "ivory-towerish" and served up undigested material of no practical value. "We are data rich but information poor," commented one line executive, complaining about receiving reams of data in the form of computer printouts that were unintelligible "to me or anybody else around here."

In performing these interviews and studies, we became a "safe vehicle" to communicate "negative surprise" information to Jake that he might not otherwise have been able to uncover himself for months. For example, we discovered that in the company culture, there was an unwritten law that you had to achieve at least a 10 percent higher profit each quarter. A manager who found himself achieving a profit higher than 10 percent one quarter often concluded he was handicapping himself for the next quar-ter if he allowed the results to stand, since—if the higher profit was the result of an unusual circumstance—he would fall woefully short next quarter if he didn't squirrel away his current quarter's "excess" profit.

Consequently, profits "over budget" were hidden or "nested" so they could be drawn on, like a line of credit, in quarters or years when results fell short. Another favorite tactic was to "blow" over-budget profits on advertising to prevent them from showing up on the bottom line.

One executive explained the system this way: "The name of the game is to meet your budgets—10 percent higher each quarter—without creating an even higher base that will trip you up down the pike. . . . By making more money than you project, you're defeating yourself in the end, and that's what's to be avoided *at all costs.*"

As critical as these studies were, even more critical was an analysis of the product portfolio that Jake undertook. The analysis measured the profit contribution, growth potential, and responsiveness to advertising and sales promotion of each product line. It also measured the relationship between media spending and actual company sales compared with competitors.

The findings were revealing. They confirmed that the company was not spending its media dollars wisely. In fact, it was spending more money to generate each dollar of sales than all but one of its competitors. Reasons:

- Each division had its own advertising agency and developed its own media plan while paying lip service to coordination. In total, the company had used *nine* agencies the previous year!

- Some divisions in the company had products with similar brand names but different properties. "It's like having two McDonald's restaurants—

one an inexpensive fast-food place and the other a luxurious restaurant,"
remarked Jake. "The consumer is confused. He doesn't know what we
stand for."

- Three times as much advertising and sales promotion was budgeted to
  be spent on the largest-volume product line than on any other. But this
  line was contributing significantly less profitability than three other lines,
  and the trend in that product category was downward.

- One product, with a 20 percent share of market, was budgeted for $14
  million in advertising and sales promotion. When marketing expenditures
  were increased 50 percent, market share increased less than 1 percentage
  point—and the product lost $2.8 million.

The portfolio analysis documented the need to concentrate marketing
dollars behind those product lines with the highest growth and profit potential—to concentrate marketing resources where the company could achieve
the most "bang for its bucks."

At a series of conferences we helped organize for this management team,
all product lines were separated into four basic strategic categories, as follows:

1. Aggressively build
2. Hold/maintain (market share)
3. Exploit/harvest
4. Divest

In deciding which product lines to place in each category, the group
developed criteria for evaluation. These included:

1. Profit potential
2. Probable life cycle
3. Existing clout in the market category
4. Price of entry into this category
5. Price of continued support
6. Opportunity for innovation—"a consumer point of difference"
7. Length of time to payout
8. Potential for leadership and market domination

With our help, managers broke into interdisciplinary task forces to analyze
both existing products and products in the new-product pipeline on the
basis of these criteria. One task force analyzed the most successful new
products over the past decade to determine the reasons for their success;
another reviewed all the significant consumer research available and industry
trend projections.

Still another task force developed a set of "future marketing principles," which the group refined and which became the basis of the company's subsequent marketing efforts. Among the points:

1. Test-market no product in which we don't have the advantage in one or more of the following areas:
   a. Quality
   b. Packaging
   c. Convenience
   d. Mode of distribution
2. Advertising should stress one specific performance characteristic that gives us a "leading edge" over the competition.
3. Do not test with an inferior product or even a parity product unless we're number one in that category.
4. If a brand exceeds its sales targets, the added profits should be reinvested in the product or others under the control of its managers.

The work of the task forces resulted in a group recommendation, in which Jake heartily concurred, that 80 percent of the existing products should receive some further funding, but only 15 percent held sufficient promise to form a "critical mass" behind which the company should put major funding.

The group reduced the number of advertising agencies from nine to three, decreed certain well-accepted brands to be "umbrella brands" carrying certain properties that the public identified with them, and changed the names of some product entries to suggest the same qualities.

Other marketing innovations introduced included a policy manual for test marketing, greater use of interview "focus groups" for new products, and broader use of media other than television to carry its message (radio, magazines, even billboards).

By this disciplined approach to portfolio management, performed collaboratively with his key poeple, Jake Bemis was able to revamp his marketing strategy to compete more effectively in the marketplace. He tightened budgeting and planning procedures, established companywide media strategies, and made a number of organizational changes aimed at increasing distribution and selling effectiveness. He also fought for, and won, corporate backing for an end to self-defeating "stop-go" media practices.

"By demonstrating to them through our analysis how they were 'robbing Peter to pay Paul,' " Jake said, "we got them to play 'hands-off' once they had agreed to the media budget."

The managers also altered the philosophy of sales promotion. Instead of promoting without regard to growth potential or profitability, they provided that products should receive heavy promotion *only* to achieve one or more of the following objectives:

1. To induce trial use (for new products and product restagings)

2. To maintain superior shelf position

3. To reduce heavy retail stocks

Other products were to be promoted minimally or not at all. The major emphasis would be not on promotional-type "push" tactics (providing incentives for distributors and dealers to push their products), but on a "pull" strategy, in which advertising and other means would be used to induce consumers to pull their products off the shelf.

Using the criteria developed for screening existing products, research and development got to work on its new product portfolio, weighing each for "affordability," "potential for leadership and market domination," etc.

As a result of these changes, within 2 years Jake was able to redirect his marketing efforts and reallocate resources from "products that were going nowhere" to "products going where we want to go." In that time period, three out of four product lines turned around!

Jake's secret lay in:

- Heavy involvement of line management
- Honestly confronting the conflicts between marketing and marketing services
- *Objectively* examining the complete product portfolio
- Recognizing that his experience elsewhere might—or might not—give him the right answers in his new company, and being willing to test his perceptions against those held by people who knew the company best
- Following the forces he set in motion to their logical conclusion—a radical restructuring of his marketing strategy, letting the chips fall where they may

There were other ways he might have proceeded instead. He might have sought to impose the methods of his old company, as many new managers instinctively do. Or he might have called in an outside expert to recommend the course of action to be followed. Either way would have meant imposing on an organization a solution that might or might not be appropriate, but certainly would not have the full support and commitment of his managers.

Instead, he chose to work with his people, using an outside *diagnostician* and *catalyst* to save time, overcome conflicts, and choose the course of action that was both demonstrably superior and capable of generating the enthusiastic "buy-in" of the people in the organization (since it was their solution).

Chapter 16
"Why Didn't You Tell Me?"
(Avoiding Unpleasant Surprises)

Information is the lifeline of any organization. The art (or science) of effective decision making ultimately depends on the accuracy and timeliness of the information upon which decisions are based.

A senior executive in a new assignment faces distinctive difficulties in developing the knowledge base and the information pipelines he needs to meet his challenges. This chapter deals with the organizational barriers to effective information gathering and suggests methods that a newcomer to a company or division—or any executive, for that matter—can employ to break down the barriers and assure effective two-way communications.

A few years ago, the research department of a large business machine company developed a new concept in office photocopiers. "How soon can it be in production?" asked the president, anxious for a new product line to boost sales, which had been lagging. The question was transmitted down the line to the production department, where the answer given was "2 years." But as the answer was relayed upward, each layer of management shaved a few months off the estimate it received from below to demonstrate its commitment to getting the job done.

There was still no machine in existence when the president, following the telescoped timetable he had been given, announced he would visit the laboratory to inspect the prototype. Working day and night, the staff managed to construct one machine and get it operating on the very morning of the president's visit. It worked beautifully for one cycle while he watched. The president, his face beaming, congratulated the crew and returned to his office, having received assurances that the photocopier was "ready to roll."

Moments after he left the lab, the machine caught fire and was destroyed, but he wasn't told. That same week, *The Wall Street Journal* carried a large ad announcing introduction of the new machine—at a time when the company did not even own an operating prototype.

This president was the victim of an organizational cover-up, a benign conspiracy to hide bad news. To one extent or another, it is an illness that afflicts most organizations large and small. What executive has not been heard to complain, upon finally learning of some unpleasant truth of company life:

"If I had only known in time. . . . Why didn't anyone tell me? . . . Didn't anyone know this was happening? . . . Why am I always the last to know? . . ."

The Problem

The circumstances may vary but the pattern is always the same: Something is wrong. Some people know it is wrong. The people with the power to correct it are not told. By the time the problem is brought to their attention, it is often a much bigger—and more costly—problem.

Like most illnesses, this one is curable. But, as in medicine, proper treatment depends upon proper diagnosis. There are many strains of the disease. Here are examples of some common forms:

- A cereal company rushes to market with a new breakfast food. It bombs out. Only later does a confidential report come to the attention of upper management warning that the product will probably meet consumer resistance unless taste and texture are improved. In that report, market researchers point out that the cereal has been tested only by home economists, never by ordinary consumers; they call for a delay in product introduction to allow marketplace testing.

  Why didn't the report surface earlier? Marketing managers had no interest in circulating it since they decided against more tests (on the grounds that testing might give competitors time to develop a competing product). The researchers declined to circulate it for fear of being branded disloyal to the "marketing team." (Better, they may have reasoned, to be able to say, "We told you so" if the worst came to pass—as it did.)

  Lessons: Many organizations provide neither system nor incentive for calling attention to danger signals if those to whom the danger is reported choose to ignore them. The case also demonstrates a common organizational conflict of loyalties—i.e., the welfare of the company versus protection of the function or department.

- The vice president of a West Coast electronics company discovers that quarterly sales and shipment figures have been falsified. Shipments that were to be made in the first 10 days of the next quarter are reported as having been made in the current quarter. The deception was made in an effort to meet budgeted sales goals, which increase quarter by quarter. Managers judged it was safer to disguise the actual sales situation than to admit failure to meet budgeted sales.

Lessons: Managers were victims of a sales-projection system that requires increased quotas each quarter. The company's emphasis on "making the numbers" discourages reporting of information that doesn't conform to plans.

- The group president of a major consumer goods company protests that the targets he's been asked to reach are unrealistically high. "I'd have to swing the ax to reach those goals," he tells the corporate president, adding that compliance would require cutting head-count, short-terming products, cutting back advertising and sales promotion, and starving new-product development. It is patiently explained to him that the numbers have been "maxi-stretched" to convince stockholders and the financial community that the company is "on the move." "You find a way to reach the goals," he is advised. "We need your commitment." A colleague suggests, "You can always send up lots of magnesium flares so that if you fall short, you have a plausible explanation."

  When the executive, after stretching his goals to the limit he considers realistic, still insists he can't "meet the numbers" he's been given, the corporate president tells him there are others in the company who would be happy to make such a commitment if he won't. After several such incidents, the executive resigns.

  Lessons: Top management is purposely shading the truth; it doesn't want a realistic assessment of the state of the business. Corporate integrity is subordinated to relations with the financial community. Those who won't play the game aren't welcome.

Almost any group of managers can compile a list of notable business mistakes stemming from faulty organizational feedback—inferior merchandise, bad investments, new-product failures, and the like. Although business, and ultimately consumers, pay for such misjudgments in the cost of goods and services—the sum must total in the billions of dollars annually—suprisingly little attention has been paid by business and industry to correcting the problem.

It is axiomatic that the effectiveness of any enterprise depends on the existence of an accurate and timely information system that serves up both the good and the bad with equal impartiality. In fact, however, most organizations operate according to a set of cultural norms and work incentives that encourage reporting of positive or reinforcing truths while discouraging the communication of unpleasant or nonreinforcing truths.

What is needed is both a *vehicle* to facilitate the communicaton of unpleasant truths and a *management climate* conducive to that communication. Creating both the vehicle and the climate requires an understanding of how prevailing cultural norms and work incentives typically operate.

Reasons for the Problem

Management is generally denied useful organizatonal feedback for one of two reasons, which, for convenience, we shall label type A and type B.

- Type A: Those who should know aren't told.
- Type B: Those who should know don't really want to know.

Type A: Those Who Should Know Aren't Told

Organizational complacency   Many organizations provide powerful discouragement to rocking the boat or sticking one's neck out, and little reward for such conduct. Like the couriers in ancient Persia who risked losing their heads for bringing the king bad news, today's "bad news bearers" can also suffer for the tidings they bring. Organizations have ways of retaliating against "troublemakers" at performance-review time or in those quiet offhand comments by which so many futures are decided. "You know that guy, there's something about him that bothers me. He's always finding fault, have you noticed?"

Fear of disloyalty   An equally persuasive inhibitor of frank organizational feedback is the fear that "blowing the whistle" is somehow disloyal. Sometimes, as in the case of the market researchers who withheld news of a new product's inadequacies, managers face a moral dilemma in implicating or embarrassing colleagues with whom they form a team. Related to this fear is the "Achilles' heel syndrome"—the fear that "If I blow the whistle on these people for this, they may blow it on me for something else."

Mock trust   A third constraint on "telling it like it is" is the convenient excuse, "Someone up there must know what he's doing, even if it doesn't make sense to me." While sometimes meant sincerely, more often such statements are an attempt to shirk responsibility for alerting those who should know. Persons who will second-guess every management decision will refuse to report a snafu with a shrug of the shoulders and the comment "Ours is not to reason why." Related to mock trust is the infighter's refrain, which we saw demonstrated by the colleague of the senior executive who refused to play a phony numbers game: "If we work hard enough, cross our fingers and send up some flares, then when the failure finally is recognized, at least they'll know we tried."

Type B: Those Who Should Know Don't Really Want to Know

"Only good news welcomed here"   The pressure for positive results—the sine qua non for high performance in any organization—often creates an atmosphere in which good news is seen as reinforcing, uplifting, and morale building, while bad news is confused with defeatism or "making excuses." Although few organizatons would admit to discouraging candid feedback, some managers in our experience have confessed to being told: "The boss doesn't want to hear about problems. He says he has enough already."

Positive thinking that ignores relevant but nonreinforcing information is nothing more than an exercise in wishful thinking. Often, however, subordinates are scapegoated before the wishful-thinking executive is recognized as such.

Hockey-stick planning   Some companies not only refuse to face facts today, but insist on projecting their wishful thinking into tomorrow. The ultimate in self-delusion is embedded in the process that we call "hockey-stick planning." Sales and profits may be declining, but the climate of the organization demands that they be projected to increase quarter by quarter. Thus the planning process resembles a hockey stick ($\checkmark$), with sales and profits currently shrinking but "projected to increase."

"Let sleeping dogs lie"   Many companies operate on the assumption that what they don't know can't hurt them. Some managers insist it's better not to know what's really happening down below. The reasoning: "If you begin kicking up the dust, we'll all choke from the dust storm." In such an atmosphere, frank communication is not only discouraged but suspect. The real story may surface only by accident—if poor morale should lead to a wholesale exodus, or a newspaper should smell a scandal, or an investment house gets wind of trouble.

Limitations of Conventional Solutions

Open-door policy   Many executives try to encourage subordinates to level with them by stressing their accessibility. "I'm always there if you need me," they will say. Many subordinates nonetheless think twice before running to their boss with unsettling news, particularly if he tends to react with apparent distress—either verbally or nonverbally. An executive may think his door is always open, but if his subordinates have things to say that may depress him, they may not walk in.

Group meetings   Conventional business meetings, by their very nature, are rarely ideal forums for exploding bombshells or even unveiling unhappy surprises. Often organized around a tight agenda and narrowly focused on immediate issues, they provide little opportunity for raising unwelcome, unscheduled matters. Moreover, the manager who finds it hard to tell his superior unpleasant news when seeing him alone may find it doubly hard to do so when seeing him in a group, for fear the superior either will be embarrassed or, if the complaint is backed up by others, may feel that his authority is being challenged.

The interoffice memo The omnipresent memo, while a versatile vehicle for communicating unpleasant truths downward, is generally useless to communicate such truths upward. Bad news, if passed through the hands of intermediaries, is often ambushed en route to the top, or its contents watered down to make it more palatable.

Getting "out of the office and onto the floor" Many executives make earnest efforts to "test the waters" by either developing independent pipelines in their organizations or periodically meeting with the troops. Generals going back to the time of Thucydides have understood the benefits of a battlefield inspection. But the amount of information that can be divulged under such conditions is, of necessity, limited, and impressions formed are likely to be superficial. Moreover, in today's modern organization, top executives who make a habit of "seeing for themselves" create insecurity among middle managers who feel themselves bypassed. Some middle managers encourage their subordinates to cooperate fully with senior management but also insist, to keep themselves informed, that such contact and conversations be reported fully to themselves. For fear of "ticking off" the boss, subordinates often decide to hold their tongues, thus frustrating senior management's attempts to obtain direct feedback.

Organizational improvement sessions In an attempt to improve interaction and smoke out hidden issues, some managers periodically remove their key people for a weekend of stock taking and self-examination. Such retreats are usually convened with little preparation, and the experience of seeking common objectives in a relaxed setting (with the help of some liquid stimulants) is often more successful in "opening Pandora's box" than in resolving issues. Often such sessions do have an uplifting effect on morale and produce a spirit of rededication and camaraderie, which are important benefits in themselves. But the challenge of sustaining these gains in the face of day-to-day pressures of the work environment often proves over whelming, as was noted by Chris Argyris in "Double Loop Learning in Organizations."[1]

Suggested New Solutions

Corrective action, as noted above, requires establishing both a climate conducive to frank feedback and new channels in the work environment to facilitate

[1] Chris Argyris, "Double Loop Learning in Organizations," *Harvard Business Review.* September-October 1977.

its flow. Our experience suggests that the two objectives are closely related and should be addressed as part of a systematic, coordinated effort. The essential ingredients of such an effort are a senior management committed to honest organizational feedback, the full participation of relevant managers in the process, and effective follow-through.

Here's the outline of a three-stage process that has proved effective in generating and capitalizing on frank organizational feedback.

Phase 1: Confidential Interviews

A professional outside resource conducts penetrating, confidential 1½- to 2-hour "open-answer" interviews,[2] following an interview process jointly designed by the counselor and management. The aim: To identify the real problems, "gut" issues, opportunities, myths, sacred cows, skeletons, and conflicts (both personal and organizational) that may be hampering effectiveness.

Interviewees typically include company (or departmental) executives and managers, and others who know the organization intimately and whose views are important to its success. These may include customers, suppliers, trade sources, financial analysts and columnists, bankers, associations, government agencies, possibly former executives whose views are respected, and even competitors.

Although company personnel departments sometimes volunteer to conduct "insider" interviews, the task is best left to a professional outsider. The reason: Managers and other insiders are more apt to open up to an impartial outsider who is pledged to protect their identity, confiding information that they will not share with "company men" who might have their own agenda and who control their pay and promotion prospects—or are answerable to those who do. While outsiders aren't concerned about jeopardizing pay and promotion, of course, they do worry about hurting the feelings of friends and other valued contacts within the company, and thus are more candid in expressing their judgments and concerns when talking to a professional third-party interviewer than when talking to a company representative who is not, after all, a disinterested observer.

Some executives worry that soliciting the views of outsiders will weaken the company image, but experience suggests that customers, bankers, and others whose input is sought tend to see the exercise as evidence that the company is "on the move" (i.e., "any company that values our opinion enough that they want to know what we truly think must really be interested in self-improvement!").

The information obtained from these interviews is distilled and presented

[2] In open-answer interviews, the respondents are asked structured questions but no attempt is made to restrict their answers to predetermined response categories as is done in multiple-choice exercises. Interviews therefore generally produce more specific information and more revealing insights than answers obtained by multiple choice.

to the client in a confidential feedback report that describes the situation as seen through the eyes of those who know it best—minus, of course, the informants' names.

Interviews of one company revealed skepticism of the wisdom of constructing a $45 million facility, which had already been approved by the board of directors and announced by the chief executive officer to the public. The respondents maintained that the projected cost was out of proportion to the benefits that could reasonably be expected from the facility. On the basis of the data transmitted in the feedback report, the board reconsidered its decision and found that its needs could be met by a different strategy, organizational structure, and facility costing only $22 million. Net savings: $23 million.

In another company, interviews revealed that a company's bonus-incentive plan, which tied remuneration to quarterly sales and profit figures, was prodding managers to short-term the business, producing immediate profits at the expense of long-term growth. In one department, managers who boasted to their superiors about their increased market share confided to interviewers that all their major products were in declining markets. They also complained about a lack of strategic planning (for results, see below).

Phase 2: The Survey Questionnaire

Although survey questionnaires are well-established among wage earners, they have not yet come into general use among managers, presumably because many top executives believe—often wrongly—they already know what their managers are thinking. As a supplement to in-depth interviews, surveys can provide important measures of many of the intangibles that impact organizational effectiveness, such as basic business values, sensitivity to external influences, management climate, functional interaction, and responsiveness to change. In addition, surveys are helpful in testing the effects (and effectiveness) of corrective action.

In assessing the management climate, for example, one survey asks such questions as: Once goals are set, are they very difficult to change? Is criticism dispensed more regularly than positive feedback? Do you often have the feeling it's not clear why decisions affecting you have been made? Do you usually have to rely on the grapevine to find out what's going on? Does top management seem genuinely interested in improving the way important decisions are made? Does your organization do a good job of identifying new opportunities? Does it encourage managers to take the time to seek out opportunities?

A Business Values Survey was employed in conjunction with a series of confidential interviews in the case of a U.S.-based multinational corporation that was dissatisfied with the business performance of a key overseas subsidiary. The parent corporation had been prodding European regional headquarters and the subsidiary for "maximum profits," while the subsidiary was insisting that national standards of "corporate citizenship" entailed costly obligations to workers and customers that made U.S.-level profit objectives unrealistic.

The survey asked executives of the U.S. parent, the European regional headquarters, and the subsidiary to rank the importance of 14 business objectives in both strategic and day-to-day decisions of the U.S. parent. They were next asked to rank the importance of the same objectives in both strategic and day-to-day decisions of the subsidiary company. Finally, they were asked how the 14 should rank in the subsidiary's future decision making.

Objectives listed included profitability, management integrity, product innovation, realistic planning, social responsibilities, open communications, and quality of products and service. The survey indicated that beneath this surface sparring, the three groups of executives were in basic agreement about business priorities. Specifically, they agreed that profitability should be uppermost in the subsidiary's future business plans.

The survey served to cut through the underbrush of misunderstanding and misperception that had kept the groups at odds; it allowed a task force of executives from the three organizations, comprising six nationalities, to zero in on the real issues: what specific profit targets are realistic in the subsidiary's environment; and what changes in its strategic planning, product mix, pricing and marketing policy, organizational structure, operating procedures, etc., are necessary to achieve them. So successfully were these issues resolved that the task force chairman was promoted to executive vice president of European operations.

Phase 3: Intensive Work Conference

The outside resource—who collects and distills information in phases 1 and 2—now becomes catalyst and decision counselor. Information from the feedback report and relevant surveys become the basis for a 3- to 4-day intensive residential "common vision/work-the-issues" conference of top managers. They submit the report's findings to "reality testing," develop an inventory of key issues and opportunities to be analyzed, and establish criteria for resolving them.

This resource focuses the group's attention on each element of the decision-making process, structures their analysis, summarizes decisions reached, and guides the managers in developing a results plan with specific, time-phased action steps, accountabilities, performance standards, and mechanisms to track progress against plan. The participation of managers in the entire process—from interview to analysis to resolution—gives them *ownership* of the results and a commitment to the success of the plan. With continuing guidance from the resource, implementation of the plan is closely monitored to ensure that decisions of the conference are built into the day-to-day operations of the organization.

In the organization where short-terming was identified as a priority issue, conference participants revamped the bonus-incentive plan to discourage what one member called "decisions for our wallet, not for the welfare of the business." The problem of shrinking markets was traced in part to a legacy of restrictive departmental charters, which prevented managers from capitalizing on new growth-sector opportunities. Charters were revised and a reorganization initiated to define the businesses not in terms of technology or distribution channels (as they had been previously) but in terms of strategic sectors.

At another company, feedback revealed that U.S. headquarters was burdening the Latin American region with demands for 42 financial reports a month, many of which sought identical data in different forms. At the conference, representatives from headquarters and the Latin American region jointly established a set of financial reporting objectives by means of which they were able to prune the number of monthly reports down to only 8. The sense of ownership and commitment was so strong that conferees devised a creative new financing scheme to reduce receivables, established a new shipping system that pruned material inventory requirements without sacrificing order-response time, reduced indirect overhead to the level of 3 years earlier despite a doubling of sales and promotion volume, and developed a strategy that won the company a $90 million contract—largest in the entire international division's history.

Changing the Climate

Managers report good news, at least in part, because they think the organization expects them to. They suppress bad news, at least in part, because they think the organization expects them to. Altering what's expected of them requires concerted action.

Installing an "Early Warning System" Mentality

In staff meetings, an executive stresses that each manager is responsible for reporting information that even potentially impacts business effectiveness (either positively or negatively) or that could cause embarrassment to the company or function. "Every one of you," he might say, "mans an outpost in the company's Early Warning System. When trouble happens, you have a duty to alert us. Unpleasant surprises are part of the life of every organiza-

tion. We can take them. What we can't take—what we won't stand for—
are unpleasant surprises that other people have been hiding from us."

Such instructions should be reinforced by written memos to each department that set forth procedures for the kinds of information to be reported,
to whom, in what form, and with what follow-up steps if no action is taken.
The company manual and work rules might be revised to include such a
statement too.

Sometimes, a reporting deadline is advisable. The president of a capital
goods company arrived at work one morning to find that a projected $5
million quarterly profit had turned into a $1.5 million deficit. Investigation
revealed that a general manager had learned of a serious shortfall in sales
2 weeks previously but had put off informing his boss for fear of upsetting
him. Company policy stipulated that all deviations from plan—either positive
or negative—be clearly noted and explained in monthly reports, but the
manager felt no obligation to report this information sooner.

As a result of this experience, the department was put on notice that
all plan deviations of more than a certain percentage had to be reported
within 48 hours. Observed the president: "The only thing worse than discovering a shortfall is discovering that someone knew of a shortfall and didn't
tell you. No business can operate without accurate numbers. If the numbers
change and we don't find out about it, we're in real trouble."

The above suggestions don't *guarantee* that management won't be surprised by unpleasant developments. They *do* assure that managers who withhold information can expect to be dealt with harshly. That awareness itself
should reduce the incidence of information cover-ups.

One executive who impressed his staff with the need for early warning
found that, as he put it, "Some people were running to me every time
they had a problem. They wanted me to do their thinking for them." His
solution was to stipulate that any problem brought to his attention must
be accompanied by a recommendation for solution. While this procedure
was effective in reducing the number of problems his people presented
him with, it has serious shortcomings.

For one thing, there are certain developments a superior must know
about—the aforementioned sales shortfall, for example—regardless of any
opinion as to what to do about it. Moreover, the requirement for a recommendation may impede timely reporting. ("Gee, boss, I was going to tell
you but I still hadn't decided how I thought we should handle it.")

More sensible is a policy that requires prompt reporting under specified
circumstances, with a recommended course of action if possible.

Establishing Information Criteria

Some executives and their management teams find it helpful to establish
a set of specific criteria that managers should apply in determining whether

or not to bring a situation to the attention of their superior. The criteria may vary from one company to another, and even from one department within a company to another. As an illustration, however, such a checklist might include any situation that potentially:

• Endangers the health or safety of workers or customers
• Represents a violation of law or company policy
• Impedes attainment of planned goals
• Affects adversely consumer acceptance of any company product
• Represents a breach of accepted standards of integrity
• Embarasses the company or tarnishes the corporate image

Status Reports

In addition to the periodic status reports they may already submit, managers are asked to review their major responsibilities and give a 1- to 2-page answer to questions such as these:

• What's going especially well?
  Why?
  How do we know?
  What are we doing to "bake it" in the system (replicate the results)?
• What's not going especially well?
  Why?
  What are we doing to correct it?
  How will it be prevented in the future?
• Any new problems you see on the horizon?
• Any new opportunities?

Asking managers to make a weekly or bimonthly "well/not well" analysis of their business tends to force unpleasant news out into the open (i.e., managers know that written attempts to cover up the truth may come back to haunt them). Similarly, in their verbal inquiries to subordinates, managers are encouraged to ask "What's going well?" and "What's not going well?" rather than the usual "How are things going?" The more specific questions will elicit much more meaningful information than the general question— if the organization, either on its own or with the help of an outside resource, has established the appropriate climate.

Staff Meetings

Meetings run or controlled by the boss rarely provide a climate conducive to raising unpleasant truths. Superiors tend to feel threatened and react defensively when subordinates unveil negative surprises publicly. They wonder about the questioner's motives: Why did he say that? Why didn't he tell me before? Is he trying to embarrass me? Similarly, no matter how well-intentioned, meetings in which "everyone is urged to participate" often become aimless discussions in which participants are more intent on making their views known than listening to the judgments of others.

While the boss-subordinate relationship can never be completely forgotten, its inhibiting effects on dialogue can be largely overcome if an impartial outside catalyst is used to periodically monitor, structure, and cochair such meetings. The catalyst's combination of interactive and analytical skills enables him to draw people out, make critical judgmental calls (distinguishing fact from opinion, issues from personalities, defensive from open reactions, etc.), distill information, and direct the discussion toward a collective search—by executives and their teams—for solutions, all without arousing suspicions that he may have hidden motives.

At one company, managers of marketing and manufacturing were consistently crossing swords at staff meetings. Each saw the meetings as a test of wills—an exercise in "one-upsmanship." So intent were the two on besting one another that they often ignored the perspectives of other participants, such as the directors of finance and administration, personnel, and research and engineering. With the participation of all members of the group, the outside resource set ground rules for staff meetings, which include time limits on individual statements (which the group could lift) and payment of a token fine for interrupting a speaker or using "killer" phrases and other "idea stoppers" (e.g., "That's ridiculous!").

One technique a catalyst may use to stimulate frank yet nonthreatening communication is to focus the group's attention (boss and subordinates) initially on a basic area of commonality—such as defining realistic objectives for the session. Once consensus is reached on objectives, he works backward to issues that need to be resolved to achieve the objectives, analysis for cause, criteria for successful resolution, generation and weighing of alternatives, etc. The process tends to create from the initial "circle of consensus" a ripple effect of widening agreement.

Confidential Communications

The old-fashioned suggestion box has largely gone the way of the horse and buggy. It responded to a legitimate organizational need—to communicate directly and often confidentially with top management—but it became trivialized as a result of management neglect and employee uncertainty about its mission. (Was its purpose to complain about working conditions? Suggest ways of saving money? Report wrongdoing? Or all three?) No single mechanism has taken its place, but the need for direct and confidential communications remains.

One executive holds a monthly 1-hour meeting with all 600 employees of his department. Fifty minutes is devoted to his explanation of company or departmental news and plans, the other 10 minutes to taking questions. The meetings themselves don't provide bottom-up communication, but they help set the climate for it. At one meeting, he announced, "If you have any suggestions for topics we should discuss, or ideas for profit improvement, I want to know them. And if you find yourself really distressed about something that's happening, and your superior either can't or won't do anything about it, I want to know that too. But you'd better be ready to substantiate your case." Sometimes he receives scribbled suggestions like the following: "The fellows down in Department X are having a hell of a time trying to do Y. This may be something you want to discuss at a monthly meeting or maybe look into."

A more direct approach to information feedback is employed by one chief executive officer, who periodically calls people down in the bowels of the organization to get an uncensored view of "how the war's going." Lyndon Johnson used his White House telephone to get frontline reports from the federal bureaucracy in much the same way, striking terror in the hearts of civil servants with his questions. The advantage of the direct approach is that it does indeed provide direct, confidential feedback. On the other hand, such calls tend to undermine the authority and self-confidence of managers and may provide distorted information since the caller generally is not in a position to judge how accurate or representative his informants' views are.

Company Newsletters

Most newsletters are public relations megaphones, transmitting pronouncements from the top down. They make only the feeblest attempt to facilitate bottom-up communication. If they solicited information about problem areas (offering, for example, to "withhold names on request" as editors of mass media publications do routinely), company newsletters could bring important developments into the open and might also become lively forums for the exchange of ideas, which many are not now.

Visible Rewards

Bonuses, letters of appreciation, and other tokens of recognition are a standard part of a corporation's incentive system for rewarding valuable service. Calling the attention of appropriate corporate officers to neglected problems or unpleasant truths and recommended solutions is itself a valuable service entitled to similar treatment. Tangible recognition is the best assurance that a company will receive the kind of organizational feedback it needs to meet its challenges.

Conclusion

Every organization is a network of information pipelines. Occasionally some of these pipelines become blocked. The challenge of organizational feedback is threefold: To recognize the source and reasons for blockage; to remove it; and to design measures that discourage its recurrence.

Increasingly, organizations committed to *excellence* will have to find ways of unclogging information pipelines. This chapter offers a variety of techniques for doing so. Not all techniques are applicable to all situations. But every organization can benefit from some of them.

It may be argued that such innovations as rewards for whistle blowers and assurances of anonymity will undermine managerial authority, hurt morale, and even impede the work effort. On the contrary, the participation of managers in identifying and resolving issues—through interviews, feedback, and issue-resolution work conferences—has precisely the opposite effect: It gives managers a commitment to frank and open communication and a dedication to success that probably has previously been lacking.

In addition, by assuring that shortcomings are promptly brought to top management attention, the techniques discussed herein facilitate the removal of obstacles to corporate objectives. In a word, they are powerful incentives to renewed organizational commitment and improved performance.

Chapter 17
"How Can I Help?"
(Getting Results through People)

It all comes down to people. People whose help and support you need to do your job. People who need your help and support to do theirs. People will measure your effectiveness and determine your success or failure with the company or organization.

Four groups of people will determine your future here:

1. Your superiors (boss, others in the chain of command, influential board members)
2. Your peers (colleagues in the organization)
3. Your subordinates
4. Your key publics (customers, suppliers, trade reps, regulators, opinion makers, bankers, financial analysts, influential stockholders)

Each of these groups requires—and sometimes indeed demands—careful attention. It may not always be possible to satisfy all members of these groups at any one time. But having a strategy toward each group, based on a shrewd assessment of their concerns and your objectives, is possible. Where do you begin?

Your Boss

Let's begin with your superiors—your boss and anyone else you report to directly or indirectly. They are the people who hold your immediate future in their hands.

Your principal concern here, of course, is with the perception of your performance—what specific results you are held accountable for, in what time frame, etc. (The key, in organizations, is not so much results as the

199

perception of results in the opinion of the people who really count, whether it be your boss, the CEO, COO, CFO, influential board members, etc.) But while that is the scale on which you may be judged primarily, it is by no means the only basis for assessing your performance or, more specifically, your potential.

In an earlier chapter, we discussed the importance of coming to a clear understanding with your boss of where your responsibility begins and ends, and the mechanics of your interaction (how often you see each other, where, for what purpose, telephone communication, hours, availability, etc.). But those are the basics. Attending to all these necessities may earn you his *respect*—assuming your performance meets his expectations—but it does not win you his *allegiance.* Without his allegiance, you may end up echoing the comments of many passed-over executives, whose careers became stalemated not for lack of competence or self-confidence, but for lack of *compatibility.*

The secret to success in most organizations lies in a combination of *performance* and *comfort level*—of being "our sort of guy," whatever that term might mean in the context of your company's distinctive culture. There are exceptions, to be sure: companies that are floundering, that take a disastrous turn, or that are otherwise seeking new leadership; companies that are looking for particular expertise or managerial experience (witness the success of the managerial "whiz kids"—Robert McNamara at Ford, etc.— in the early 1960s). Generally, however, your climb up the company ladder depends on excelling at your job, proving your dedication and loyalty, and being generally regarded by those who make the decisions as "one of us."

You don't have to eat cottage cheese with ketchup for lunch simply because your boss does (though H. R. Haldeman aped Richard Nixon in this regard), or live where he suggests for prestige and contact purposes, or join his exclusive club. You *do* have to be someone the boss feels he can trust: the possessor of skills he admires, who shares a set of common assumptions about the business world and a compatability of basic values. In addition, you must be perceived as approachable rather than forbidding— the kind of person the Italians would call *sympatico.*

Machiavelli, it's true, counseled that it's better to be feared than loved, but he was giving advice to a sitting ruler—a king, not (to quote a recent movie title) *The Man Who* Would Be *King.*

When we help a client strategize his key relationships, we are not, however, being Machiavellian. We try to help a client identify the world as he sees it and as his boss sees it, and identify ways of matching up the two visions. This helps him to become more responsive to the boss's concerns, as well as to better do his job and obtain support for his own objectives.

We want our clients to excell at their jobs. We also want them to become recognized for doing so. Thus we help them draw up a periodic "contributions scorecard" showing the measurable results achieved by their leadership.

Here are a number of suggestions that have worked for many of our clients. Some or all may be applicable to your own situation:

List the major areas of your responsibility. Opposite each area listed, rate your performance, either in a few words or with a number. In our own work we often use a 10-high scale, measuring from 10 to 1 in descending order of excellence.

Next, record how you think the boss rates your performance (*not* how you think he *should* rate it). Now compare the two ratings for each area. If there are any discrepancies, jot down ways in which you can narrow the gap and act on them.

CHART 6-A

Primary results for which I am accountable	How I rate my own performance	How I think my superior rates my performance	Key reason for any differences	Best ways to close any gaps
1.				
2.				
3.				
4.				

Another helpful exercise might be to list your boss's major concerns and problems. Supplement this list by jotting down your own thoughts about things that *should* concern him or the company. Study the list to determine if any of these needs or concerns represent potential opportunities for you (i.e., areas that you could pursue on his behalf where the chances for making a significant contribution outweigh the risks of becoming involved).

One client—accustomed to hearing his boss complain about lack of dedication and organizational apathy—suggested that the CEO prepare some thoughts on the nature of corporate excellence and how to achieve it. "I don't mean to suggest that I am dedicated to excellence and nobody else is," he demurred, "but it might serve as a thought-starter to get people thinking about what they can do in their own shops to help shape things up." Also, he provided a thought-starter list for his superior.

The CEO thought this was a splendid idea. In addition to articulating a need that the CEO had felt but not focused upon specifically, the executive's initiative carried a message that here was a man concerned with issues of corporate excellence.

Another potential opportunity lies in profit improvement. Regardless of how much attention a corporation gives to this question, there is always room for one more voice. The client who suggested that his department's successful profit improvement program might be adaptable to other parts of the corporation found a willing listener in the chief executive officer. His suggestion also helped establish him in the boss's mind as a man whose thinking went beyond the narrow confines of his own department. He has since been granted expanded responsibilities.

One client saw an opportunity in his boss's remark that another division didn't seem to have the vaguest idea of what customers wanted. The division was headed by a former research man, not a marketer. In fact, the client was the only man from a marketing background on the senior management committee. He suggested that he would be happy to prepare a list of questions that the division might seek to answer as a means of better pinpointing the needs of its customers and increasing its market share, which was slipping. The boss thought it would be a splendid idea.

The client, one of the most astute marketers we know, did his homework, drafted his report, and made his presentation to the senior management committee, after first—as a courtesy to reduce any feeling of threat—seeking out the divisional general manager and going over the report with him page by page.

In another instance, a new vice president, joining a company whose work involved grain trading, found himself the only top officer with a background in commodity trading. To demonstrate his professional and managing acumen as soon as possible to his boss, he and I strategized a way to make a series of trading decisions within the full view of his superiors. He set up Monday morning meetings from 8:30 to 9:00 among the key trading managers representing his company on the floor of the Commodity Exchange in Chicago and invited the executive vice president and the CEO to attend these sessions for their own information.

Every morning, both men attend the sessions. While the CEO rarely says anything, the exercise keeps him abreast of what's happening in the marketplace, enables him to assess our client's trading skill, and also educates the two superiors in the commodity trading business. As a result of his performance at these sessions, plus his own success in turning around a formerly unprofitable enterprise, the client is now a leading candidate to become COO when that job becomes vacant.

Your Board of Directors

Aside from your boss and anyone else you may report to indirectly, ask yourself what other people could be crucial to your future? The answer might include the CEO, COO, the company's chief financial officer, and other internal "approval authorities." In addition, determine who are the influential members of the board of directors and how you might go about demonstrating your "value-added" contribution to them. These may include a former CEO now kicked upstairs in retirement to chairman; perhaps some relatives of the founder with large holdings; outside board members representing banks with a financial stake in the company; businessmen and lawyers whose experience or name lends prestige or entree to your company.

Increasingly, outside board members include representatives of minority and consumer groups concerned less with traditional profit-and-loss considerations than with the social or public impact of company policies.

In assessing the potential influence of each member, try to answer these questions:

1. Why is each person on the board?

2. How long has each been on the board?

3. What degree of influence on major decisions and plans does each have?

4. What is his/her primary interest?

5. What is your boss's perception of each (i.e., "pain in the ass," "really knowledgeable," "figurehead," "particularly good in area of acquisitions and diversifications," etc.)?

6. What are their "hot buttons?"

7. On what other boards does each member sit?

8. Whom do you know who might know them through another company affiliation?

Influencing the board requires the same sort of careful courtship that we have discussed with the CEO or boss. Chart 6-B illustrates one way this can be done.

Presentations to the Board

Try to become a regular fixture at board meetings because of your involvement in issues of concern to it. We try to help our clients devise ways of making presentations at each and every board meeting. We also help them assure that these are effective presentations. The visibility that these meetings afford are of utmost importance to the future of any ambitious, achieving senior executive.

In deciding how to position yourself with the board, you might ask yourself the following questions:

- What concerns or needs does the company have that are *not* being attended to now or *not* being attended to effectively?

- Which of these are of highest potential payoff for the company? (For me?)

CHART 6-B Cultivating the Board

A. Inside influentials	B. Relations with your boss	C. Primary interests/concerns	D. Hot buttons	E. View of my performance/capability (10-high scale)	F. Things in common	G. Actions to take
1. Scott Anslem (Pres. & CEO)						
2. Elmer Hanscomb Exec. VP						
3. Henry Malcolm VP—Finance						
4. Francis McGarry VP—Res. & Eng.						
B. Outside influentials						
1. Osgood Mannheim Ch.Bd. (retired CEO)						
2. Ernest Wolverine Legal Counsel						
3. Leonard Ferber (Banker)						
4. Mabel South (Widow of founder)						
5. Rev. Andrew Wyrack (Community Rep.)						
6. Ruth Rehnquist (housewife, consumer activist)						

(Warning: The easier these issues are to convert into bottom-line results, the more potential payoff there is from your involvement. On the other hand, if you should fail in resolving them, the more obvious your failure will be if you don't produce results.)

- What distinctive experience or knowledge do I have that might make me a valuable resource to the board or company?
- Aside from substantive issues, are there any management process issues suffering from neglect or in need of updating?
- For whatever issues I choose, how can I accomplish these in such a way as to best assure their success while avoiding giving offense to people or stepping on toes any more than is absolutely necessary?

One client, noting that one division got 75 percent of the funding and virtually all of the glory at board of director meetings, analyzed the company's various businesses and became convinced that some other divisions could dramatically improve their share-of-market business and contribution to company profits if a small amount of those funds were diverted from their "flagship business" to his own department. He developed a series of charts showing the likely impact of various strategies on the overall position of the company under various operating assumptions. It was clear from his presentation at the board meeting that the company would, under the most reasonable assumptions, benefit from some diversion of funds. While the head of the department from which funds were being diverted was naturally unhappy with the decision, he could not fault the logic on which it was based.

The exercise demonstrated to the board members not only the thorough professionalism of the executive who made the study, but also his concern and detailed familiarity with sophisticated strategic business concepts. He came to be relied on more and more in discussions of strategic plans throughout the company.

Another client was so successful in his initial presentations to the board—both in identifying problem areas and in the professionalism of his presentations—that he became a regular feature at board meetings. His presentations were short, sweet, and to the point. They included humor, were always accompanied by overhead projections, and never lasted more than 10 minutes. They were models of logic, structured around answers to simple questions such as "why?" "what?" and "how?" and usually provoked considerable discussion—and favorable comment.

Our client became convinced soon after joining the company that the board was committed to a course that our study suggested was unnecessary and unwise. It involved an announced expenditure of more than $40 million for a new research facility. Nevertheless, as the new kid on the block whose reputation was still to be established, he could not directly oppose the project without raising questions of his own motives.

Accordingly, after having done his homework, he presented to the CEO, then to the senior management committee, and ultimately to the board our analysis of the research facility issue, which led him—"tentatively," he said—to conclude that the company would benefit more from a smaller research facility, given the dimensions of the task it was to perform. However, rather than call for a reversal of the decision, he suggested—in view of his own fallibility as a human being, and his lack of knowledge of all the factors that might have gone into the decision before he joined the company—that the decision merely be deferred and that another outside resource be hired to study in great depth the future of the facility. This was done, and the consultant's findings corroborated our own; the executive was prudent enough not to seek credit for this accomplishment.

Many boards resemble that old definition of an elephant: a mouse designed by a committee. Many of the senior executives we counsel dread meetings of the board (some others complain about senior management committee meetings), because the culture is one that inhibits free expression and puts a premium on not "sticking your neck out."

"The secret of our board meetings," says one executive, "is to be able to say both 'yes' and 'no' in a single sentence and make it look like you really are committing yourself when you are not." This particular executive has earned a reputation for being a "bull in a china shop" simply because he does not believe in trying to be "all things to all people." The problem, I should emphasize, is not that he is tactless, but that he regards it as a virtue to think clearly, express himself clearly, and make decisions without waiting to "see which way the wind blows." Fortunately, boards are coming to recognize the benefits of open, synergetic discussion and to encourage bold, creative thinkers like this executive—rather than platitudes and "fence-straddling."

Relations with Your Peers

Any ambitious executive is in competition with his peers. Rivalry is inevitable. But its adverse effects can often be minimized by foresight, diplomacy, and courtesy.

Earlier in this chapter, we discussed the case of an executive who volunteered to write a market research plan for the division of a colleague for presentation at the senior management committee. It was a logical assignment for him to take on. He was the only member of the senior management committee with a marketing background and the colleague's division was losing market share. It could also have turned into a direct confrontation if he had allowed himself to be portrayed as invading a colleague's turf. By practicing foresight and courtesy—going to the colleague to personally preview the report—he was able to win the colleague's support for the plan. Consequently, his presentation to the senior management committee raised none of the defensive reactions that often accompany such presentations. (He was also careful to make the presentation sitting down at a table with his peers, thus avoiding any appearance of trying to lecture them.)

In handling relations with your peers, always give credit where credit is due. Never seek to hog the spotlight. Avoid putdowns and carping comments. *Be a gossip-stopper, not a gossipmonger.* Avoid the temptation to try to make yourself look good at the expense of others.

One client, who was enjoying a string of successes with his latest assignment, made a presentation at the senior management committee meeting that analyzed his own division and several other company divisions in terms of four possible avenues of growth: sales, capital investment, geographical expansion, and profit improvement. His matrix showed that only his own department was growing in each of the four areas.

Instead of rave reviews, his performance earned him a chorus of criticism, some of it unjustified, but all of it avoidable if he had made his presentation in a less threatening manner. One after another, senior management committee members criticized him, arguing that the chart was contrived specifically to make his own operation look good and their own look bad. This was not the client's intent at all. He had taken what appeared to him to be a "perfectly logical approach visualizing succinctly relevant information about growth opportunities."

Stung by the criticism, he revised his presentation before taking it to the board of directors. There, he showed on a slide the four ways of increasing business growth and indicated that one division was doing it through sales, another through sales and investment, and that his operation had chosen to pursue all four routes. Essentially, it was the same presentation, minus the implicit value judgment that the more routes pursued, the better for the operation.

In strategizing the first presentation of another client to the senior management committee, we first tried to identify where each member would stand relative to the subject of the presentation: what might be his concerns, questions, criticisms. We then explored the potential impact of the proposed plan on each operation. Then the client went through a dry run of his presentation, which I critiqued in detail both as to style and substance. On the basis of our critique, the client drew up a list of impressions he wanted the presentation to leave. It looked like this:

I want my presentation to be one that leads people to see me:

As	Not as
• Deep, professional, and balanced	• A smartass
• Analytical and committed	• A hip-shooter or flip
• Striving to change where change is needed, but also interested in preserving what is useful	• Constantly critical
	• A revolutionist
• An evolutionist	• Simply a production manager
• A broad-gauged manager	• A loner
• A good team player	• A "grandstander"
• A leader willing to give credit to others for really outstanding work	• A meddler
	• Insensitive to "people problems"
• A leader	• Smug or believing that I can fix anything at the snap of my fingers
• Warm, sensitive, and perceptive	
• Justifiably self-confidant, but realistic in assessing the odds against success	• Overly dramatic
	• Someone "not on our wavelength," a "foreigner"
• Measured, controlled	
• "One of us"—someone who we can be comfortable with, who shares our philosophy, values, feelings, hopes, and goals	

Bucking for Promotion

Career counselors used to teach that if you want a promotion, make a list of the qualities that the job requires and measure yourself against them. If you discover any gaps, develop ways of overcoming them. Every step, in our experience, is valid—except the first.

Often the qualities you think the job logically requires are *not* those upon which it is ultimately decided. Here, for example, are the criteria one executive believed would be used in choosing the next company president:

- Excellent leadership
- Strategic planner
- Problem solver
- Broad business background
- Doer/thinker
- Articulate spokesman
- Organizer

- Depth of successful relevant experience
- Existence of a successor management plan and good, "high potential" backup management
- A change agent
- Demonstrated superior results
- Commitment to excellence

Here are the criteria that apparently were used in choosing the president:

- Long tenure
- Knowledge of company
- Awareness of the company's culture, problems, and people
- Impressive record in running one operation for 20 years
- Successor management in place
- Comfort level with CEO
- Superior standing in the community
- Friendships with influential board members

In short, the company chose someone who was easier to live with rather than someone who might send it in challenging new directions. The lesson— and the example could be duplicated in hundreds of companies—is this: Given all that you can discover about the attitudes, values, and motivations of those who will make the key promotion decision, list the criteria you believe *will be* (not *should be*) employed in making the choice. Then measure both yourself and whomever you consider your nearest rival or rivals for the position against these criteria. Wherever you come up short, devise ways of overcoming the deficiency, whether it is real or perceived.

Chapter 18
"What Do They Want from Me?"
(Tough Problems with Superiors)

The group president is a relatively new function in the annals of professional management. It was created to provide greater coordination of company operations in matters that do not require the direct attention of the chief executive or chief operating officer.

With responsibility for two or more divisions, a group president can often recognize management problems and identify potential synergies that cut across divisional lines. His bird's-eye view gives him a valuable perspective not always shared by individual divisional managers concerned with their own programs and priorities.

But the position carries frustrations as well—not only for many who carry the title but also for those who are their subordinates. The group president is often a "doer" who suddenly finds himself responsible for results without being able to control the operational details by which those results can be achieved. A division president or executive vice president who reports to a group president often feels himself held on a tight leash, receiving instructions, demands, guidelines, and requests for information that he may interpret as misguided at best, and, at worst, undercutting his authority and frustrating his plans.

This is precisely the situation that faced one of our clients, the president of a division that made component parts for video display terminals.

Case 1

Dick Jensen, president of the Video Components Division, felt he had made a smooth transition from his former job as manufacturing vice president to running the entire division. Six weeks later, it was announced that his and another division would henceforth report to a new group vice president. Charles Lee, his new boss, had an impressive operations background overseas, and had served as assistant to the corporate CEO for the past 2 years.

Lee was a handsome, athletic former linebacker for Notre Dame, a "take-charge" man who described himself at their first meeting as "the kind of guy who likes to push a button and see things happen." Dick was to find out what that meant almost immediately.

Although the two had agreed that Jensen would continue to run the division on a day-to-day basis, within 1 week Lee began asking for information directly from Jensen's subordinates and issuing instructions concerning specific details of plant operations.

Lee set a deadline for submitting the division's annual operating plan that, Jensen protested, required setting goals for the following year 9 months before it began and long before a firm sales trend could be established. Lee also asked to review all product development programs and told Jensen that no marketing plan could be accepted without his personal approval. The straw that broke the camel's back was Lee's insistence on attending all meetings of Jensen's management committee.

The attendance issue was first raised when Jensen arranged to take his team away for a 3-day work conference, which he called "Operation Opportunity." Shortly after taking over, Jensen had called us in because he had heard how we can help executives in new assignments "shrink time" in capitalizing on opportunities and welding their key subordinates into a smooth-functioning management team.

In the course of our confidential interviews with key subordinates, we had learned that Jensen's predecessor had begun negotiations with a Japanese company that wanted to buy electronic components produced by Video under a 2-year contract at fixed prices. The predecessor had rejected the contract on the grounds that fixed prices were undesirable in an inflationary era and that the volume of component parts the company wanted to buy would tax Video's existing production facilities and prevent the division from meeting a possible surge in domestic demand. Since that decision 9 months ago, the company had purchased the production plant of a bankrupt Video competitor. The plant had capacity enough to meet the needs of the Japanese without sacrificing any new domestic orders.

Thus, when our interviewers routinely asked, in the course of their questioning, whether there were "any new business opportunities" that Video was not exploring because of the pressure of ongoing business, more than half the respondents mentioned "the Far East contract." On the basis of our feedback, Jensen contacted the Japanese company's New York office and ascertained that the company was interested in reopening negotiations with Video and that its basic demands were unchanged.

Accordingly, Jensen asked us to design a conference that would help "land that Far East contract." It would be built, in part, around a seminar we offer, entitled "Mining the Future," which helps managers develop an *opportunity* orientation. As approved by Jensen, there would be three objectives for the conference:

1. To develop an opportunity orientation that would carry over into the daily activities of each of the managers
2. To create among the men a feeling of interdependence and cooperation—in a word, teamwork
3. To draft the outlines of a contract proposal that would be both profitable for the company and highly likely to be acceptable to the Japanese firm

Now Lee was throwing a monkey wrench into the plans. In a short, crisp memo, following Jensen's announcement of the conference, Lee informed Jensen he wanted to attend the conference himself and bring along his chief financial officer, Ned Isaacs. Ned, he wrote, "will have a number of important questions concerning your business that you should be prepared to deal with."

To Jensen, the demand was unacceptable. First, to have these two "corporate observers" at the conference would make the men much less candid in voicing their opinions and feelings. Second, to allow Ned Isaacs—or his boss—to go on a "fishing expedition" at the conference would defeat the whole purpose of the meeting.

Jensen phoned us, and we discussed how he might respond to Lee's memo. Meeting with us 2 days later, Jensen listed what he wanted to achieve, preserve, and avoid in his response to Lee. His list included these objectives:

Achieve:

1. Continued support for the "Operation Opportunity" conference
2. Lee's understanding of why it would *not* be desirable for him to attend the whole conference
3. His feeling that we are not trying to "cut him out" or question his legitimate authority
4. His understanding of why no extraneous issues should be raised and no nondivisional people should attend
5. Benefit of Lee's experience abroad in designing the contract (if relevant)

Preserve:

6. The men's confidence that *I* am running this company
7. My reputation with Lee for objective and aboveboard dealings
8. My integrity

9. The positive beginning I have already made in the division

10. The feeling among the men that we indeed can control our destiny—
if we're smart enough and work effectively together

Avoid:

11. Making Lee feel that we're "working behind his back" or undercutting his authority

12. Making him feel that we resent him and don't want his help

13. Having him attend the session (except possibly briefly to take advantage of any expertise he might have to offer)

14. Any diversion from our purpose

15. Having the men feel I'm not in control of my division (i.e., wondering "who's really boss?")

On the basis of these objectives, Jensen drafted a memo to Lee that Lee himself later characterized as "a model of evenhanded professionalism."

The letter began by thanking the group president for his support "of this important project for our future," and added, "We look forward to your participation at an appropriate time during the conference so that we might take advantage of your international experience in devising the best contract proposal."

The letter went on to say that since the purpose of the conference was to attack a specific opportunity and help build a cohesive team, "I feel strongly that no one should attend the entire conference, except for myself and my team. I'm afraid to have others attend—whether they be you, Ned, or anyone else—might put unnecessary pressures on the members, so that they would become unduly concerned about how they're "coming across." It might also raise questions about who's really running this division, which both you and I know would be counterproductive."

The letter conceded that Ned Isaacs "probably has some very good questions that we should be thinking about very seriously, and I want to give him every opportunity to raise them with my people. But I think the appropriate forum to do that is a management committee meeting sometimes *after* the conference—not at the conference itself." He proposed, therefore, that the week following the conference, Lee, the financial man, and "anyone else you might want to involve" should be invited to a management committee meeting to discuss any aspect of the business.

The letter invited Lee to attend a "working lunch" at noon on the last day of the conference to discuss and critique the outlines of the strategy the group would be developing. "Any changes you might suggest at that time would be very helpful in finalizing our proposal at the conference," he added.

Finally, the letter said that after Lee had a chance to digest its contents, Jensen would appreciate the opportunity to discuss it with him.

Two days later, he had his meeting with Lee, who agreed to each of the requests made. Lee did show up on the last day for lunch, asked some very good questions, made some quite perceptive suggestions to improve the contract, and left after saying that he felt that the meeting "is in good hands."

Details of the strategy the men developed go beyond the scope of this chapter, or indeed this book. Suffice it to say that the group's objective was to devise a contract that would represent a "win" for the Japanese and also a "win" for Video. The Japanese wanted assured supply for at least 2 years, at predictable prices. The company wanted to use its excess capacity during the 2- to 3-year period before domestic demand reached a level that would utilize it. It also wanted to avoid getting locked into a rigid price schedule that might force it to pass up more profitable business opportunities.

The group devised a strategy that gave the Japanese an assured supply for 3 years, rather than 2, which was to the Japanese company's advantage. At the same time, it insulated Video from inflationary pressures by proposing a price formula setting forth under what economic conditions prices would be increased, and by how much. This enabled the Japanese to crank contingency prices into their planning schedule.

On the basis of this strategy, successfully developed at Jensen's work conference, the Video Components Division landed an $88 million contract. When the inflationary spiral in the mid 1970s began, it invoked the inflationary clause in the contract, ultimately achieving well over $100 million in sales from the contract.

Jensen's landing of the Japanese contract was accepted throughout the corporation as a feather in his cap. But it didn't solve Jensen's problems with his boss. For Charles Lee was a compulsive tinkerer, a man whose insistence on taking direct control earned him the nickname "Itchy Fingers Lee." Jensen continued to chafe under his overbearing presence, as did the president of the other division that also reported to Lee.

Lee, too, was frustrated by the group president's role. He eventually left the company to become COO of a larger corporation, where he could do what he liked to do best: "push a button and see things happen."

Case 2

Dick Jensen's problems with his boss centered around questions of control—a frequent source of executive conflict. Less tangible but equally laden with potential for conflict is a problem that another of our clients experienced with his superior: bad chemistry.

Our client was Harry Wilson, a brilliant executive with a reputation for integrity, who was hired by the chairman and chief executive officer of a Fortune 1000 company in the cosmetics field. The CEO, Clarence Reed, was himself a brilliant and hard-driving executive of sharp entrepreneurial instincts. In 5 years, he had transformed TYW, Inc., from an industry laggard that was losing ground in the marketplace into a modern, very profitable mini-conglomerate.

Reed's game plan had been to take the company from "the Dark Ages" and develop it into a multibillion-dollar corporation by the early 1980s, tripling revenues in his first 5 years (which he achieved) and then doubling them again in the next 4 years.

But along with admiration for his accomplishments, Clarence Reed had earned the nickname "Reel" because of his skill in manipulating people. Like a fishing reel, it was said, he dangled people like bobs on a string, reeling them in and reeling them out, twisting them this way and that, controlling their lives in ways that assured *he* was always in firm and total control, not only of the company and each of its operating units, but even, in many cases, of their personal lives.

In the bar at a convention, he would order drinks for everyone—not to pay for them but to assure that they drank what *he* wanted them to drink. Sometimes he even ordered drinks for their wives. He promised one executive one thing and another executive the same thing—asking each of them not to discuss with anyone else his conversations for fear of fostering envy. At least three subordinates were told that they had the "inside track" on the presidency when the incumbent retired. When the time came, he turned instead to an outsider and appeared astonished when the three protested he had gone back on his word!

Reed not only insisted on being informed of the most intimate details of the organization. To prevent anything of significance from escaping his attention, he had established pipelines to "loyal supporters" deep within the organization whom he would call at home for information, rumors, and juicy gossip about their superiors.

Clarence Reed was a consummate operator, a wheeler-dealer who was at the same time a brilliant empire builder and a pillar of his local community—one of the large sprawling metropolitan areas in the Northeast. He fostered competition, giving two people the same assignment and letting each know he was watching them carefully "to see who carries the ball and who doesn't." He dominated, cajoled, sometimes publicly embarrassed his subordinates—then dashed off flowery notes observing that "Of course, it was all intended for fun. . . ."

He separated people into two categories: loyal and disloyal. He identified as disloyal anyone who proved to be an independent thinker, raised questions about courses of action he was considering, or even suggested solutions to problems that he himself had not considered. A brilliant strategist with little direct operating experience, Reed had been happiest when the corporation was small enough so that he understood how everything worked. He prided himself on being "the only person around here who understands how all the pieces fit." But the more successful his diversification program became, the less he could directly control each of the constituent companies.

We first met Reed through our client, Harry Wilson, whom Reed had brought in from a company in a related field to head a perennially troubled division of his growing corporation. Wilson was a practicing Christian who preferred to think the best of everyone and was totally without guile. He took Reed at his word when the CEO told him he would be in line for the presidency if he managed to turn around his division.

We began working for Wilson 1 week after he assumed command of the division, and helped him over a period of 2 years in a series of projects that transformed every aspect of the organization—its marketing effort, its product development, its sales effort, and its planning.

Exactly when Clarence Reed became disenchanted with Harry Wilson is still a mystery. It may be that Wilson's first mistake was to buy a house in an area of the city that Reed disapproved of. When Wilson told Reed where he was bringing his family, the CEO commented, "It really would be better if you were to live out near me." His own area, Reed said, would be "more in keeping with the image of the company" and provide superior business and social contacts. He offered to have his wife help Mrs. Wilson find a suitable home in that neighborhood. Wilson thanked Reed for his offer, but said his wife had found the house she wanted after weeks of looking and the whole family had "fallen in love with it." He felt it would be inadvisable to "back out of the deal."

Or it may have been Harry's insistence on moving slowly and deliberately before making major changes, which contrasted sharply with Reed's hip-shooting style, that began to tip the scales against him in his boss's eyes. In Harry's view, as in ours, change must be carefully planned to be effective. It must be targeted against clearly defined objectives, measured against alternatives, and thoroughly troubleshot. Moreover, it must be understood and supported by the organization or it will not be effectively implemented.

Harry explained all this to Reed in a conversation in which he declared, "You get better plans, and better support of them, if you involve people in making the decisions that they have to live with. We don't have all the answers in my office."

To this Reed replied, "Hell, people don't know what to do; that's why we have leaders. We're the ones that have to come up with the answers. If they don't agree with them, the hell with them, unless they're any good, in which case they will agree!"

Wilson's insistence on careful planning paid off for the company and won him the admiration of his organization, customers, and even his chief competitor. Before he took over, volume and market share were down in every product category in which his division competed. He and his managers analyzed the business and found that the division was spending as much money to market low-margin, low-potential products as it was to market high-margin, high-potential products. They established a set of criteria for determining resource allocations and evaluated all company products against them. The result was a strategy that concentrated company resources on fewer product lines of high-potential payoff, while profit-managing or reformulating less promising product lines.

Wilson's company also introduced six new products in test markets in his first year, a record no competitor could match, and all were internally financed. In the 12-month period in which Wilson made these changes, he also managed to increase his company's profit contribution, reversing a declining profit trend, and he continued to increase profit contribution year by year.

But however dramatic the results he produced for Reed, Harry never seemed to produce them fast enough to satisfy his boss, even when he followed the timetable the CEO had agreed to.

Indeed, the more he produced, the less he seemed to have his boss's appreciation. After one meeting with Reed, at which Wilson described a major new-product success, he expected to receive glowing tributes or at least mild admiration. Instead, Reed accused him of making it appear that his was the only division making significant inroads in the marketplace. Reed also argued that his presentation of third-quarter business results was "too rosy." "I'll bet when your fourth quarter results are in, you'll have some big disappointments. You're obviously overconfident."

Dejected at having the wind taken out of his sails, Harry asked us, "What's wrong here?" We advised him, "Intellectually, Reed wants you to succeed. But emotionally and in his gut, you'd better consider and test the reality that *he really wants you to fail.*"

This was, he concluded, a painful but probably accurate assessment.

In joining the company, Wilson had been told by Reed that 18 months hence, the president would be retiring and he himself would probably move up to chairman. In the interim, he said he would watch Wilson's performance closely to see if he measured up to the responsibilities of the presidency. However, 11 months later, in a surprise move, the president resigned and the board of directors named Don Fowler, the executive vice president of another division, as corporate president. Feeling betrayed, Wilson demanded an explanation from his boss.

"The board just thought," explained Reed, "that the time had come when it had to make a change, and you haven't been here long enough for it to really pass judgment on you. The nominating committee of the board, of which I'm not a member, stressed that Fowler knows this corporation backwards and forwards. If the board had waited, Harry, I have little doubt that the choice would have been you, but it just couldn't afford to wait. We hope you understand."

Wilson was prepared to submit his resignation that day, but Reed began to talk glowingly about the changes in Wilson's department. He observed that Fowler, who was 62, "won't last forever," and added that he himself was thinking of retiring in 3 or 4 years, which would provide the opportunity that Wilson was looking for to become president. Wilson went away still disgruntled but feeling that all was not lost.

In the months that followed, the division continued to produce positive results, with the normal frustrations and setbacks from month to month that affect all organizations, but Wilson noticed an apparent cooling in Reed's attitude and relationship toward him.

One day Wilson received a memo from his CEO, expressing distress that "sound managers are leaving your division." The letter went on to say that he could not understand Wilson's business strategy, and that "one doesn't have to ask" to learn that people within the division were upset by the key person that Wilson had brought in to manage his new business strategy, Roger Foss.

The rest of the memo was devoted to an attack on Roger Foss's leadership of his department. "Whether or not he's the right man," wrote Reed, "we know he's the man you brought in. I only fear that he will detract from your accomplishments. . . . I would hate to see your fast track slowed down by your subordinate's leadership weaknesses. . . ." He concluded by suggesting that Wilson take "whatever action is necessary to ensure that no more damage is done by Foss."

It was the sharpest letter Wilson had ever received. His first reaction was to march down to the CEO's office and "have it out" with him. Instead, he decided to ask my guidance at a meeting we had scheduled for the following week.

Together, we worked the issue, "Determine the best way to respond sincerely and directly to the chairman's anxieties." We developed the following list of criteria that any course of action he took would have to satisfy.

1. Be objective, not emotional or defensive.

2. Stress the need for impartial fact finding, not jumping to conclusions.

3. Maintain my control over my operations. ("Get the CEO's nose out of my business.")

4. Get at the issue without alarming Roger or giving anyone an opportunity to undermine either him or me.

5. Request that any concerns that the CEO has stay between him and me, and not be shared (as he might be doing) with other executives or people at lower levels in the corporation.

6. Give Reed an understanding of my game plan—i.e.:
   a. I share his sense of urgency.
   b. I've already started investigating.
   c. It'll be 60 days before I've reached firm conclusions.

7. Give Roger my objective assessment of how he's doing, balancing a view of his accomplishments with concerns about his management style.

8. Point out that any new organizational change would have high potential for organizational insecurity and unwanted departures.

9. Indicate that two of three managers who recently left were actually asked to resign and did not do so voluntarily; the third did leave for a position of much greater responsibility which he had no opportunity for obtaining here, at least for some time.

On the basis of these objectives, Wilson sent Reed a personal and confidential letter that took full cognizance of the CEO's concern, declared his intention to investigate, and stressed the importance of not jumping to conclusions or doing anything to upset the organization. A paraphrase of key portions of the letter:

> . . . I am keenly aware, Clarence, of your concern about the issues you raised in your memo. . . . I will do everything I can to alleviate your concern in the immediate future.
>
> I am aware of the rumblings that have come to your attention. What I don't know is to what extent they are based on fact and to what extent they are based on emotion or possible jealousy by some of his subordinates. Separating fact from fiction will be my first order of business.
>
> In the next 60 days I will undertake a low-key investigation to determine if the concerns you alluded to are, in fact, adversely affecting our company's business and our ability to retain key people or attract new people.
>
> Of course, any organizational change may cause some people to feel disappointed and can lead to unwanted departures. All I know with certainty at this point is that no one whose services we value highly has so far submitted his resignation.
>
> It is very important, Clarence, that knowledge of this project stays *strictly* between us. Any indication that you and I are seriously concerned could have a negative impact on the organization, seriously compromise the imcumbent's position, and hurt our business. If, in the next 2 to 3 weeks, anyone

brings you additional information on this subject, please send them directly to me.

The letter ended with the promise of a full report and follow-up action within 60 days—and the following request: "Let me run the business 'til the end of the year without interference. Stop criticizing my people, and letting them have a pipeline to you. Evaluate our performance *after* your financial people sign off to our year-end results." [For results, see Chapter 19, "What Do They Want from Me?" (Tough Problems with Subordinates).]

But the CEO's perception of Roger as a problem did not disappear. Reed may have harbored lasting resentment toward Wilson for not having fired his key deputy, despite the impressive business results they both continued to achieve.

While Wilson repeatedly made attempts to repair his relations with Reed, the relationship between the two men continued to deteriorate. Their business philosophies and managing styles were too much at variance for them to be comfortable with each other. Eventually, Wilson became convinced that he had no future in the company, and left to accept a new job—as president of a smaller firm in the same industry. He began building this company's strength to do battle with Reed's company.

Case 3

We have examined ways of dealing with two kinds of common problems with superiors—problems of control and problems of chemistry. Here's a third "C" problem that many executives encounter with their boss: *coordination.*

In this case, we again served as a catalyst, this time in working out a new modus operandi between a senior executive and his superior in a privately held company, where the boss was used to making all the major decisions himself.

Jim Doyle was a salesman, a big bear of a man with a marvelous sense of humor, an inquisitive mind, and a record for cultivating customers that was the envy of his colleagues at the Walter Brigham Company, a small producer of sporting goods equipment.

Doyle also had an acute sense of insecurity, which made it necessary for him to always feel he was "where the action is." But being where the action is was not a problem at Brigham. Within a year after he joined the company, Doyle was made vice president of sales on the basis of his own sales record and his popularity with customers. An excellent motivator of men, he fired up his sales force, introduced a new training and career advancement system, and within another year was moved into the newly created position of executive vice president for sales and marketing in a reorganization that made him the top deputy to President Walter Brigham, the company founder.

Brigham had begun the company on a shoestring and devoted his life to building it. For years, he ran the business single-handedly, relinquishing control only grudgingly when it became too big for him and his health began to fail. Now approaching retirement age and without any children to carry on, he was looking for someone to take over and hoping that Doyle would measure up to the demands of the job. As a way of exposing Doyle to a larger sphere of business challenges—and also keeping a close eye on him—he created the executive-vice-presidential position and began involving Doyle in a range of business decisions.

But soon problems set in. Brigham found that to involve Doyle in major decisions often required postponing action, since the executive vice-president's heavy travel schedule did not always permit timely consultation. Moreover, Brigham discovered that Doyle was not as knowledgeable about some aspects of marketing as he had thought. He therefore began taking his inquiries and ideas directly to Doyle's marketing subordinates.

Doyle, however, worried about Brigham's reduced reliance on him and resented the president's direct dealing with his subordinates, which Doyle interpreted as undercutting his authority.

One morning, a member of my staff and I had scheduled an 8:30 A.M. meeting in our offices with both Doyle and Brigham to discuss marketing plans for a possible breakthrough in golf ball construction that would enable the company to make major inroads against its competitors. Brigham's small research department had developed a process that appeared to make the golf ball case impervious to scratchs or cracks, thus giving the ball a longevity that no competitor could match.

Much to my surprise, when I arrived at the office at 7:15 A.M.—an hour and a quarter before our scheduled meeting time—I found Doyle literally on my doorstep, looking very pale and anxious. "I need to talk to you before Walter gets here," he announced.

I invited him in, put on a pot of coffee, and we began talking. Doyle's words came haltingly and uncertainly at first, then pouring out in a mixture of rage and frustration. He couldn't sleep, he had no appetite, he was ready to hand in his resignation. Why? "Because despite everything Walter has done for me, I've obviously let him down. He looks to me for advice less and less, undercuts me with my own people, countermands my directives, and usurps my authority. Why he doesn't ask for my resignation, I can't understand, but I'm prepared to submit it to him this morning, if that's what he wants."

I asked specifically how Walter Brigham was undermining his authority, and Doyle produced from his pocket a handwritten list of 24 actions the president had taken in the past 6 weeks that Doyle interpreted as indicating a lack of confidence. They ranged from the president's phoning a candidate for a new position in the marketing department to arrange an interview without checking first with Doyle, to making unilateral changes in the marketing plan for the following year, which Doyle's marketing subordinates had developed and he had approved.

"Either I'm going to run my own shop or they don't need me in this company," he said. "If he's going to give me a job to do and then do it himself, I'm not going to stick around. There are too many useful jobs in this world to fill than to stay in one that isn't useful."

I asked Doyle if it were more important from his perspective to work on the "golf ball casing question" or help clarify where he stood with Brigham. He said until he cleared up his authority, he couldn't concentrate on anything else of substance. I therefore suggested that when Brigham arrived, Doyle raise the question of his own position with the company and ask if they could discuss that before going on to the new-product opportunity.

He agreed, and we proceeded to draw up a list of objectives he wanted to achieve, preserve, and avoid (as problems) in resolving his differences with his boss. Among them were:

Achieve:

1. A clear understanding of where my responsibilities begin and end
2. An end to his interfering in matters that are within those defined responsibilities
3. His understanding that I have no dispute or concern over his right to "run the company"
4. His feeling that I continue to support his leadership and direction of the company
5. A full airing of any issues on his mind and on mine

Preserve:

6. His faith in my leadership of marketing and sales
7. The confidence of my two departments in me

Avoid:

8. Any recriminations or ill will between us
9. Any feeling on his part that I might be power-hungry
10. Any feeling on his part that I'm a "crybaby"

11. Any feeling on his part that I expect to be consulted on matters outside marketing and sales in which he doesn't think my perspective would be helpful

Brigham arrived promptly at 8:30, and after the usual pleasantries, Doyle explained the situation and suggested that he and Brigham "hash this thing out" using us as a resource, since we had experience in helping people explicitly define accountability, roles, and relationships. Brigham readily agreed and added:

"Jim, I know you've been apprehensive lately and I frankly haven't known what to do about it. I'm glad you brought this up. As far as I'm concerned, it's more important to work out our relationship than it is to do anything else right now. If you've got a problem, I've got a problem. Let's see if we can resolve it together. Then if time permits, we'll deal with the golf ball question."

Whenever we're helping a group resolve issues that are likely to be controversial or give rise to strong opinions or emotions, we find it helpful to begin by establishing mutually acceptable ground rules. This conserves time and minimizes the chances of causing hard feelings. My associate, whom I brought in to work with us, began writing on an easel as the two men suggested ground rules that should govern our session. Among those we established were:

1. No name calling or questioning each other's motives

2. No interrupting each other

3. Each man in turn to outline the issues as he sees them and then jointly set priorities for resolving them

4. A 3-hour time limit for all discussion, after which the two men would decide whether or not to continue discussion or turn to the "golf ball question"

5. Provision made for next steps to:
   a. Follow up plans that had been agreed to
   b. Resolve any remaining differences

Walter Brigham had some generalized criticisms of Jim's performance. He faulted his deputy for submitting a marketing plan lacking in creativity, then scheduling a vacation at the time it was scheduled for Brigham's review and approval. Brigham also felt that Doyle had waited too long before replacing a product manager who both agreed was weak. Walter felt that Jim was "doing" instead of "managing"—involving himself in details rather than setting broad guidelines for his managers to follow. Finally, he had heard rumors that Jim was grumbling and complaining about Walter's leadership to others in the organization and possibly also to customers (Jim categorically denied this).

Jim was concerned because, in addition to being consulted less and less on areas outside his direct responsibility, Walter was contacting advertising agencies and making plans to visit them to work on marketing matters without Jim's prior knowledge. If such meetings interfered with Jim's travel schedule, Walter was holding them without him.

In addition, Jim said, Brigham had been contacting marketing people and giving them directions without checking with him. Although Jim did not dispute Brigham's right, as owner-president of the company, to change plans and deal directly with subordinates, he felt that he must know everything that was going on in his department, insofar as it involved the president.

Having agreed on the issues (doing it systematically took only 1½ hours), the two jointly established, with our help, a new modus operandi, which they called "Decision-Making Ground Rules for Our Work Together Regarding the Sales and Marketing Function."

It provides the following elements:

1. Walter, as president, makes final decisions on sales and marketing plans.

2. Walter makes no decisions concerning sales and marketing without prior knowledge and discussion with Jim.

3. Jim is to be consulted on all questions involving his areas of responsibility, and no directions are to be issued to sales and marketing people without his prior knowledge.

4. All marketing and sales decisions are to be *announced* by Jim.

5. There is to be no grumbling by either party to subordinates or customers.

6. Walter makes no decisions or commitments to agencies seeking company business without full prior discussion with Jim.

It was also agreed that although Walter had no obligation to discuss matters outside Jim's areas of responsibility with him, he would try to involve him "in any matters that would help [Jim] do his job better." That left it clearly up to Brigham to decide whether to consult Jim on any particular issue outside marketing and sales. Walter also said he would welcome suggestions from Jim on any aspect of the business—an opportunity Jim immediately recognized for what it was: an invitation to widen his own perspective and prove his value to his boss.

In a subsequent meeting with Jim, one of my associates helped him identify ways in which he could be helpful to Walter outside marketing and sales, and Jim proceeded to act upon these. For example, it was well known that the company's production costs were above those of several of its competitors. Jim suggested undertaking a manufacturing profit improvement program, using the services of an outside consultant to identify opportunities for greater productivity and develop a plan to realize them. Walter liked the idea so much he named Jim to head a task force (along with the vice president of manufacturing and the vice president of research and development) to explore ways of making this study. Using a set of criteria that we helped the task force design, the men recommended a particular consultant, and the study was completed, with savings of more than $1 million in the first year alone.

Jim was able to compensate for his own lack of background in marketing by recruiting the number two marketing man at one of his competitors and making him vice president of marketing at Brigham. Jim Doyle has since been designated Walter Brigham's successor and was scheduled to become president and chief executive officer when Brigham retires in 1981.

Conclusions

In all three cases cited in this chapter, new executives experiencing problems with superiors resisted the temptation to take precipitous action. They were able to choose the course of action that best suited their needs and carry it out effectively by:

- Asking themselves the ExecuTrak® objective-clarifying question: What do I want to achieve, preserve, and avoid (as problems) by *any* solution to this situation?

- Using an outside resource as sounding board and strategy adviser to design the most appropriate course of action to satisfy their objectives.

If you're a new executive facing "people problems" similar to those of these clients, you may want to follow their examples.

Chapter 19
"What Do They Want from Me?"
(Tough Problems with Subordinates)

Let's face it: Every senior executive in a new assignment is going to face serious conflict with some subordinates—and they with him. It's inevitable, it's natural, it may even be healthy for the organization—if the sources of the conflict can be identified, analyzed, and ultimately eliminated.

In the following examples, three newly promoted executives faced varying kinds of "trouble in the ranks." In the first case, the problem was management style; in the second, lack of control; in the third, a badly bruised ego.

How these executives resolved their conflicts may provide you with helpful tools to reduce the likely sources—and serious impact—of your own tough problems with subordinates.

The Man Who Did Too Much

Superman, they called him behind his back—and indeed the name fit. Roger Foss was an ex-Marine captain from the Korean conflict, a creative, witty, and hardworking manager, whose dedication knew no bounds and who achieved dramatic results in his first 3 months as vice president and general manager of the newly organized division of a Fortune 1000 company in the cosmetics field. But in so doing, Roger found himself isolated from his troops—leading a one-man parade pointing in directions that nobody but himself understood and supported. Rather than achieving the acclaim of his superiors, as he had hoped, he found himself almost out of a job. How did it happen?

As Roger looked back on it, he had done all the right things. He had taken a small efficiency apartment, just a block from the headquarters of his new company, leaving his family behind in Atlanta so that his children could finish the school year before being uprooted. He virtually lived at his office—beginning work before 7 A.M., eating lunch at his desk, leaving work to drop by the bar on the ground floor to chat with subordinates who might have stopped by for a drink or two, having a light supper, then returning to his office to rummage through files he inherited, read memos, and plan his strategy.

He rarely left the office before midnight, and worked through every other weekend—returning home on the weekends that he didn't work—demonstrating an extraordinary degree of dedication and stamina. His charge had been to "breathe new life into your division and its products." But the business had flattened, and there was little question that key subordinates were not working at their optimum.

Nor had he—as he assessed the situation—ignored the human needs of the organization. During his first 2 weeks, he had spent an hour or two individually with 30 key people, and conducted a meeting with all 1000 employees of his division—1½ hours with four groups. He had talked about the strength of the division, their understandable pride and dedication, his excitement about the challenges that lay ahead, his own need for their help, and his faith that he and his people could "join hands" to get the job done.

A model of organization, he had "calendarized" all his meetings, crammed his schedule book full of appointments, and gained—on the whole—so much insight into the business, its problems and its opportunities, its history and its performance over the previous 10 years, the trade and the competition, that a reporter from a trade magazine who interviewed him found it hard to believe he was new to the job. "Here I thought I was interviewing a new executive," the reporter told a colleague, "and instead I found a man who talked about his business as if he'd spent his life in it."

What was wrong? Partly the problem lay in the perspective of the people who worked for him. Because of his constant activity, memos, probing questions, constant suggestions—all of which had, he believed, a sound business purpose—he had communicated the idea that he wanted to be heavily involved in all major decisions. His managers came to believe he lacked faith in their judgment. As with many "take charge" senior executives, his managing style bred insecurity in the organization, hurt morale, and led his managers to take less initiative. This, in turn, forced him to become more of a "doer" and less of a manager. As a result, none of them—neither the new VP–general manager nor his managers—were making the best use of their talents.

Exaggerating these problems was the fact that by trying to do so much himself, Roger was stretching himself too thin. Subordinates complained they could never get to see him unless it was at 7 A.M. or after 6 P.M.

Bottlenecks developed, decisions piled up on his desk, and even when he was available, managers never felt they had his undivided attention.

Roger was vaguely conscious of the "people problems" he was causing, but he felt he was making "tough, solid decisions that have gone too long unmade." His boss agreed. "Somebody has got to take the bull by the horns around here," Roger told Harry Wilson, the group president, at one of their weekly luncheons to review the division's plans and progress. And Harry had to agree that Roger's advertising and sales promotion program, his judgment regarding capital expenditure requests from his department heads, and his undertaking of a profit improvement program were all necessary and long-overdue reforms.

Besides, Roger was convinced that much of the grumbling by veteran managers was caused by jealousy. There was no question that several egos had been badly bruised by his appointment in the first place. "Every organization," he told Wilson, "is composed of two groups of managers: the makers and the breakers—those who can help you do what has to be done, and those who will try to fight you every step of the way. The grumbling only suggests to me that we may have more breakers than either of us thought."

It was a warning from Wilson's boss—corporate CEO Clarence Reed—that brought matters to a head. In a sharply worded memo to Wilson, Reed warned, "You're sitting on a time bomb that's going to explode one of these days." He went on to suggest that Wilson act decisively so that "no more damage is done by Foss."

How Wilson dealt with his superior's sharply worded note is itself an example of how to deal with a superior [see Chapter 18, "What Do They Want from Me?" (Tough Problems with Superiors)]. How he dealt with Roger Foss's situation, and our own unofficial role, helped avert potential disaster for both Roger Foss and Harry Wilson—and the corporation.

Wilson immediately undertook a low-key, informal investigation of the situation. He told Roger and another division VP–general manager that he wanted to meet during the next month or so with their direct subordinates because he wanted to get more of a "feel" for that level of management, to indicate his personal interest in each man, and to get more of a sense of the "pulse" of the divisions. Both welcomed Wilson's interest, because he had a reputation for remaining remote from the operations.

During the next 4 weeks, Wilson held low-key talks with 14 of Roger's subordinates. Basically he sounded them out on what was going well in their view and what wasn't going well, what their own ideas for improving the company were; he confronted the question of Roger's management only indirectly and discreetly. It is doubtful that any of those interviewed came away feeling that the purpose of the meeting was to get feedback on Roger's performance. At the same time, Wilson informally chatted with the group directors of personnel and finance, who had daily contact with people at all levels in Roger's division.

What he found was that Roger was indeed perceived as "riding roughshod" over managers, that he countermanded many decisions, and that he was perceived as a meddler. He was impatient with people whose minds didn't work as fast as his. He would sometimes cut people off in midsentence, believing that he knew what they were going to say, or announce a decision before group opinion had been crystallized.

At the same time, there were managers who were really caught up in the excitement of the changes that Roger was making. He had reorganized the division around strategic growth sectors, each with its own specific charter, ending its previous—and largely arbitrary—breakdown around distribution channels. He introduced long-overdue management information and inventory control systems. In a word, he brought modern management techniques and new direction to an organization that had long suffered from lack of both.

Nevertheless, for every person who felt that the division was "finally getting its act together," there were others who were skeptical of the changes or critical of his management style.

I had occasion to chat with Roger once or twice a day during this period, and he was full of enthusiasm, seemingly oblivious to any problems he was creating. When I tried to broach the subject, he brushed it off by echoing Harry Truman's famous observation: "If you can't stand the smoke, get out of the kitchen." Yet I too began to pick up signals of frustration and resentment among his subordinates.

Shortly after taking over, Roger had brought into the organization a new manager of manufacturing, and I had been asked to spend a day orienting him to the division's climate, the key personalities, issues, and sacred cows, and helping him to begin defining his own initial objectives and develop a preliminary plan to attack them.

About 2 months after he joined the division, this manager of manufacturing asked if I would spend a day with his group. When I arrived, he closed the door and asked me if we could talk in complete confidence. "Of course," I said, and he proceeded to pour his heart out to me. I was alarmed at this report and asked if there were others who felt the same way. He referred me to three other managers, two who had also been hired by Roger and who had equal reason to feel personally loyal to him.

Obviously, if four key managers—three of whom Roger himself had appointed—were disgruntled with his leadership, there was real trouble in his division. I made arrangements to talk confidentially with the other three, and their reports corroborated the frustrations and concerns that had been voiced by the first manager.

The question was, what could I—and what should I—do about it?

I knew of Harry Wilson's soundings in the organization, since he had confided to me his intent. At the same time, I could not divulge to him what I had learned, since my commitment to the four men was to give Roger their direct feedback, while protecting their anonymity.

I decided to try to make an appointment with Roger to share the information with him and help him strategize how to key to the concerns that had been voiced. As a last resort, if he did not want to accept the feedback, then I might be forced to take it to Harry Wilson to protect his leadership, though I hoped this wouldn't be necessary. First and foremost, though, I had to somehow get through to Roger, even though it had been Wilson who brought me into the corporation when he himself was a parachuted-in executive.

I phoned Roger and told him that I had some disturbing information that I wanted to share with him, that it involved some concerns about his leadership, and that I'd like to see him as soon as possible because I felt he really should be aware of it. I tried to reassure him that I had no ax to grind but rather wanted to share my insights with him—*and him alone*—as a friend to whose successful leadership I was committed.

Roger did not want to hear any negative feedback. He put me off several times, and observed that he was aware of "dissatisfaction in the ranks" and was planning to hold a workshop with his key managers and their wives in Boca Raton, Florida, to "break down any barriers that may have been developing," in a month!

Roger finally—grudgingly—gave me an appointment for the week following the workshop. In advance of this appointment, but following the workshop, I again checked by phone with each of the four managers to learn if some progress had been achieved. "Not really," was the universal response. I therefore went ahead with my plans for meeting with Roger, after carefully thinking through with several of our staff my own objectives for the meeting. They were to:

Achieve:

1. His understanding that I was sharing this information with him as a friend and as someone concerned with his success and the success of his division

2. His understanding that the information was volunteered by managers who had no ax to grind, but who wanted him to succeed

3. His understanding that a lot of careful thought and preparation by us went into this feedback

Preserve:

4. My own commitment to the men to share the information with him alone

5. His respect for my firm's professionalism

Avoid having him feel:

6. That my company was motivated by "a search for new business"

7. That he was, in any sense, a failure as a manager

8. That "enemies are ganging up on me"

9. That the information was inaccurate or constituted unfair criticism

10. Resentful toward me or the informants or seeking recriminations against them for confiding in me

I rented a room on the top floor of a new hotel in the city, with a panoramic view of the downtown business district, and it was there that we met. I had drawn back the drapes in hopes that the view would set a relaxed and ego-reinforcing tone to the meeting. Even so, it was a painful meeting—for both of us.

I began by telling Roger that I had understood he was pleased with the results of the Boca Raton workshop and that he was probably asking himself, "What the hell is Arnold here for anyway? What are his real motives?"

I went on to explain, "If I weren't concerned with your success, Roger, I wouldn't be here today, because frankly there's nothing in this for me or my company. You won't hear from me again after today if you don't want to. I could also have shared with Harry Wilson what I learned, but I didn't want to do that either. You, not Wilson, are the proper client for this feedback. I made a commitment to four of your managers to bring these concerns directly to your attention, which is why I'm here."

Finally, I said that I hoped he could appreciate the personal risk the four were taking in asking me to bring this information to his attention, and that they wouldn't have done so if they weren't committed to his success.

I then shared with Roger the men's observations and concerns, which I had grouped into such categories as "Decision Making," "Priorities," "Leadership and Direction," "Meeting Management," "Internal Politics," and "Support—Above and Below." Under each category, I gave him verbatim quotes from the men, without identifying the particular sources of quotations. A sample:

Priorities:

- "He's all over the lot working on 30 different things at once. You never can get into his office to see him. . . . When he calls meetings, you've got to change your whole plan to fit his schedule."

- "He doesn't set priorities. There are lots of new people on board who don't understand what's going on. They see Roger flying all over the place, firing off 800 ideas per minute, and making them drop whatever they're doing to go follow up his ideas."

Decision Making:

- "There's no decision process. It's almost as if he listens and acts on the last good idea he hears. Someone says this, and he says, 'Fine, do it.' Someone says that, and he says, 'Fine, do it.' "
- "His decision-making process is to be sure there are lots of meetings, and lots of people listening to everybody else, and lots of ideas to think about and try out. But at some point, he has to say, 'Okay, fellas, this is the way we're going to go. Let's all get together and make it work.' "
- "I don't see decisions, I see constant wheel-spinning."

Roger listened intently and took copious notes. When I was finished, he paused and thought a long time before talking. Then he shook his head and said: "There are only a couple of things in there that I hadn't heard in some form before, but I guess I just haven't taken these problems seriously enough. I must have greatly underestimated the depth of the concern, because I felt the challenges I faced were so great. I've been trying to deal on 32 different fronts and people see this as my not acting decisively on any one front."

He asked me a few probing questions to validate the data. At no time did he try to violate the ground rule by asking "Who said what?" (He knew I wouldn't tell him.) When we were through, he thanked me for coming.

I asked if he'd like me to help him think through his next steps, and he said no. "I intend to go back and call the four together. I made sure they would all be in town today because I thought I might want to meet with them after the feedback. I think I'll thank them for their input, and ask them frankly, 'Where do you think we should go from here? What are your ideas as to what should be done?' "

Roger did precisely that, as I learned that night when I received a call from one of the four men. "I wondered if he'd meet with you," he told me. "And I wondered if you would have the courage to tell it to him straight. Well, he had courage and so did you, John, and all I can say is, I'm grateful. It must have been difficult. I don't know if I could have said those things face to face." He added that Roger handled the meeting of the four with "dignity and humility," and won the respect of all the men in doing so.

Out of that session, and his performance review by Harry Wilson, evolved a new modus operandi for the division, worked out by Roger and his key managers. Among the points it provided:

1. Each department head and I will jointly determine *what* results are to be achieved.

2. You are each responsible for determining *how* it will be achieved.

3. I hold you accountable for results we mutually agree on to be achieved with and through your people.

4. Otherwise, I will help you obtain the necessary resources to get the job done—and then get out of the way.

5. I expect superior performance from you at all times (e.g., no cover-ups of "disappointing numbers" or costly mistakes).

The procedure also specified that Roger would:

6. Get involved only in the key elements of the decision-making/planning/ review process (i.e., setting objectives, reviewing plans, attending key agency and sales meetings, visiting every factory at least twice a year, some contact with major customers, occasional visits to field sales offices).

7. Be available to you 24 hours a day, 7 days a week.

In retrospect, Roger's facing up to the negative impact of his management style—demonstrating to his subordinates that he had heard them, and involving them in problem-solving what to do about the concerns—marked a turning point in his leadership.

Six months later, Harry Wilson indicated that Roger Foss was performing beautifully, delivering the numbers with no apparent serious "people problems," and that the CEO had gained a new-found respect for him.

The Man Who Did Too Little

Ken McAdams was the new president of a division of a conglomerate that made steel and concrete pipes for utility companies and heavy industry. He was also the most likable executive I've ever known. Warm, honest, generous, and humble, he was possessed of all the Boy Scout virtues— but he was clearly floundering in his new position. The former operations director of a small steel company, for the first time in his life he now found himself unable to exert firm control.

The sales vice president was the first cousin of the corporate president. He never accepted Ken's leadership. Marketing was a mystery to him. Only the manufacturing department seemed willing to accept his leadership and give full cooperation, but with the two other departments going their own way, Ken was stymied.

To get away from his in-house problems, he found himself spending more and more time at outlying plants, chairing engineering and manufacturing association meetings, and listening increasingly to the strident voice of his operation's vice president against the sales and marketing people.

When Ken called us, it seemed out of sheer desperation.

"I need some kind of vehicle to get my team going in the same direction and pulling together," he said. "And I've got to get some of these concerns that are being bottled up or expressed to me privately out into the open so that we can deal with them as a team."

Ken McAdams had learned of us through his former boss at the steel company, who had engaged our help in improving marketing effectiveness. He felt that using us as an impartial outsider to identify the concerns, anxieties, and business issues that stood in the way of the division's success could help bring his people together and develop some badly needed forward momentum.

"I have to find out what's really going on both in the marketplace and in the bowels of my own organization. After 6 months on this job, quite frankly, I feel I'm still on 'square one.' There are walls between functions, and when plans are made, they never seem to come off. I suppose I could be putting myself in the eyes of the sniper's gun by hiring you to find out what I haven't been able to find out, but dammit, there's got to be a way to make the right things happen around here and I'm going to do my damnedest to be the one to do it."

On the basis of our strictly confidential, probing interviews of 60 people within the organization at all management levels—including supervisors, foremen, and several hourly employees and union representatives—we identified a host of concerns: organizational, marketplace, and leadership.

Four weeks later, we presented Ken McAdams with our preliminary feedback, and scheduled our usual work conference with the key managers to work through the problems identified. McAdams felt more immediate action was necessary. Thus, we strategized with him a talk that he should give at the very next weekly management committee meeting, to provide preliminary feedback and get a head start in coming to grips with the issues that were impeding the division's effectiveness.

At the outset of the meeting, he announced that after the regular business was completed, he would like to give the men some preliminary feedback from the project. "Why is that?" asked the sales VP. "I thought we wouldn't have the feedback completed until the work conference next month?"

"That's right," McAdams replied, "but I think there are a number of points that have already been developed, of sufficient importance to justify out time and attention at this meeting."

Piped up the marketing VP: "If that's the case, I agree. We should hear about it now. It might affect everything else that we do, so wouldn't we benefit by having the issues brought out on the table first?" His comment brought affirmative headshaking from other members of the management committee, so Ken pushed on.

Okay, here it is: As you all know, we hired ExecuTrak® Systems, Inc., to try to help us bring out what's on everybody's mind—the issues, the concerns, and the opportunities that we face. They've given me some advance feedback, and I've got to tell you—we've got some big problems. We can face them together and solve them, or we can continue to bury our heads in the sand and work against each other, which is what I think we've been doing for the last 6 months, and God knows how long before that.

I want to save this company, I want to build this company, and anyone of you who isn't committed to those two goals doesn't belong at this table or in this company. If anyone wants to leave now, be my guest. But, if you're going to remain here, I'm going to expect—dammit, I'm going to demand!— your full cooperation. Does anyone want to leave?

No one spoke or moved, so Ken continued.

First, this is—in ExecuTrak's words,—"a sleepy company," a "status quo company." They say there's no "sense of urgency" here. People "run for their lives" as soon as 4:30 arrives. That, gentlemen, has got to stop.

Second, there's a lack of cohesiveness and commitment to working together. I think we can all recognize that as a problem. We are not a well-knit team. Hell, we are not a team at all! ExecuTrak® was told any number of times that there's a lot of finger-pointing going on, people writing little memos "to cover their ass" so that when things go wrong, it won't look like they're to blame. Well, gentlemen, when things go wrong, we're *all* to blame and no "cover-your-ass memo" is going to relieve you of your responsibilities.

Third, there are a lot of concerns about *my* leadership—and I have to say, in all humility, that *I think they're justified!* People complain that I'm traveling too much, that I'm not around when they need me. I wasn't aware that's a problem, but apparently it is, and I'm going to correct that starting right now. I'm going to be available to every man in this room any time you want me for at least the next 4 weeks. I want to be consulted on all major decisions, I want to be informed of all major changes or developments in your department, I want to know what all your problems are and how I might help you resolve them. I'm not going to do your jobs for you, but I'm going to see to it that *you* do your jobs.

There's also been a number of instances in which people have been working around me, going to corporate with problems and plans. That's going to stop. Any time anyone from corporate contacts you, I want to know it within 24 hours. Any time you want to contact them, I want to know about it before you act so that we can mutually decide if you should do it.

Lastly, *I* am running this company and as long as I am, everyone is going to be working for me. That's got to be clearly understood and accepted. I've made a lot of mistakes, and some of you may have made a few also; but from now on, I want to correct those mistakes and do everything I can to avoid making new mistakes. And for that, I'll need the help of every person in this room.

Finally, between tomorrow and the end of the week, I want to meet individually and confidentially with every one of you to discuss what your concerns are, what are the things that I can be doing to help you do your jobs, and what suggestions you have to improve the functioning of the organization and the communication between departments. We're one company, and we're going to sink or swim together. So let's begin tearing down the walls that are separating us and preventing us from doing what we're all here to do. Any questions?

The sales vice president—the cousin of the president—was the first to speak. "I don't know quite how to say this, Ken, but I think I've probably been less enthusiastic than some of the others about a lot of the things that have been going on here since you joined. I may even be part of your problem. But I want you to know that I think what you just said is right on the mark. It hits me where I hurt, and I think I probably deserve to hurt a little bit at this time. And I want you to know that I, for one, am willing to climb on board and see if we can't get this thing accomplished together."

Several others in turn added their support to Ken's remarks, and expressed their appreciation for his attempt to get the issues out in the open and deal with them. The group conducted its regular business, and concluded on a note of greater optimism than Ken told us he had ever seen in his 6 months with the company.

When the feedback report was presented 4 weeks later, it was accepted enthusiastically, and the work conference imbued the men with a spirit of cooperation and dedication. Ken McAdams went on to become a strong and vigorous president, reversing his division's 5 years of declining sales and profits.

The Passed-over Executive

Larry Goff and Tom Shearer—each a vice president and general manager of a major division—hoped to get the new group-vice-presidential position created when the Merriweather Corporation reorganized its Plasticon subsidiary and combined the two divisions.

Instead, their boss, Plasticon President Gary Ireland, recruited a well-respected manager from another Merriweather subsidiary for the new position, Paul Langford, a British-trained engineer with advanced degrees in business management and organizational behavior. Langford had successfully merged two divisions after joining Merriweather 3 years before, following management experience with a major competitor.

Ireland knew that both Goff and Shearer would be deeply disappointed at being passed over, and he carefully planned his meetings with each of them to break the news. He hoped that Langford's credentials would help persuade them of the wisdom of his decision, and that the fact that each of them would have new and challenging responsibilities would further ease their disappointment. There were two jobs he was prepared to offer: one was vice president–general manager of a new acquisition, Synthenetics, Inc.; the second, vice president–general manager of a new business development department that would be charged with identifying and screening new companies for acquisition.

In reviewing the performance of both men, Ireland concluded that while either of them could fill either of the two positions, Goff was the more astute manager; therefore, he would offer Goff first choice of either. Whichever one Goff didn't choose would then be offered to Tom Shearer. This strategy risked the possibility that either or both men would choose to resign, but that was a risk that Ireland had accepted in naming an outsider to the position that both men coveted. What happened was something that Ireland had not anticipated.

Ireland's strategy for breaking the news, developed with help and trouble-shooting from us, involved asking each man to meet with him separately for a "general low-key discussion of the company's future." He suggested that the meeting be in the man's office, rather than his own, and that it be held before or after business hours "so that neither of us should feel at all rushed." He arranged to hold them both on the same day—one at 7:30 A.M. and the other at 5:30—on the day before Langford's appointment was to be announced. Neither man was told Ireland was meeting with the other.

Here is the outline Ireland followed in each discussion:

A. My needs/your needs:

    1. Each of us has certain needs and desires—both in our business life and in our personal lives. Ideally these should be fully compatible. In real life, sometimes they are not.

    2. Everyone here knows you take tremendous pride in your work, that it gives you satisfaction and industry stature, in addition to monetary reward.

    3. I have thought very much, very hard, and very long about your needs and how we can best satisfy them.

    4. I have needs too, of course. One of the most important is to carry out the mission I was hired to perform.

    5. This is not as easy task, as you well know. It involves making many difficult decisions, some of them dealing with sensitive personnel matters.

B. Organization realignment:

    6. I'm confronting one of them now in determining how to staff up our newly reorganized subsidiary.

7. You know the kinds of pressure I am under to produce results from this reorganization. You know what the strengths and weaknesses of the organization are. You have been, and I hope will continue to be, an integral part of that organization's leadership.

8. In undertaking this reorganization, I believe that we need an experienced reorganizer at the helm, someone whose management background demonstrates a successful track record in recognizing potential synergies, overcoming sensitive "people problems," and minimizing any loss of time during the changeover.

9. A further consideration is that the chairman has urged me to have in place by year-end a possible management successor in the event that I should, for some reason, no longer continue to be president of this group.

C. My decision:

10. Over the past month, I have given very serious deliberation to this issue, and have reluctantly concluded that there is nobody within the company who could be my successor that soon. In another 18 to 24 months, possibly. But my mandate from the chairman is only 7 or 8 months—at the outside—to get a successor "in place."

11. For all the above reasons, I've decided to bring in a very respected executive from outside our company as the new group vice president responsible for both divisions. [There followed a description of Langford's background and qualifications.]

12. I know that this must be deeply disappointing to you. The fact that I have thought long and hard before coming to this conclusion probably isn't much comfort to you at this time.

13. I made this decision after consulting with several key executives of the parent corporation. They concur with it.

D. What next?

14. I have suffered disappointments, as you may know, in my own career, and have recovered from them and gone on to reach higher goals. I hope you will be able to take the same viewpoint after you've had some time to think about things.

15. I respect your work and feel you've made a tremendous contribution to Plasticon over the years. Your reputation, as you know, is topnotch. I hope we will be able to still count on you.

At this point, Ireland gave Goff and Shearer time to express their feelings and then briefly described some of the specifics that had led to this conclusion. He referred to shortcomings of each man discussed in previous performance reviews (Shearer—a "short-terming mentality"; Goff—an autocratic style that made him hard to work for). Then came some questions and further discussion.

Ireland went on to describe the two jobs to Goff, told him he was well qualified for either of them, and suggested he consider both. Goff, who had sat glumly throughout the discussion, composed himself enough to ask a series of probing questions about the two positions. He seemed particularly impressed with Ireland's statement that the company was about to take a much more aggressive acquisitions posture, and that a third or more of future growth would probably come from acquisitions. Goff concluded the meeting by saying:

"Hell, I'm not a guy to agonize over things or beat on myself. The first acquisition is small potatoes, but the job to plan future acquisition strategy would give me an opportunity to really help the company grow. I'll take it."

Ireland then met with Tom Shearer, followed the same outline, and offered him the job as head of Synthenetics, a small company in a nearby state that produced synthetic fibers for decorator fabrics and rugs. Shearer was visibly shaken. And his spirits weren't raised much by the thought that he could run Synthenetics, which was to become a division within Plasticon. He said he would have to think it over.

In the next 2 days, Shearer offered his resignation three times in 1 hour to three different people—to Ireland, to Langford (when Ireland arranged a meeting between the two men), and to Merriweather's president, Arthur Conaroe. All three told him that they valued his ability and asked him to take more time before reaching a final decision.

On the third day, Shearer had a 4-hour talk with Langford, whom he hardly knew. They discussed Shearer's disappointment, Langford's own new challenges, what little each of them knew about Synthenetics, possible difficulties they would have in working together and how to overcome them. At the conclusion of the talk, Shearer announced: "I think I can work for you. It will be hard to swallow my pride, but I'm willing to try. Who knows, Synthenetics may end up being the most challenging assignment I ever faced.

Both Goff and Shearer were designated vice president–general manager—Goff for new-business development and Shearer for the new Synthenetics Division. They moved from fifth-floor offices to larger, adjoining offices on the seventh floor. Articles in the company newsletter portrayed the two as receiving promotions carrying added responsibilities.

Three months later, in a surprise corporatewide reorganization, Synthenetics was made a separate subsidiary within Merriweather and Tom Shearer was appointed its president. Shearer moved to the executive floor—the tenth—to an office two doors down from Gary Ireland, his former boss. Larry Goff stayed on the seventh floor, reporting to Paul Langford, who continued to report to Ireland.

Trouble set in almost immediately. Langford noticed it first when Goff showed up at a staff meeting looking pale and not wearing a tie. Usually eager to share his ideas with others, he sat silent, arms folded, looking thoroughly bored. When Langford made a point about customer relations, Goff was overheard to remark, "Boy, does he have a lot to learn!"

After the meeting, Langford sought Goff out and tried to engage him in conversation. Goff cut him off abruptly, saying, "Some other time, maybe. I'm busy," and bolted from the room.

In the weeks that followed, other managers began grumbling about "Goff's negative attitude" and his "carping comments." At one staff meeting he mumbled, "If I were running this division, we'd be number one by now." He began spending more and more time away from the office. It took him several weeks to draft a recommended acquisitions policy statement and a step-by-step plan to identify, screen, and evaluate likely acquisition targets.

Langford tried to get Goff to open up about what was bothering him, but he shrugged it off and said, "It doesn't matter." A sales training specialist, an old friend of Goff's, also tried to smoke out his concerns. He reported to Langford, "Despite every door I tried to open with him, all I heard was, 'There are no problems here,' 'I'm on top of things,' and finally, 'It's none of your damn business.' "

Eventually, at Langford's urging, Ireland summoned Goff to his office, and "read the riot act" to him.

"Look here, Larry," he said, "you've done a helluva lot for Plasticon over the years, and everyone here knows it and respects you for it. But lately, you're acting like a thumb-sucker and a crybaby. You're drowning your troubles in tears, and that's not like you. Now I don't want to give you my 'shape up or ship out' speech. But something's wrong. What is it? What's the problem? I'd like to help you and so would a lot of other people, but we can't unless you level with us. What do you say?"

Goff's eyes filled up. "You known damn well what's bothering me," he began. "I feel like I've been shunted aside. First, you bring this outsider, Langford, in to run my department. Then you take Shearer, a guy with less on the ball than I have, and make him president of a company. I'm building castles in the sand, which may or may not pan out, while everyone else is building a business. It's goddamn humiliating."

Ireland nodded empathetically. "I suspected that was the trouble, but I wasn't sure. I think I can understand how you feel."

He began to gently probe the source of Goff's frustration. "Do you feel that you should have been chosen to integrate the two divisions instead of Langford?" began Ireland.

"Well, I can't deny I wanted the job. Of course, he's done this kind of thing before, which is why you picked him. But it's not easy to accept, just the same."

"I'm sure it isn't," said Ireland. "And having to report to him while Shearer doesn't may also be tough for you."

"You're damn right it's tough on me," said Goff, "Boy, did I ever make the wrong decision on that Synthenetics job. If I'd only known."

"Known what?" asked Ireland.

"Known that the corporation was going to reorganize and make the head of Synthenetics a president in his own right. Some people really have all the luck."

"You mean Shearer?" interjected Ireland.

"Yeah, but I don't mean Shearer isn't a good man. Don't get me wrong."

"But you wish you were the president of Synthenetics right now?"

"Damn right! Why shouldn't I? It could have been me." And he made a fist with his right hand and dug it into the palm of his left.

"Believe me," said Ireland, "I didn't know about the reorganization and the upgrading of Synthenetics either. It was as big a surprise to me as it was to you. Nobody knew."

"I understand that," said Goff. "I just have to accept the fact that circumstances changed and stop kicking myself for it. I've got to get on with my new job."

"And what about that new job?" asked Ireland. "When you say you're building sand castles when everyone else is building businesses, what do you mean?"

"What I mean is, I'm doing speculative things: identifying acquisition targets, some of which might pan out and most of which probably won't."

"Well, that's one way to look at it," said Ireland. "But isn't a lot of our future growth going to come from acquisitions? As I see it, what you're doing is building the foundations for this company's future. Isn't that true?"

"Yes, I know that," conceded Goff.

"Could it be," continued Ireland, "that you're frustrated because the foundation you're building is still below ground, so you're not seeing the actual fruits of your labor yet?"

"I think you're right about that," conceded Goff.

"Maybe, too, you're thinking so hard about the jobs you wish you had that you can't concentrate on the job you have."

Goff signaled his acknowledgement with a smile and a nod of his head.

"Well, then," said Ireland, "If I can try to sum things up, the problem *isn't* that Langford is running the merged division but that you aren't. And the problem *isn't* that Shearer is *heading* Synthenetics but that he's *president* of Synthenetics. And the problem in your new job *isn't* the job itself but your attitude toward the job. Now, *if* that is a valid summary of your situation, what does it tell you about the present state of affairs?"

There was a long pause as Goff let Ireland's summation sink in. Ireland sat back in his armchair, arms folded on his chest, waiting for the other man to speak. Finally, Goff leaned forward. When he spoke, the edginess had disappeared from his voice.

"Well, Gary," he said, "What I think it tells me is that you're right when you say I've been crying in my beer. Hell, I guess I've been a first-rate pain in the ass. I've been feeling sorry for myself—boy, have I ever!—and I've taken my frustrations out on everybody I could. I've seen this happen to other people during my career. Now it's happened to me, and I didn't really realize it."

He gulped, and his voice cracked as he continued: "Well, I'm going to have to cut out this chip-on-the-shoulder stuff, starting right now. I've always said anyone who wants to walk around with a chip on his shoulder has no right walking around in my shop. It goes for me too. Gary, I'm glad we had this little talk. Thanks a lot. I think it's helped me just to talk things out with you. I appreciate your patience, and your understanding."

There was a moment of silence as both men let the truth of Goff's admission sink in. Then Ireland asked: "Larry, is anything else bothering you?"

"Yes, there is one more thing. I don't know quite how to say this, but there isn't anybody in the world who knows more about my former division than I do—its problems, its products, its customers, its opportunities. I think I could help Langford speed up his own learning process and avoid mistakes if I could spend some time with him. I feel I've been cut off, that the investment the company has made in me over the years is being squandered. If my experience means anything, it ought to be made available to Langford. Do you know what I mean?"

"I know exactly what you mean," said Ireland, "and I'm sure you're right. Let me give it some thought."

"I don't want Langford to think he has to take my advice," asked Goff, "but I think he ought to be aware that I do have some expertise and some contacts that might be useful."

After Goff left, Ireland called Langford and filled him in on the conversation, emphasizing his own feeling that Goff's perspective might be helpful to Langford in meeting some of his own challenges—and in bringing Goff "back to the fold." "Why don't you invite him to lunch, get to know him a little better, and explore what areas in particular he might be able to help you in," Ireland suggested.

Langford took the opportunity to repair his relations with his balky lieutenant. A week after his first lunch with Goff, he asked for a second, and later a third. He made a point to call Goff on the phone to ask his advice on certain types of matters on which he felt Goff had unusual insight and good judgment.

Langford established a good working relationship with Goff, and Goff overcame his own frustrations to become a fully participating member of the Plasticon team again. If he still feels he chose the wrong job, he no longer berates himself for it. The keys to his change were:

1. Ireland's sensitive attempt to smoke out the sources of his frustration

2. Goff's recognition that management did value him, and his own determination to put disappointment behind him and make a "go" of his new assignment

3. Langford's decision to risk appearing to need Goff's help and to tap his expertise

Conclusion

Managing relationships with passed-over managers calls for unusual sensitivity on the part of a new executive. It becomes more important than ever to make the man recognize that his performance and services are valued, and to show evidence of that feeling by sounding him out on areas of his expertise.

There is often a period of adjustment following disappointment, in which "patience" should be your watchword. But if all else fails, there comes a time when a man simply must be told the score. At that point, either he begins to "shape up" or the organization must make alternate plans.

In thinking through your own relationships with subordinates, it is often helpful to try to put yourself in their shoes. Gary Ireland's sensitive probing of Larry Goff suggests that he had thought through Larry's situation from Larry's perspective; he knew how his subordinate must feel. Roger Foss, on the other hand, was so concerned with bringing about long-needed changes in his company that he was unconcerned with how his actions were perceived by others—until he got our feedback. Ken McAdams was sensitive to his impact on others; he just needed help in identifying the basic sources of conflict and overcoming the subtle, psychological barriers between departments.

Whatever your own tough problems with subordinates may be, avoid the twin temptations to act precipitously or sweep them under the rug. Specify the problem as accurately as possible, and identify your objectives by asking, "What do I want to achieve, preserve, and avoid (as problems) by any solution?"

In fashioning the course of action that best meets those criteria or objectives, try to integrate what the logic or facts of the situation indicate should be done with a *genuine* concern for the welfare of the individual.

Chapter 20
"How Am I Doing?"
(Assessing Your First Year)

At some point near the end of your first year, you and your boss should mutually assess your progress. Although the meeting may come at his initiative, it is probably to your advantage to suggest it first. This way, you demonstrate responsibility for your leadership. (Besides, he may forget when your year is up!)

If you have implemented the "first-year management" process outlined in this book, you will long since have developed—and obtained your superior's agreement to—your overall mission (your charge or "marching orders" from him), your key performance areas (major areas of responsibility), your primary objectives (what you're committed to accomplish in each area), and your performance criteria (standards of measurement). Periodically—perhaps once a month—you should evaluate how you think you're doing on each.

To put their best foot forward at this important meeting, we advise our clients to develop an ExecuTrak® "Contributions Scorecard," clearly spelling out their accomplishments from the *company's* point of view. In drafting this ExecuTrak® Scorecard, clients often find it helpful to involve an objective third party skilled in helping executives "display their wares" to maximum advantage.

This chapter will tell how to design your contributions scorecard and how to plan and troubleshoot your career discussion with your boss.

There are three benefits *to you* in drafting a contributions scorecard for this discussion:

1. It presents your boss with a clear analysis of what you believe is the "significant value added" that you have contributed to *his* function's achievement and the company.

2. It can serve as the focal point for a performance—and even a career—discussion, assuring that this begins on the most favorable terms to you.

3. It demonstrates your professionalism and foresight, since a systematic approach to assessing progress is not generally practiced, despite its obvious wisdom.

Such a contributions scorecard is also helpful to your boss. It saves him time and energy, because he can react to the assessment you've prepared rather than prepare his own assessment from scratch.

The kind of contributions scorecard we have in mind consists of:

- An ExecuTrak® "Wheel of Fortune" segmented into the major areas that represent, in your view, your accomplishments

- A written backup scorecard, explaining in a sentence or two the impact and/or benefit of each accomplishment *to the company*

- A short cover letter for both documents setting the climate that you hope will characterize the meeting

How the president of a packaged goods company designed his Wheel of Fortune for his superior on his first anniversary is shown on page 247.

The Wheel of Fortune summarizes your accomplishments. The contributions scorecard details them. Excerpts of this client's scorecard are shown on page 248. Note that each number on the scorecard corresponds to a wedge on the wheel.

Because it focuses on significant *benefits to the company,* we believe this scorecard is a better measure of your effectiveness than the list of "major activities" that many executives submit for use as a basis for periodic evaluations.

Usually, we suggest that you make the request for a 12-month progress review up to a month before your actual anniversary date, thereby demonstrating that you are thinking ahead and are indeed concerned about assuring that you and your superior are "on the same wavelength" regarding your performance results.

You might introduce the subject by casually mentioning to your boss that your anniversary date is coming up in a few weeks and requesting some time on his calendar to discuss how you're doing. A minimum of 1 hour should be set aside for that purpose.

To begin setting the climate for a thoughtful and productive dialogue, a week or so before the actual meeting date you might send him a memo like this:

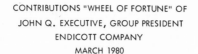

CONTRIBUTIONS "WHEEL OF FORTUNE" OF
JOHN Q. EXECUTIVE, GROUP PRESIDENT
ENDICOTT COMPANY
MARCH 1980

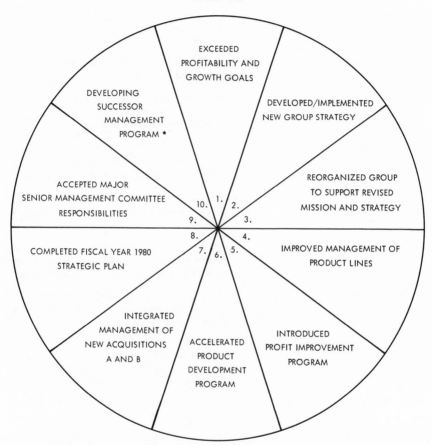

*NOTE THAT THIS ACCOMPLISHMENT IS NOT YET COMPLETE. NO MATTER; IF IT
REPRESENTS A MAJOR ACCOMPLISHMENT IN-THE-MAKING, IT SHOULD BE LISTED.

George:

I'm very much looking forward to reviewing the record of my first 12 months at Endicott with you on [date]. To help save time at the meeting, I'm summarizing my own thoughts about my contributions to the company, which might serve as a basis for our discussion. If you'd like to have a copy in advance of our discussion, I'd be happy to supply it.

We believe that *offering* to furnish these materials in advance is better than either submitting them routinely in advance or simply "springing" them

Contributions Scorecard of John Q. Executive, Group President, Endicott Company, March 1980

Contribution area	Impact
1. Profitability and growth	• Achieved profit before taxes of $58 million, or an increase of 32% over last year. Includes $2.8 million over budgeted contribution.
	• Increased our share of corporate profit before taxes to 41% this year from 38% average of last 3 years.
3. Group reorganization	• No valued key executive resigned of his own volition in any department during or since companywide reorganization.
	• Met every deadline in annual plan.
	• New systems for decision making and communications established and working smoothly.
5. Profit improvement program	• Introduced new program targeted to save $10 million. Actual 12-month savings will run close to $20 million.
6. Product development	• Test-marketed more new products than in any single year before; went national with 2 of 6 products *ahead* of schedule, with positive initial results.
9. Senior management committee	• Was moving force in resolving corporate conflict over new construction. Avoided $30 million capital expense by solution chosen.
	• Entrusted with special task-force assignments that led to revamped market strategy for X Division; recommended policy regarding sponsorship of "TV violence" that avoided corporate embarrassment and possible annual meeting boycott.

on your boss at the meeting itself. The routine submission of the materials in advance might make the boss feel you are being overly "pushy." Waiting until the meeting to share your assessment might make him feel he is being pressured. By giving him the option, you are offering him the benefit of your own analysis at *his* convenience—and he'll "get the message" that possibly he should be thinking about your accomplishments also.

There are, of course, other forms a contributions scorecard can take. One division president received a major corporate promotion on the strength of his record of performance, which the corporate president knew was outstanding. What the corporate president didn't know was the personal hardship and dedication our client had to undergo to achieve that record. Although it is often not to an executive's advantage to stress the personal and family cost of his contributions, in this case we believed it would be important, and helped him to "spell it out." The reason: In offering him the new position, the corporate president offered only a token increase in his salary and benefits.

The client wanted to go back to the president with a scorecard that would demonstrate the truly remarkable dedication he had shown to the company in the past—and would continue to show in the future. On the strength of that demonstrated dedication, we believed that the president would appreciate to a far greater extent this man's unique contribution and might well increase the size and composition of the renumeration package accompanying the promotion.

The man considered the alternative of simply requesting a larger compensation package without such a scorecard. But he worried that in the absence of strong supporting evidence, such as the scorecard could supply, he would probably be turned down or the discussion might degenerate into an argument. Excerpts from his scorecard are shown on page 250.

We were asked to be present when this executive presented his contributions scorecard to the corporate president. As often occurs in such discussions, the president was genuinely surprised at how much his operating executive had achieved. (Our client also had been surprised at how significant several of his own accomplishments were when we jogged his recognition of them.)

After verifying the accomplishments to his own satisfaction, the president increased the executive's total compensation package substantially. Later, the grateful executive confided: "Including additional stock options, I figure your counsel of my scorecard was worth $180,000 to $200,000 to me!"

As already noted, the Wheel of Fortune and contributions scorecard provide a summary of how you think you're doing. They help you put your best foot forward. Your boss may not always agree—nor should you necessarily expect him to. What they do assure is that if he disagrees, the burden of proof rests on him, since you, presumably, have done your homework and collected your documentation to support each contribution you enumerate.

To prevent a boss from feeling the scorecard represents a "stacked deck" in your favor, we often suggest that the scorecard contain several columns, as follows:

- Contribution Area
- Measurable Impact (My Assessment)
- Measurable Impact (Your Assessment)
- Reason for Any Gap?
- How to Reconcile?

Division President's Contributions Scorecard

Action	Impact	Personal investment
1. Achieved agreement with contractor on new quality specifications.	Enabled us to make commercial version of basic product without projected $1.5 million investment while avoiding anticipated 2- to 3-year delay. Result: Profits rose from anticipated $200,000- to $300,000-per-month level to over $600,000 per month.	Spent two-thirds of 1980 vacation developing and then implementing strategy, including visits to manufacturer's home office in successful effort to persuade him to relax specifications.
2. Terminated long-standing vice president after documenting performance shortcomings that clearly were impeding company progress.	Operations efficiency improved dramatically (production runs rose 22% within 3 months).	In addition to my own responsibilities I had to assume his for more than 6 months until a qualified replacement could be trained; in the process, corporate staff executives who did not know the problems felt I was "insensitive" and a "hard-nosed SOB."
3. Negotiated satisfactory base raw material contracts with suppliers.	Assured adequate supplies at economical cost for 1980–81, without which viability of key operating unit would have been questionable.	Had to "hang tough" with suppliers and battle unsupportive home-office staff which had failed to secure economical contracts over previous 3 years.
4. Designed strategy for winning court case that resulted in lowering of tariff barrier.	Tariff reduction will yield company $8 to 10 million over 20 years.	Devised strategy based on my personal review of over 5000 pages of legal briefs and testimony; all work performed in my "free time" (evenings and weekends).

Reconciling any divergent views may require verifying records, checking with other executives, or waiting until a particular audit report is published. The important thing is to know where you stand, and the contributions scorecard is a superior vehicle for finding out.

Similarly, to the extent that the 12-month review with your boss discloses shortcomings in your performance (while you've been working on your list, after all, he may have been working on one of his own), you can seek to *jointly* establish cause for deviations and acceptable standards of future performance.

Up to this point in your 12-month assessment, we have been concerned with helping you and your boss agree on "where you are." But the 12-month review also gives you an opportunity to sketch out with him "where you want to go" in the *next* 12 months. Accordingly, we often counsel clients to couple their contributions scorecard with an outline of their objectives for the next year and to flesh out these areas in collaboration with their boss. Some excerpts from one client's contributions scorecard for the previous 12 months *and* objectives for the next 12 months are shown on page 252.

As a logical extension of your outline of objectives for the next year, you may want to encourage a discussion of your longer-term objectives with the company and ask your superior what he thinks your future prospects are. Or you may want to suggest a separate follow-up meeting—if all goes well at this one—to discuss your career goals and how they can best be satisfied with the company.

As with all other important meetings, your preparations for this review are not complete without giving some thought to "What could go wrong?" A thought-starter list of pitfalls and action you might take to prevent or minimize any adverse impact is presented on page 253.

Independent of the assessment you make with your boss, your year-end review might be a time for reassessing your own operating practices, especially those that you suspect may represent a less-than-optimal use of your time. To aid you in making this assessment, it may be helpful to log all significant expenditures of your time over a 3- to 6-week period. You may be able to construct this from reviewing your calendar, if it is a sufficiently detailed and accurate reflection of your work activities.

Analyze this log or calendar to see how your use of time conforms to your key performance areas. Ask yourself these questions:

1. Are you indeed spending appropriate amounts of time on the areas that *primarily* determine your business success? If not, what activities are taking a *disproportionate* share of your time—and how can you curtail them?

2. How much of your time is discretionary—and how much is beyond your control?

Excerpts from Client's Contributions Scorecard

Major 1980 contributions	Impact on business	Key 1981 objectives
1. Improvement in overall business performance under my leadership.	Sales rose from $140 million to $185 million; operating profit contribution rose from $10.9 million to $13.5 million.	Achieve sales of $240 million; operating profit contribution of $16.2 million.
2. Implemented first sales training program, new-customer promotion.	a. Increased the percentage of our business represented by new accounts (30 months or less) from 15% of total business to 25% of total business. This represents *double* the highest new-account increase of any year for the past 5. (Note: One of our goals is to broaden customer base.)	a. Raise new-account ratio to 30%, while re-negotiating contracts of old accounts to eliminate "grandfather" clauses made un-profitable by inflation.
	b. Improved customer satisfaction as measured by 15% increase in average size of orders and by consultant evaluation.	b. Achieve another 15% increase in average order size by implementing new bulk-order incentive rates, payment terms, etc.
3. Established Western Canadian Region.	None yet. Gives us potential franchise in fast-growing area where competitors are beginning to stake out claims.	Expect $5 million in sales in year 1; potential to achieve $40 million in sales, $6 million profit contribution to operating profit by end of year 3.

List of Pitfalls and Action

Potential pitfalls	Action to be taken
1. He may be preoccupied and not give me his full attention.	Try to catch him before or after normal business hours. Would an evening session with a relaxed dinner be appropriate?
2. He may zero in on areas where I'm vulnerable.	Identify my vulnerabilities myself. Be willing to concede mistakes if he calls attention to them and explain how I'm working to correct—or prevent a recurrence of—each of them.
3. He may disagree with the credit I claim for some of my accomplishments.	Identify which of my accomplishments he is likely to question. Am I truly responsible? Be ready with documentation.
4. He may feel I'm doing his job in assessing my own performance, and resent me for it.	Explain at the outset that the list is intended to facilitate our discussion, not close it off, and that I welcome his perceptions of the job I'm doing.
5. He may want me to outline my perception of my shortcomings to supplement or balance the list of accomplishments.	If this reaction is likely, prepare a list of "Areas in Need of Improvement" for his review at the meeting and ask him to comment on it with suggestions for how I can improve such performance.

3. How can you increase your discretionary time? (You might want to discuss this question with your secretary, who should have some insights into improving the way you invest your time.)

4. How much of your workload can be delegated under what guidelines, and to whom?

5. How much of your time is spent in meetings that resolve too little to justify your participation?

6. How much time do you spend in "opportunity thinking"—regularly exploring, with your colleagues and alone, what else the company might be doing? What it could do better and how? What is it doing that it shouldn't be doing? What changing consumer trends are at work to which you might respond? How can your managers be more highly motivated and productive? Etc.

The review of your first 12 months in a new job, then, is a time for looking forward as well as looking backward, a time for stock taking, for strategizing, for examining how well you did—and how you can do even better in order to achieve a "win-win" resolution of the business challenges you're paid to resolve: "win" for the company and "win" for you!

Chapter 21
"So What Does It All Mean?"

(Your Creative Power and Future)

It all comes down to this: An executive in a new assignment must:

1. *Identify*—quickly and accurately—the key issues and opportunities he faces
2. *Establish* clear—and clearly understood—direction and goals
3. *Mobilize* all the human, material, and monetary resources at his command to follow that direction and achieve those goals

The preceding chapters outline a *process* that has proved successful time and again in mastering these three new-assignment challenges. The process is participative. It is systematic. It is integrative.

It is *participative* in that it provides a mechanism by which you can crystallize the best thinking of those who know the business, both in your own organization and outside it.

It is *systematic* in that it enables you to filter—by a series of questions—the *why, what,* and *how* of your organizational purpose and plans, and to determine what changes should be made *after* carefully weighing all feasible alternatives.

It is *integrative* in that it stresses the necessity to crank into the decision-making process not only the facts, or logic, of a situation but also the feelings and attitudes that impinge on the situation, including the feelings of those whose support is necessary for successful implementation.

This chapter relates these principles to the larger society and suggests ways in which your application of the concepts and tools outlined in this book can become a *way of life* with you and those you lead.

Let's begin with the concept of Spaceship Earth. We are all, in a sense, bound together, whether we be executives, workers, politicians, scientists, students, clergymen, retired, or whatever. Where we are ultimately bound, none of us can know. All we can say with certainty is that the future is uncertain and that the choices we make, for good or for ill, should help influence our *collective* destiny.

Although this book is concerned with individual and organizational destiny—matters over which we can, if we are wise, exercise considerable influence—ultimately our decisions have a ripple effect on the larger society. As technology and communications shrink the spaces that separate continents and peoples, the implications of our managerial acts become inextricably linked with the welfare of our fellow man.

Executives in the future are going to have to be increasingly concerned with using their power in ways that are both *creative* and *socially constructive.* Let's take each of these in turn.

What do I mean by creative power? Lord Acton was seeing only the negative attributes of power when he pronounced his now-famous maxim "Power corrupts, and absolute power corrupts absolutely."

Unquestionably, power can corrupt. But power can also create. Indeed, there can be no creativity without power.

It is the power of his imagination and discipline that permits an artist to create a canvas that enriches our lives. Ideas gain power and influence as they capture our imagination and extend our vision and understanding.

In my view, using power creatively—and using it effectively—are synonymous.

Using power creatively means recognizing that there is no such thing in this world as absolute power. All power is limited in today's business—and even political—world. Your own ability to maneuver will be circumscribed by restrictions both legal and ethical, by the scrutiny of your superiors, by the necessity to maintain the support of your subordinates and the other constituencies upon whom your success depends (customers, trade, the public), and perhaps most important of all, by your own conscience.

Using power creatively means questioning the prevailing assumptions of your organization and even your business. Every business exists on assumptions; indeed, no business can operate without them. But periodically all assumptions need to be reorganized and reevaluated. The best way to challenge them is to ask each of your subordinates for a list of the assumptions that underlie the present business, and then to inquire of each one, "How do we know that this assumption is valid?" (It's especially helpful to employ an outside resource to identify organizational myths, sacred cows, and taboos that are hampering business effectiveness in ways that insiders—being part of "the system"—often perceive either dimly or not at all.)

The beer industry took it as a "given" that consumers would not buy a light beer—until Miller was bought out by Philip Morris, and some shrewd cigarette marketing men, having weaned smokers away from "full-flavor" brands, began questioning the market research on which the beer business had been built. Their questioning revealed that growing consumer concern with caloric intake had created a climate conducive to a low-calorie beer at a time when technology had progressed to the point that a beer both low in calories and good-tasting could be produced. The result was a revolution that transformed the beer industry—and made Miller one of the premier beer companies in the world.

In your own business, be alert for lifestyle and other industry trends that have potential application to your own business, and ask periodically: "What are the assumptions on which we're operating, and how do we know they're still valid?"

Using power creatively means encouraging your subordinates to ask the same questions you do about *what* they're doing, *why* they're doing it, and *how* else it might be done (or *what else* they might be doing). By encouraging a questioning—indeed, a challenging—atmosphere, you do more than provoke healthy discussion of your business future. Equally important, you move strategic thinking *down* in the organization, thus helping assure that people "keep their eye on the ball" and consciously key what they're doing to the larger organizational purpose.

Using power creatively means understanding that, in any organization, *perceptions are the reality you have to deal with.* Your own perceptions, and those of others about you and the business, will affect how you act toward your colleagues, and how they act toward you. Each of us often finds himself in situations in which his intent is very different from the impact he actually has. The difference between *intention* and *reality*—or *perception* and *reality*—creates a gap that may persist without being recognized and corrected. In this respect too, an outside resource, who can tap perceptions without the implicit threat that your attempt to tap them on your own would generate, can play a significant role.

The result of attempting to identify the gap between perception and reality, both within and outside the organization, is to give you as the boss the ability to "stand outside yourself" and learn what needs to be done. As the nineteenth-century Scottish poet Robert Burns so eloquently stated:

> Oh, what gift the giftee gi' us
> To see ourselves as others see us.

Using power creatively means motivating your people rather than dictating to them—by inviting their ideas, challenging their imaginations, and encouraging them to shoulder increasing responsibilities.

One of the greatest satisfactions of my company's work is being able to watch people blossom as our process takes hold in an organization. People relegated to roles as "doers" ("You're not paid to think; you're paid to do!"), when encouraged and *supported* to think creatively, can become a new reservoir of talent for any company. Unfortunately, most organizations are so structured as to stifle, rather than to realize, the potential of their managers and employees.

Moreover, by giving your subordinates a task to do, and leaving it up to them to determine *how* to do it, you encourage them to take responsibility for the results. If, on the other hand, you are dictating *how* they are to achieve *what* they're to achieve, not only are you inhibiting their initiative, you're also supplying them with a convenient excuse for nonperformance ("If only the boss had let me do it my way!").

If yours is the office where "the buck stops," then you can also help make it the office where "the buck starts" (i.e., where responsibility is delegated). One of the most persistent mistakes many managers make is to underestimate the potential for growth of their subordinates. To the extent that you can achieve your objectives through the work of others, you can devote your own time to the truly important things that deserve your attention.

Using your power creatively means periodically taking the pulse of the organization and its external publics to determine what it's doing well, and *not* so well, and what it should be doing that perhaps it is not. Many executives find it helpful to take these soundings within the first 2 or 3 months of their tenure, and again at the end of their first year, so that they can judge what has and hasn't changed, what remains to be done, and what possible unintended consequences have flowed from the changes they have undertaken.

These soundings are not only a vehicle of communication, which is important in itself, but also a way of demonstrating to your managers and your outside publics the importance of their insight to the organization's self-improvement.

The further up the organizational ladder you climb, the easier it is to lose touch with "what's really happening down below." Executives who fly first-class, who mix socially and professionally principally with others of like status, can become removed from the concerns that motivate their customers and employees. The trappings of power can literally become a trap. *Using power creatively* means avoiding self-entrapment by providing *mechanisms* by which you can indeed remain "tuned in" to the sensitivities of your colleagues, superiors, and subordinates, to the needs of your customers and to trends, and to the problems of society.

Using power creatively in the future will increasingly mean using power in ways that are socially constructive. Government will require it, consumers will demand it, and the survival of our way of life on Spaceship Earth may provide us no alternative.

Obviously, there are several dimensions to the demands that weigh increasingly on corporations to be, in the European phrase, "good corporate citizens." In some European countries, managers routinely exercise the social obligation of providing continuity of employment to their employees. In others, workers share in the reins of power through participation in works' councils and even on boards of directors.

In the United States, social responsibility is taking a different turn. Anti-pollution controls, measures to ensure the safety and effectiveness of products, workplace protections, contributions—monetary and otherwise—to the welfare of local communities, and leaves of absence to perform public service to local, state, and federal government are all examples of responsibilities that U.S. executives are beginning to shoulder as a matter of course.

Unquestionably, many of the new social requirements incumbent upon business add to the costs of doing business. But any failure by industry to meet social responsibilities will cost even more dearly in weakened public support and strengthened government regulation.

The executive of one company was asked about a material used in some major consumer products that was alleged to be carcinogenic. His answer was that, although tests indicated a possible health risk, the Food and Drug Administration had not yet banned the chemical. "Besides," he added, "all our competitors use it."

Blind commitment to profitability may reap a company short-term gains, but to the extent that it creates an unhealthy environment, it will only hurt the company—and the country—in the longer run. Executives concerned about their longer-term livelihood, the longevity of their children, and Spaceship Earth cannot afford to adopt such an attitude. What we tell our children—"I don't care if your friends are all doing it; that's no excuse!"—should apply to ourselves and our companies as well.

As the world grows smaller and consumers more sophisticated—as the press, government, and board-of-director scrutiny of corporate ethics becomes more widespread—*service,* not lip service, will become the key to survival. Executives too often work in a microcosm, each in his or her own specialized sphere, concerned with how actions affect only that microcosm. If you should find yourself beginning to feel uneasy—if "what's best for my company" is in conflict with "what's best for my children"—you should perhaps be asking some searching questions of yourself and your superiors. Or looking for another job.

Similarly, public patience is wearing thin for executives who enjoy the rewards of lucrative contracts while professing shock or ignorance upon learning that they were obtained by bribes or other questionable means. Obviously, no executive can know everything. But executives can go a long way toward ensuring ethical practices if they draw up, and require each manager to indicate in writing his agreement with, a code of ethics governing all company contacts.

In our experience, most executives claiming surprise at revelations about illegal activities engaged in by members of their organizations *are* genuinely surprised. But we suspect the reason executives often don't know is because *they don't want to know*. Often too, something they've said, or some action they've taken, has set the climate in which such activities are accepted.

So what does it all mean?

It means that the basic questions you should seek to answer in your new assignment are questions like these:

- What do I want to contribute?
- How do I want to be remembered?
- How can I best use the resources at my command to fulfill my own objectives, ensure my company's viability and growth, and contribute to the welfare of the larger society of which we are only a tiny part?

There are some who would argue that the answers to these questions are not necessarily compatible. I submit that they *must* be compatible—or they cannot be effective. Your new assignment presents the unique opportunity to demonstrate not just your leadership, but your *humanistic* leadership—to provide focus to your own creative energies, to create a developmental environment for your people, to grow your business profitably, and to contribute to the well-being and progress of mankind.

Index